MW00824346

COOLI⊓UDE

AN ANTHOLOGY OF THE
INDIAN LABOUR DIASPORA

COOLITUDE

AN ANTHOLOGY OF THE INDIAN LABOUR DIASPORA

Marina Carter and
Khal Torabully

Anthem Press

Anthem Press is an imprint of
Wimbledon Publishing Company
PO Box 9779
London
SW19 7QA

This edition first published by
Wimbledon Publishing Company 2002

© Marina Carter and Khal Torabully

All rights reserved.
No part of this publication may be reproduced,
stored in a retrieval system, or transmitted, in any form
or by any means, without the prior permission in writing of
Wimbledon Publishing Company, or as expressly permitted
by law, or under terms agreed with the appropriate
reprographics rights organization.

British Library Cataloguing in Publication Data
Data available

Library of Congress Cataloging in Publication Data
A catalog record has been applied for

ISBN Hb 1 84331 003 1
ISBN Pb 1 84331 006 6

1 3 5 7 9 10 8 6 4 2

Contents

Introduction   1

The Coolie Odyssey: A Voyage In Time And Space   17

Thrice Victimized: Casting The Coolie   45

Surviving Indenture   88

Reclaiming The 'Other': Diaspora Indians
    And The Coolie Heritage   117

Some Theoretical Premises Of Coolitude   143

Conclusion: Revoicing the Coolie   214

Poetic And Critical Texts Of Coolitude   217

Notes   227

Bibliography   240

Introduction

The forced diaspora of African slaves has generated a veritable media industry. The imagery of the chained man, of the brutalized woman, of the kidnapped child has held our attention for several centuries. The dehumanization of the slave cast its shadow over succeeding generations, whose attempt to refashion their own history is illustrated in the 'négritude' movement. However, the recognition of a black identity did not fully take into account the ethnic complexity of post abolition societies that developed in the Caribbean and Indian Ocean. Creolité, antillanité and Indienocéanisme are among the more ethnically inclusive movements that have emerged to replace négritude. The dissemination of Indian labour throughout the nineteenth century British Empire has lacked a defining element until now. The concept of coolitude is designed to fill that lacuna, to describe and encapsulate the distinctive characteristics of the streams of indentured migration which have decisively shaped modern nations such as Mauritius, Trinidad, Guyana, Fiji and influenced others like Guadeloupe, Martinique, East and South Africa.

From *Négritude* to *Créolité*

Black US intellectuals like W E B Du Bois and Booker T Washington are credited with the commencement of black studies. Activists, like Marcus Garvey, took up their work whose stand against discrimination and injustice gave a new drive to the movement of black consciousness. *Négritude* is the francophone equivalent, and dates from the launch of *L'Etudiant Noir* in 1934 by Aimé Césaire, Léopold Sedar Sengor and Léon Gontran Damas. Senghor explicitly credited the Harlem Negro Renaissance movement of the 1920s for influencing *négritude*: '*le mouvement de la Négritude – la découverte des valeurs noires et la prise de conscience pour le Nègre de sa situation – est né aux Etats-Unis d'Amérique* (the *Négritude* movement – the discovery of black values and the conscientization of the black- was born in the USA).'[1]

Négritude has subsequently been defined as 'a theory of the distinc-
tiveness of African personality and culture'. The movement, and the
work it developed, 'took as its territory not only Africa but the whole of
diasporic African culture'. However, since *négritude* implied that all
people of negro descent shared inalienable essential characteristics, the
movement has been criticised as 'both essentialist and nativist'. What
made the *négritude* movement distinct was 'its attempt to extend perceptions of the negro as possessing a distinctive personality into all
spheres of life, intellectual, emotional and physical'.[2]

The movement was an important rallying point for all those who
believed they had been the victims of discrimination, and who wished to
underscore, as Aimé Césaire wrote, that 'no race possesses the monopoly
of beauty, of intelligence, of strength, and there is a place for all at the
rendezvous of victory . . .' C L R James has commented, in relation to
Césaire and his work, '*Négritude* is what one race brings to the common
rendezvous where all will strive for the new world of the poet's vision'.[3]

Numerous black diasporic writers were inspired by *négritude*. In
Mauritius, René Noyau and André Legallant, sang 'the echoes of black
blood from Africa', together with Emmanuel Juste and Pierre Renaud.
Edouard Maunick, a Mauritian then established in Paris, who, according
to critic Jean Georges Prosper *'y trouva le masque de la négritude et
l'éspousa* (who discovered there the mask of *négritude* and espoused it),
was highly rated by Senghor who prefaced his 1976 volume *Ensoleillé vif,*
with these words; *'peu de poètes nègres nous présentent une vision aussi
neuve et profonde du monde que Maunick* (Few black poets have demonstrated such a new and profound vision as Maunick.)'

In *Les Manèges de la Mer*, Maunick described himself as a product of
many races, but a 'nègre' by preference:

> . . . *enfant de mille races*
> *pétri d'Europe et des Indes*
> *taillé plus profondément*
> *dans le cri du Mozambique*
>
> *reconnaissant les racines*
> *je me tais en signe de deuil*
> *sur la part non partagée*
> *je suis nègre de préférence.*

. . . child of numerous races
framed by Europe and the Indies
more deeply carved
in Mozambican cries

when identifying my roots
I am silent to say my grief
on the unshared part of my self
I profess to be a negro by preference.

The influence of *Négritude* in the francophone world can be inferred from the fact that many diasporic writers – not necessarily black themselves – were drawn to portray and extol black music, art and language. Thus, Senghor defined the white Mauritian author and artist Malcolm de Chazal as an African painter, and Chazal himself, in his novel Petrusmok embraced African culture, stating that '*le langage du Noir est allégorique, délicieusement symbolique, analogique et illumine* (The language of the black is allegorical, deliciously symbolic, analogical and illuminated).'[4]

Danse Negre

J'ai préféré à tout système philosophique
Ce piétinement sur la plage
Cette ombre noire sur ce sable blanc
Cette voix rauque dans ce soir doux.

Edmée Le Breton, *Ressacs*, 1947.

To all philosophical systems
I have preferred this dance on the beach
This dark shadow on the white sand
This raucous voice in the sweet night.

La Vierge Noire

Le noir serait-il beau
Partout où il se trouve
Excepté sur ta peau?

Alain Le Breton, *Insulaires*, 1978.

Would black be more beautiful
Everywhere else,
Except on your skin?

Whilst Maunick's poetry evokes '*la douloureuse quête identitaire du poète et son aspiration à la liberté* (the poet's painful quest for identity, and aspiration to freedom)'[5], his writing did not take *négritude*, as a whole, to a less essentialist stance.

It was Emmanuel Juste – the great poet of *métissage* in the fifties – and Marcel Cabon who took up the mantle of the more ethnically inclusive message of *métissage*.

Like the black pride movement, *métissage*, or a mixed origin, is rediscovered as a source of pride. Alain Le Breton, a Mauritian writer, describes one of the characters in his novel as having inherited a range of qualities from his mixed ancestry: '*Un brin de galanterie française s'alliait chez lui au puissant génie de l'Afrique* (A drop of French gallantry was combined in him with the powerful genius of Africa)'.[6]

Dans la mémoire du monde
Le métis a la peau dure.
Il n'a ni talons, ni dos.
Dans la mémoire du monde
Un fruit martèle rouge un
panier de soleil.

Emmanuel Juste, *Mots Martéles*.

In the memory of the world
The métis never kneels.
He no longer has back or heels.
In the memory of the earth
A red fruit hammers
A basket full of suns.

Alain Lorraine was another advocate of *négritude* in Réunion, where, in the 1950s, Jean Albany, from the same island, living in Paris, took the notion of a unique island culture one stage further, adopting the term '*créolie*' which represented for him '*le paysage mental qui le rattache à son île et l'art de vivre qu'il en a hérité* (The mental landscape which attaches him to his island and the art of living which he has inherited from it)'.

The term became a symbol for later poets, one of whom, Gilbert Aubry, published 'Hymne a la créolie' in 1978. For him, *créolie* is '*dans la recherche et le respect des racines propres aux divers groupes, c'est l'ensemble qui prend les cultures des quatre horizons pour en faire son trésor et son partage quotidien* (the search and respect for the real roots of diverse groups, it is the whole which takes the cultures of the four continents to make of them a treasure and a daily dividend)'.[7]

Earlier, Marius and Ary Leblond, Goncourt Prize winners in the 30s, attempted the portrayal 'of the intimacy of the races and souls of the settlers and the indigenous population'. With the usual archetypes of the colonial novel, they wrote interesting short stories of which *La Marche Sur le Feu* is a good example of the theme of fascination and repulsion of the coolie. In Mauritius, the writing of Jean Georges Prosper was also blossoming from *négritude* into a vision of a creole society in which discrimination would be at an end. In the words of Chiniah: '*l'apocalypse prospérienne révelera le martyre nègre, le martyre créole, et la prophétie annoncera la fin de la discrimination sociale et l'émergence de l'identité créole, grâce a la dignité reconquise* (The Prosperian apocalypse reveals the martyrdom of the negro, of the Creole, and prophesies the end of social discrimination and the emergence of a creole identity, thanks to a reconquered dignity).'

Prosper, the lyricist of the Mauritian national hymn, shared with

Cabon, Chazal and Hart, though the latter expressed his desire to be part of the French literary tradition 'outre-France', the intense idealist quest of a meeting of cultures and the need to go beyond cultural and racial barriers for the elaboration of an authentic Mauritian culture. Prosper's poetry blends several influences on a cosmic plane and his creolised *négritude* carries poignant overtones of a new Mauritian identity at work: 'Carrousel des races et des civilisations maintenant immobilisé. Réar étant descendu de son char spatial, est maintenant entré dans le nirvana auréolé d'un matin blanc (The meeting point of races and civilisations is now stationary. Réar having come down from his spatial chariot, has now entered the haloed nirvana of a clear morning)'.[8]

Emmanuel Juste and Edouard J Maunick, developing the theme of the richness of Mauritian cultural *métissage*, proclaimed that the descendants of immigrants – as all Mauritians are – had a mission to propagate the notion of 'exile' within the mother country: 'Nos aïeux venaient tous de quelque part; nous avons pour mission de continuer leur exil dans un lieu devenu pays natal (Our forefathers all came from somewhere; our mission is to continue their exile in a place which has become our motherland)'.

This concept of exile was evident in the pre-Independence Mauritian literature. However, writers like Cabon and Chasle made attempts to blend Indian, African and other cultural references to go beyond 'exile' and delineate 'enracinement' on an island where a national identity was evolving. Their work undoubtedly reflects a further step in the process of maturation both on the level of identity-construction and literary development. Exile, in the new literary awareness, has led to more pertinent questions of how to cope with the cultural variety at hand, which was often negated or misused in social and political combats, and how to create, in the new land of adoption, a new vision meeting the modern needs of a society emerging from colonialism.

Writers from these Indian Ocean societies, under the visionary auspices of Camille de Rauville, collaborated in the evolution of a movement known as *indienocéanisme*, which reflected the composition of their plural societies. The principal characteristics of *l'indienocéanisme* have been defined as the following:

- Hinduism, interest in the mysteries of Asian traditions; nirvana
- Lemuria – the mythical continent as visualised by Jules Hermann of Réunion, Robert Edward Hart and Malcolm de Chazal in Mauritius

- Nature in the tropics – flaming and blossoming
- Rousseauesque re-civilization
- The French speaking community
- The island community.[9]

> 'Enfant de corsaire, enfant d'esclave, descendant d'immigré, venu de trois continents, né sur une île de sang-mêlé et de sang-à-mêler'.
>
> Raymond Chasle, *L'Etoile et la Clef*, 1975.

Child of corsairs, child of slaves, offspring of three continents, born on an island of mixed bloods and bloods to mix.

> 'Il aimait cette atmosphère du samedi soir, le va-et-vient des chalands, ces odeurs mêlées, – de poisson salé, d'épices, d'arack, (lui qui détestait tous les tord-boyaux), ces humbles commerces qui s'installaient sous le lafouche pour l'après-midi: les marchands de bazar, la vieille Minatchi qui vendait des pistaches grillées (et elle avait la bouche toute rouge de bétel), Soukdéo qui vendait des gâteaux-piments, le barbier . . .
>
> C'était le jour de la paye et Cassim était là, lui aussi, venu chercher l'argent de ses clients . . . Et ce braillard de Manilal, avec le bâton et le parasol, emblèmes de son rang, et la grosse montre qu'il tirait à chaque instant de dessous sa veste pour bien montrer son importance.
>
> Il était le sirdar, celui qui commandait au champ. Sirdar encore par les moustaches et le ventre. Dès qu'il paraissait, chacun en était averti à dix lieux à la ronde.'
>
> Marcel Cabon, *Namasté*, 1965.

He liked this atmosphere of Saturday night, the movements of customers, those mixed smells – of salted fish, spices, arak, (he who hated strong alcohol), those humble stalls which were set up under the banian tree for the afternoon: the vegetable sellers, the old Minatchi who sold roasted peanuts (her mouth was all red with betel leaves), Soukdéo who sold chili cakes, the barber . . .

> It was payday and Cassim was there too. He had come to fetch
> money from his customers . . . And unruly Manilal, holding a stick
> and an umbrella, emblems of his rank, and the large watch which he
> incessantly pulled out of his jacket to show his importance.
>
> He was the sirdar, who commanded in the field. Sirdar also by his
> moustache and his belly. As soon as he appeared, everyone was
> warned from far ahead . . .

On Martinique and Guadeloupe, *Créolité* emerged as the inheritor of the
Négritude movement. The movement dates from the publication of its
manifesto, *Eloge de la Créolité* (1989) translated as *In Praise of Creoleness*,
(1993), written by Martinicans Patrick Chamoiseau, Raphael Confiant
and Jean Bernabé. Inspired by Edouard Glissant's notion of *antillanité*
(Caribbeanness), but explicitly including non-Caribbean islands, such as
Reunion in the Indian Ocean in their movement, they argue that
Caribbean or Creole identity resides precisely in the mixing or creolization of the numerous ethnic groups of the islands. They contend that the
process of creolization has so marked the Caribbean that no single identity has emerged as dominant, in spite of France's one-time policy of
cultural assimilation. For the authors, it is precisely this unstable identity
that must be cultivated.

The créolité movement has been chiefly concerned with the transmis-
sion of the Creole sensibility through literature. Some of Confiant's works
have been in French Creole, as this language is itself considered to be a
reflection of the multiple cultural and linguistic influences on the islands,
but French remains the chief literary expression of the movement.
Chamoiseau's *Texaco* (1992) effectively blends French with Creole, and
on a thematic level, the *Créolité* writers, particularly Confiant, seek to represent all ethnic groups present on Creole islands and to highlight the
complexity of interactions which this cultural diversity engenders.

Maryse Condé, also a French Caribbean writer, has remained apart
from the movement, which has been considered to be overly Caribbean-
centred. Indeed the *Créolité* vision is deeply rooted in the French Creole
Caribbean heritage. Confiant cites an anecdote from his childhood, when
a teacher warned him: '*Raphael, le créole est un patois de nègres sauvages
et de coulis malpropres*' (Raphael, creole is a patois spoken by savage

negroes and dirty coolies)' to explain his commitment to the use of his mother tongue.[10]

Edouard Glissant has demonstrated that the *métissage* of cultural forms has led to the recovery of such occulted histories. He has shown that New World populations were unable to take possession of their social and material environment because of domination by the 'other'. This cultural domination moreover involved a hidden process of insidious assimilation – an urge to mimic the 'other'. It is precisely for this reason that the French Caribbean writers explicitly rejected a single ethnic origin in favour of the inclusive 'creole' status: '*Ni Européen, ni Africain, ni Asiatique, nous nous proclamons Créoles* (Neither European, nor African, nor Asian, we proclaim ourselves Creoles).'[11]

A Creole charter drawn up in 1992 recognized 'the existence of a Creole matrix that transcends the diversity of Creole languages and cultures [and] establishes a direct parentage between Creoleness and black identity, more specifically its Francophone version, *négritude*'. In the words of the original charter '*la créolité est le fondement et le prolongement d'une négritude authentiquement humaniste* (*Créolité* is the foundation and prolongation of an authentically humanist *négritude*)'.[12]

By emphasizing the plural nature of Creoleness, these writers recognized that complexity – and not clarity – was key. As Francoise Lionnet explains 'in the effort to recover their unrecorded past, contemporary writers and critics have come to the realization that opacity and obscurity are necessarily the precious ingredients of all authentic communication'.[13]

Hookoomsingh has noted that 'the difficulty of attempting to grasp the concept of Creoleness lies . . . in distinguishing between the dynamic process of contact and interaction and the resulting product, that is, Creole identity'. This can vary greatly from island to island. In Mauritius, for example, where more than two thirds of the population are of Indian origin, the fact of speaking a Creole is distinguished from an ethnic Creole identity.[14]

The geographical dispersal of the Creole islands and the social specificities that arise from their varied locations do not preclude the cultural similiarities that link them. These dissonant characteristics have led French anthropologist Jean Benoist to collectively describe them as an '*archipel inachevé*'. He adds: '*Si la constellation des îles Créoles était rassemblée dans un même océan, elle s'imposerait par le rayonnement d'une culture et d'une civilisation originale. Mais écartelée entre la Caraïbe, les terres*

d'Amérique et l'océan Indien, mêlée de façon ambiguë à bien des entrecroise-
ments de civilisations, soumise à de puissantes forces centrifuges, elle évoque
plutôt les restes d'un univers éclaté (If the constellation of Creole islands
were gathered in the same ocean, it would assert itself as a dynamic original culture and civilization. But divided between the Caribbean, the
Americas, and the Indian Ocean, mixed in an ambiguous fashion through
the intersections of different civilizations, subject to powerful centrifugal
forces, it conjures up, above all, the remains of a shattered universe).'[15]

Creolization

'The process of intermixing and cultural change that produces a
Creole society.'

Diaspora

'Diaspora, the voluntary or forcible movement of peoples from
their homelands into new regions, is a central historical fact of colonization . . . the practices of slavery and indenture . . . resulted in
worldwide colonial diasporas.

The descendants of the diasporic movements generated by colonialism have developed their own distinctive cultures, which both
preserve and often extend and develop their originary cultures.
Creolized versions of their own practices evolved, modifying (and
being modified by) indigenous cultures with which they came into
contact . . . The development of diasporic cultures necessarily questions essentialist models, interrogating the ideology of a unified,
'natural' cultural norm, one that underpins the centre/margin model of
colonialist discourse. . . . The most recent and most socially significant
diasporic movements have been those of colonized peoples back to
the metropolitan centres. In countries such as Britain and France, the
population now has substantial minorities of diasporic ex-colonial
peoples. In recent times, many writers have adopted the notion of a
'diasporic identity' as a positive affirmation of their hybridity.

Ashcroft, B et al, *Key Concepts in Post Colonial Studies*,
London, 1998. p. 58, p. 68–70.

Redefining the Indian Diaspora:
Towards Coolitude

Créolité

An interpretation of creolization that blends diverse sources and is essentially an unfinished process by which human groups blend their histories and imaginaires.

Coolitude

'It is impossible to understand the essence of coolitude without charting the coolies' voyage across the seas. That decisive experience, that coolie odyssey, left an indelible stamp on the imaginary landscape of coolitude'.

K Torabully, 'The Coolies' Odyssey', *The Unesco Courier*,
Paris, October 1996, p. 13.

In tandem with the *créolité* writers, Stuart Hall has defined the diaspora experience as one characterized 'not by essence and purity, but by the recognition of a necessary heterogeneity and diversity; by a conception of "identity" that lives with and through, not despite, difference; by hybridity. Diaspora identities are those which are constantly producing and reproducing themselves anew, through transformation and difference'. Identity in diaspora is not seen, therefore, as static or fixed but rather as 'subject to the continuous play of history, culture and power'.[16] This definition is similar to that of creolization by Edouard Glissant, for whom it is the 'thought of chaos'.

From a more individualistic perspective, Parekh has also defined the Indian in diaspora as a person with multiple identities:

'Different overseas Hindu communities, and within them different social groups, developed along different lines and evolved distinct identities that marked them off both from each other and their counterparts in India. Over time little and large "Indias", each with a distinct history, social structure and mode of self-conception, sprang up all over the world. The diasporic Hindu was no longer a Hindu happening to live abroad, but one deeply transformed by his diasporic experiences. The

Hindu diaspora then contains multiple identities, all sharing some common features but relating them differently and additionally having distinct features of their own'.[17]

The significance of the *créolité* movement was that every ethnic segment of Creole society, whether of African, European, Indian or Chinese origin, was considered crucial to the elaboration of a *'commune créolité'*. Thus as Burton has noted: *'L'indianité s'inscrit au centre d'une problématique de la Créolité, tant à cause des modifications qu'elle a dû subir en milieu Créole que parce qu'elle a pu propager d'elle-même en ce même milieu* (*Indianité* lies at the heart of the *créolité* problimatic, as much because of the modifications which it has to undergo in the Creole milieu as through its self-propagation in this same milieu).'[18]

At the same time, the size of the Indian component in the various Creole societies in our purview has inevitably influenced the degree of importance attached to the recovery of an Indian identity. Referring to the 45,000 Indians who settled on Guadeloupe, and the recent attempts of the Indian elite there to rediscover their Indian identity, or *'indianité'*, Schnepel questions whether the development or process of reformulation of an Antillean national consciousness is likely to take place parallel to, rather than to include the rehabilitation of the East Indian component of those societies.[19]

The difficulty of integrating Indians into a broader Caribbean Creole identity stems, at least in part, from a historic antagonism between the Indian who came as an indentured immigrant, and the ex-slave, whom he supplanted on the plantations of the sugar colonies. The Indian was perceived, consequently, as a lackey of capitalism whose presence perpetuated coercive, unequal labour relations and inhibited the growth of an independent peasantry. The long term stigma attached to the Indo-Caribbean has been well summarized by Jean Benoist:

'Longtemps stigmatisée par le fait d'être venue prendre le relais de l'esclavage, et d'avoir été ainsi la complice, involontaire mais complice quand même, de la permanence de la société coloniale après l'abolition de l'esclavage, l'immigration indienne a été à la fois étrangère, méprisée et fondamentalement exclue. Le temps de la Négritude l'a ignorée. L'Indien était le coolie, socialement inexistant . . . fondamentalement à l'écart (Long stigmatized from the fact of having taken over the reins from slavery, and of having thus been complicit, albeit involuntarily, in the perpetuation of a colonial form of society after the abolition of slavery, the

Indian immigrant has been at one and the same time a despised foreign
and fundamentally excluded. The negritude era ignored the Indian
who was the coolie, socially non-existent . . . fundamentally on the
margins).'[20]

The negative stereotype of the diaspora Indian has been perpetuated
by some of its most famous offspring. V S Naipaul, himself an Indo-
Caribbean, uses the character of Ganesh in *The Mystic Masseur* to rip
into the overseas Indian mentality. For Naipaul the Trinidad Indian is 'a
complete colonial, even more philistine than the white', and his ilk are
dismissed by Ganesh as 'A peasant-minded, money-minded community
spiritually static because cut off from its roots, its religion reduced to rites
without philosophy, set in a materialist colonial society'. Naipaul sees the
overseas Indian as 'peripheral' and the chief themes identified in his
characterization of Indo-Caribbeans have been described as 'destitution
and derivativeness'.[21]

Naipaul, and Neil Bissoondath, an Indo-Caribbean writer settled in
Canada, see their island birthplaces as fundamentally limiting. For
Bissoondath, Caribbean history is 'just a big black hole'. One of his
characters decries 'small places, places of limited scope, of brutal past,
hesitant present and uncertain future'.[22] The overseas Indians portrayed in Bissoondath's books are perpetually isolated, living in 'self
imposed exile' because they 'neither give up their past nor accept the
present.'[23]

The social conservatism and apparent cultural vacuousness of the
diasporic Indian deplored by Naipaul and Bissoondath and remarked
upon by a host of other writers has been linked, by Salman Rushdie,
to the more generalized sense of loss and the urge for reclamation
which is prevalent among exiles. In *Imaginary Homelands*, he predicts
that he and his fellow rootless migrants will be constantly in quest of
the irreclaimable; 'we will not be capable of reclaiming precisely the
thing that was lost . . . We will, in short, create fictions, not actual
cities or villages, but invisible ones, imaginary homelands, Indias of the
mind'.[24]

The works of those writers who interpret the indentured labour diaspora, or who themselves are the descendants of one of these several
'subaltern diasporic movements forced by colonial circumstances', have
been particularly characterized by 'cultural anxiety' and by forms of
seeming cultural fragmentation.[25]

In practice, however, the eclecticism, some might say chaos, of such diasporic writing is often central to the meaning and symbolism of the text. Jain has noted that the dynamics of language is important to the diasporic writer who 'often deliberately disrupts his narrative to include words and expressions from his native language . . . This strategy succeeds in large measure in defining generic boundaries'. For Bakhtin, the language of the diasporic writer is itself a form of contestation. Language becomes double-accented and double-styled because this reflects the multiple identities of the writer. In other words it represents the essence and the expression of the concept of hybridity that is itself central to the discourse of diasporic writing.[26]

In formulating the concept of 'coolitude', writer Khal Torabully has drawn upon these emerging traditions of diasporic writing. His own research, with its distinctive original poetic vision, goes beyond the traditional definitions of creolization and *indienocéanisme* and rests, to summarize, on 2 pillars:

> 'Firstly, the reconstitution of a memory, which veers between an
> imagination drawn back to the atavistic homeland – Indianness as
> a set of inalienable values bequeathed by India since the
> beginning of time – and the constellation of signs spawned by the
> uneasy interaction of the exiled Indian's values with the cultures
> of the host country. Secondly, the contribution of a poetics based
> on the Indian element and shaped by the fact that the coolie was
> chronologically the last arrival to contribute to the making of
> diversified societies.'
>
>   K Torabully, 1996.

The poetry of Coolitude – the concept defined and worked out by Torabully – is embodied chiefly in two volumes, *Cale d'Etoiles* and *Chair Corail, Fragment Coolies*, and expanded in *Palabres à Parole*, in a reappraisal of the poet's reservoir of signs, quoting intertextual references of exoticism, and redefining them poetically so as to underline the importance of language constructions and deconstructions in coolitude. In *Dialogue de l'Eau et du Sel*, Torabully reinvests meditative poetry through the birth of the sea and reinvents the mythical creation of the island, while *Roulis sur le Malecon*, is a forceful encounter with the *métissage* of Cuba where 'psychic *métissage*' points to the poet's desired identity, and

L'Ombre Rouge des Gazelles, is a text on Algeria in the great tradition of Arab poetry.

Cale d'Etoiles, the founding text of coolitude, has been described by Jean-Georges Prosper as:

'*une odyssée, une épopée d'envergure vient exorciser la douloureuse mémoire de l'immigration de l'engagisme, à l'Ile Maurice, de l'Indien coolie! D'ou l'écriture hallucinée, désaxée, d'un texte chargé de tragiques références, évocations et réminiscences; avec la prédominance de l'isotopie des tribulations indiennes de la deuxieme moitié du XIXème siècle mauricien. Douloureuse mémoire reprise en charge par le poète dans une nouvelle pensée créatrice dénommée Coolitude, sorte de Négritude a l'Indienne.* (An odyssey, a forceful epic came to exorcize the unhappy memory of immigration, of indenture, in Mauritius, and of the Indian as coolie. From this derives the hallucinatory, disjointed Mauritian writing of a text replete with tragic references and reminiscences, with the predominant isotopy stressing the tribulations of the Indians of the late nineteenth-century in Mauritius. Unhappy memories that have been reclaimed by the poet in a new form of creative thinking called Coolitude, a sort of Indian version of Négritude.)'[27]

Whilst *Négritude* and Coolitude have much in common, *Cale d'Etoiles* devises an original language blending different visions of the world, moulded into poetry. Khal Torabully never lapses into an essentialist philosophy. Indeed, he does away with exile, and clearly reveals in *Cale d'Etoiles* that the key-text is the 'Book of the Voyage', giving the sea voyage an essential function in his poetry. It is to be understood as a place of destruction and creation of identity, which is a preliminary to the '*enracinement*' in the host country, itself comprehended as a dynamic space of the diversity of perceptions and cultures. This nodal point has been explained by Véronique Bragard, a Belgian researcher: 'Coolitude is not based on Coolie as such but relies on the nightmare transoceanic journey of Coolies, as both a historical migration and a metonymy of cultural encounters. The crossing of the *Kala Pani* constitutes the first movement of a series of abusive and culturally stifling situations. By making the crossing central, Coolitude avoids any essentialism and connection with an idealized Mother India, which is clearly left behind. It discloses the Coolie's story which has been shipwrecked ('erased') in the ocean of a Western-made historical discourse as well as a world of publication and criticism'.[28]

No doubt, Coolitude is the song of a forgotten voyage. But it is also more: the coolie odyssey is the ultimate voyage: the essence of journeys and the essence of Man. The struggles of the coolie, his disappointments and his hopes, are the echoes of a universal human experience. *Créolité, indienocéanisme* and Caribbean *créolité* are enriched and redefined when related to coolitude, which gives them new venues of meaning and perspectives in many fields. Coolitude thus entails a fresh attitude and new definitions, capable of giving these theories a new impetus and unprecedented configurations.

1

The Coolie Odyssey:
A Voyage in Time and Space

'The Beyond is, first of all, for the coolie who settles, a confused poetics,
pregnant with silence, looks, unsaid words. This last-comer was forced to
situate himself in this new cultural challenge where the other is an ambiguous
figure, bearer of signs of reconnaissance and annihilation, and capable of
wrecking symbols. The game of anomy, based on the absence of social
landmarks, pushed the coolie to the bottom of the ladder, out of speech.'

K Torabully, *Coolitude*, 1996, p. 59.

*The metaphor of the voyage was played out throughout the coolie's life. From
the first crossing of the kala pani – that forbidden sea journey – the migrant
was cast in the dual role of adventurer and victim. Coolitude explores the
concept of the ocean as a nodal moment of migration, a space for destruction
of identity, yet also one of regeneration, when an aesthetics of migration was
created. This chapter revisits the recruitment of the coolie and the experience
of sea-crossing, detailing the expectations and experiences of the overseas
migrant, the raw emotion of transition and upheaval, of uncertainty and
struggle, the evolution of another identity beyond India.*

The Moment of Departure –
Coolie Choices and Voices

The testimonies of migrants frequently bear witness to a pre-existing
decision to look for work away from their native village, to join the
armies of rural Indians tramping the roads looking for seasonal employment, before the fateful meeting with a recruiter that was to lead them
much further afield, to a distant colony. Ekhadosee reported having left
his home in Midnapur to look for work at Calcutta when he met a man
who promised him a monthly wage of ten rupees. The man lodged him
at Bam Bazar for a week before tutoring him as to how to pass the

registration: 'I was taken to a Saheb but before that was tutored to say that I was going of my own free will and accord – six rupees was given to me, out of this two was taken by the Duffadours, who for two rupees purchased for me a chest and some chorelis, two rupees remained with me which I used in purchasing necessaries while on board for my subsistence – I seldom ever got food from the ship's people – I would never venture to go on board ship to the Mauritius – the promised service was in Calcutta and not the Mauritius.'

The Many-faced Recruit

Je suis chamar des plaines du Gange Pallan Palli
Déjà esclave du Canara –
A Andhra je ployais sous le joug du Misradar Tiouurel
Prêt a quitter la terre brûlée de Meerut
Je me déclarai aventurier assoiffé de l'or des colonies
Pour me consumer dans les cannaies de Saint Alary
Je suis le mutin des révoltes des Sipayes
Le brahmane vaincu du royaume d'Oude

K Torabully, *Chair Corail, Fragments Coolies*, p. 53.

I am a chamar from the plains of the Ganges Pallan Palli
Already a slave from Canara
At Andhra I struggled under the yoke of Misradar Tiourel
Ready to leave the burnt earth of Meerut
I declared myself an adventurer, thirsty for the gold of the colonies
To be consumed among the canes of Saint Alary
I am the mutineer from the Sepoy Revolt
The vanquished Brahmin from the kingdom of Oudh

An early recruit to Mauritius, the Bengali woman Djoram, recounted a typical story of immiseration and mobility within India. Already a migrant to Calcutta, she was there convinced by a recruiter to embark on a ship to take service – only once aboard did she, and many other migrants who made these pioneer journeys in the 1830s, become aware of how far their new employments were from India:

'I was born at the village of Amtah about three days' journey south of Midnapore. I left my home at Amtah about four and a half years ago, and came to Calcutta for service; about two years after my leaving home, my father was drowned in an inundation, and my mother came to Calcutta with my two brothers; we lived together at Khidderpore; I lived with an ayah for one year, cooking for her and serving her on two rupees per month; finding she could not support me, she taught me ayah's work, and I served a Mr Martin for about a year, when Mr Martin left for some other country; I was then out of employ; I remained two months, and then took service for the Mauritius; this is about two and a half years ago; a baboo, whose name I do not know, and a duffadar called Jungli Havildar entertained me . . . I was sitting in a tailor's shop at Bhowanipore when this Junglee Haldar and the baboo came to me . . . I was told I could get ten rupees a month wages, food and clothing, and that I was to serve a gentleman and lady who were proceeding in the ship I was to embark on; I asked how far Meritch was; they said five days' journey, and that if I pleased I could remain in service there or return; they thus deceived me and got me on board.'[1]

Karoo was enticed to Calcutta with the promise of work on road repairs, and when the promised job did not materialize, was, like many others, inveigled into the emigration depot:

'A man of the name of Golam Ally, who is a duffadar, went to my country. He gathered fifteen men and brought them down to Calcutta, he had three men with him with badges on. He asked us "What are you doing in the jungle? Come to Calcutta, and you will get employment for repairing roads, for which you will receive pay at the rate of four rupees per month, besides diet" . . . When we arrived here, he told us that no employment on the roads could be got; "You had better go forward and you will find plenty of employment." He mentioned that we should go to the Mauritius.'[2]

Vulnerable individuals, especially women who had left their homes after a dispute, as in the case of Ratna, interviewed in Fiji, were easy fodder for unscrupulous recruiters:

'My man left the house after he had been rebuked by my father-in-law. I took my child and went looking for him in Ajodaji. I spent five or six days there, I did not know where to go and where to look for him. I was told that my husband had gone to Calcutta. I went to Calcutta by train in search for him. I was told that he had already left two or three days earlier. I went to the wharf and there I saw a steamer, some people took my son off me, and threatened me. I was put into the depot with my child and stayed there for two or three days before embarking on the ship.'

Calcutta-born Maharani later told interviewers that she escaped to Trinidad after being abused by her husband's family in India.[3]

A Natal Indian, Aboo Bakr, testified to personal knowledge of coolies recruited under false pretences:

'I know an Indian woman, a Brahmin, she belonged to Lucknow; through a quarrel with her mother she made a pilgrimage to Allahabad; when there she met a man who told her that if she would work, she would be able to get twenty-five rupees a month in a European family, by taking care of the baby of a lady who lived about six hours' sea journey from Calcutta; she went on board and, instead of taking her to the place proposed she was brought to Natal.'[4]

Even into the twentieth century, when migration overseas was a well-known phenomenon for the socially disaffected and economically marginalized, it was still possible for recruiters to trick individuals into migrating, including young men of relatively affluent backgrounds. In some cases their parents, particularly if literate and well-known, were able to raise the alarm fairly quickly, and institute the mechanisms of British bureaucracy on their side. Thus, when the son of Gopinath Pandey, a village headmaster from Uttar Pradesh, was tricked into going to Natal and embarked on the steamship *Pongola*, his father wrote a letter to the port emigration authorities. The letter reveals his disgust and distress at the manner of his son's embarkation for Natal. Gyapershad, the son, was a 17-year-old student, described by his father as 'a promising lad':

'. . . on the occasion of attending to some ceremonies at his
maternal uncle's house he was decoyed and criminally
misrepresented by some recruiters of professional roguery at
Cawnpur to join the Coolie Depot preparing emigrants for the
Colonies.

That the affection which I as an old father bear to him has
almost not only paralysed me but also his old mother and young
wife recently married, on account of his having been snatched
away from our paternal care and guardianship . . .

Under the circumstances I am constrained to reach your
honour in the sanguine expectation of your being gracious
pleased of adopting prompt measures for stopping the said
Gyapershad my son at any of the intervening stations available to
the SS *Pongola* in transit from Calcutta to Natal and for taking
him back to Calcutta to me and for thus saving his old parents'
critical life.

P.S. It is sickening to hear that I am a Brahmin and my son
Gyapershad has been misrepresented to be Rajput (Thakur) for
sheerly serving the evil purposes of the recruiter.'[5]

Even where migrants had a good understanding of their destination,
resentments and misrepresentations as to working conditions and wage
rates could still occur. In 1914 a group of Punjabi migrants to Fiji
reported that they had left India:

'. . . on the inducement and representations of Wali Mohamed
and Atta Mohamed, castes Sayed, residents of Karnana, tahsil
Nawanshar, District Jullundur, Punjab. They have been sending
our people during the last five years and on each steamer 45 or
46 men are being emigrated while they take Rs 35 as their
commission for each individual . . . we were made to understand
that in Fiji we can get work on daily wages at 5/- but regret to say
that even 2/- can be hardly earned – thus we have been suffering
much. We had no previous experience of such tricks and they are
deceiving to the people and are also against the law.'[6]

Folksongs from the colonies of Indian settlement testify to the resentment felt at deceptive recruiters:

Oh recruiter, your heart is deceitful,
Your speech is full of lies!
Tender may be your voice, articulate and seemingly logical,
But it is all used to defame and destroy
The good names of people.[7]

A song from Fiji curses the arkatis, or subordinate recruiters:

I hoe all day and cannot sleep at night,
Today my whole body aches,
Damnation to you, arkatis.[8]

If early migrants were deceived as to the real distance of their destination, and later indentured recruits disappointed in the opportunities proffered, in the peak years of migration, during the mid-nineteenth century, would-be emigrants could find themselves the prey of rival recruiting agencies that thwarted their attempts to go to a particular colony where they may have had friends or relations. Chummun left his village intending to go to Mauritius, around 1860, with a relative who had already been to the colony when, at Raniganj, they were met by a munshi 'who advised us to go to Bourbon and offered to take us to the Bourbon Depot. He succeeded in inducing my companions to follow him. He said that Mauritius had become a bad place for Coolies and that Bourbon was much better. He said that Mr Caird had gone away and that the Mauritius Depot was locked up.'[9]

Jhurry gave a statement to the Calcutta Magistrate in April 1861 that revealed that he had instigated a chain migration to Mauritius, but that his own brother had been unable to accompany him, having been lured to the Trinidad depot by a recruiter:

'I was ten years at Mauritius. My masters were Hart and Bissy, of Grand Port district. As they were very kind to me, I came back to recruit Coolies for them. I have five men with me now, who are disposed to accompany me. They come from Arrah Zillah. My brother left Arrah to come and join me. He was enticed away by an arkotty who took him to the Trinidad depot. I endeavoured to communicate with my brother, but was prevented by the arkotty who had charge of him. I have heard that my brother has been sent away to Trinidad.'

Another recruit, who had friends in Mauritius, left Sherghotty to go to that island but was taken by a duffadar to a place called the 'new Mauritius depot'. Only after he had been registered as an emigrant did he find that it was the Demerara depot:[10]

'When an inspector of emigration visited Thanjavur in 1866, he found numerous abuses of their position by recruiters. Mootoosamy Pillay had a sign in front of his house inviting would-be migrants for Mauritius to enter his premises. On investigation, he was found to have a licence for Ceylon. In a reversal of earlier deceits, which saw recruits intending to work inland, being taken overseas, Ramalingum, a recruiter ostensibly working for the Mauritius depot in Madras, was dismissed from his post in 1871 when he was found to have been taking recruits to the local Godavery works instead.'[11]

The various stories that lay behind migration decisions are encapsulated in Mahadai Das' poem:

They Came in Ships

Some came with dreams of milk-and-honey riches,
Fleeing famine and death:
Dancing girls,
Rajput soldiers, determined, tall,
Escaping penalty of pride.
Stolen wives, afraid and despondent,
Crossing black waters,
Brahmin, Chammar, alike,
Hearts brimful of hope.
 'They Came In Ships' by Mahadai Das in Dabydeen & Samaroo
 (eds), *India in the Caribbean*, 1987, p. 288.

Children were particularly vulnerable to entrapment, and as indenture contracts could be signed from the age of ten years and upwards, minors could find themselves engaged to an estate overseas for lengthy periods. In 1882, a small boy, Dawoodharree, was found to have been recruited from India for the Sans Souci estate in Mauritius, along with a group of men. He pleaded with the Protector of Immigrants to cancel the engagement, but the estate manager was unrelenting, claiming that:

> 'Dawoodharree was engaged at the same time as five or six other men who came from India with him, that he was aware that he was going to Mauritius to contract an engagement for five years, that his passage as well as the passage of the others, had been paid by the sirdar of 'Sans Souci' estate, and that the amount disbursed for this purpose by the sirdar had been refunded by the estate.'

The Protector initially ordered the estate to provide a certificate of discharge for the boy together with a cheque for forty rupees to provide for his repatriation, but after enquiring into the case, concluded that Dawoodharree should be made to work for one year, after which his engagement could be cancelled if he so wished.[12]

It was also common practice for recruiters to station themselves on the roads leading to centres of pilgrimage. Luckless travellers finding themselves without funds were another source of labour for the arkatis and duffadars. Mootoosamy Pillay left his home to attend the Kundri festival held in the mosque of Meera Sahib. On his return, at Karrical, he met a recruiter who induced him to emigrate. Vitilinga Naicken was travelling to Madras to see his sister when he became ill at Pondicherry. Taking lodgings there, he was assisted by a stranger who 'came thither and gave me some hot water. He took care of me two days, and then led me to his own house where he kept me about a month and cured my sickness. He then heard my story and said . . . that if I went to Bourbon I could acquire money and return home, and that he would also accompany me.' Nagamootoo Padiatchy's stated reason for emigrating was almost banal: 'About eleven years ago a quarrel ensued between myself and my father. Displeased with my father, I thought of going to the Mauritius, and accordingly went to the bazaar street of my village.' Inevitably, he there met a recruiter's agent who was only too happy to undertake the necessary formalities on his behalf.

Come, you from the Grand Peninsula
Into the small isle of France.
Come to dance the immense twilight,
To purify your face and your senses.
Here is Money island Rupee island.

Just lift a stone and be rich.
Here the master is a friend
Come for all the gold of Dwipa Aropi.

The envoys told me
Come to Mauritius
And take Savannah and the Gunner's Quoin

To cover the ocean of the Indies
Our vessel will glide ten days only,
Nearer to you than the beat of blood.
The ocean? Worry not: sweet like the lover
When our vessel will reach the last breakers.

And I knew after two moons in drowning
Time was the consumption of times.
And I anchored in Durban, Dina Morgabine,
Singapore, Fiji, the West Indies, in the dust of waves.
To be scattered in the gales of continents.
In the currents of colonies.

K Torabully, *Cale d'Etoiles, Coolitude.*

Some migrants were deceived into going overseas in the mistaken belief that they were being recruited by the East India Company. Ramdeen stated:

'I was a syce at Barrackpore; Juggernauth, another syce, induced me to go to Mauritius. Juggernauth also went and died there. He told us Gillanders & Co were sending men to Mauritius, and induced us to go to get service. I came by myself to Calcutta, and the others were collected from other parts near Calcutta, where they had come in search of employ; fifty out of two hundred and fifty were Dangahs . . . There were some Ooreahs also . . . We were told that we were engaged to do the Company's work.'

When Ramdeen was asked what he understood by 'company', he replied that he knew of only one company, 'the government of this country'. He declared that he and his fellow migrants would not have gone if they had known it was not for company service.[13]

> You have learned the legendary store
> of men lost in the orchard of gales,
> fallen in water like five black cents.
>
> And the monsoon has reaped you in its ropes
> when the last pagla of the village spoke
> of a book as strange as a shipwreck.
>
> <div align="right">K Torabully, <i>Cale d'Etoiles, Coolitude</i></div>

The Indian Government officially took a neutral stance on the emigration question, but the misleading notices posted by emigration officials in the pay of the overseas colonies at major Indian ports seemed to give the impression that the local government was the employer because they stipulated that migrants were under the protection of the 'Company'. In 1852, for example, the Emigration Agent of Mauritius at Madras circulated a notice in the Tamil and Telegu languages which asserted that recruits could earn good pay, and be well fed, housed and clothed at Mauritius, thereby being able save all the wages earned over five years, with a free return passage at the end of that time. The notice concluded 'These are the advantages that a kind Government secures to all those who are desirous to proceed to the Mauritius, and emigrants are strongly advised to select this colony rather than the foreign settlement of Bourbon where the Honourable Company cannot look after their interests.'[14]

A considerable number of individuals were attracted by the idea of Company service. Contrary to traditional views of the Indian tied to his village, researchers have established that 'population mobility was inherent in the social order and the peasantry lived in a state of flux.'[15] Kolff has demonstrated the existence of a military labour market in India even in the pre-capitalist period, with sultans, rajahs and Mughal emperors all recruiting for large state armies from among marginal peasants. By the nineteenth century, it had become common practice for inhabitants of certain districts to supply the new rulers – the British – with military recruits. Yang's study of Saran district in Bihar, for example, reveals that the district had provided the British Army with 10,000 sepoy recruits by the mid-nineteenth century. He shows that where migratory trends developed, various types of labour, including seasonal work and overseas indenture, would be taken up and concludes that the rural migrant displayed considerable skill and sophistication in his migratory choices: 'Whether he moved, where he went, and what he did all testify to his capacity to operate under some degree of risk and uncertainty in order to create a safe investment . . . there has always been movement in response to better opportunities'.[16] It was money which lured villagers like Tirvengadum and Marooda to the French Indian Ocean island of Reunion. At Pondicherry Tirvengadum was assured by the recruiter Carpayee that overseas labourers returned 'with plenty of money'. Madooda was told that he too, would become wealthy, if he went abroad.

The Disenchanted Sepoy

Je suis une non-valeur
Inapte au travail de la terre
Sheik est mon nom grinçant contre la graisse
De porc dans les cartouches ennemies
Paria crachant la graisse de vache dans le barillet
D'Enfield.

K Torabully, *Chair Corail, Fragments Coolies*, p. 55.

I am without value
Unsuited for field labour
Sheik is my name, grimacing in the face of grease
Of pigs in the enemy's cartridges
A Paria spitting cow's grease into the barrel
Of an Enfield.

Accustomed to travel for and with their work, sepoys were among the first to take up the challenge of overseas labour. Rengasamy Naicken, who went to Mauritius with the first batches of recruits in the 1830s, described his background thus:

> 'I was formerly employed as a sepoy under the Danish Government of Tranquebar. After the annexation of that settlement to the company territories, I obtained a Vesharipoogarship in the Tranquebar talook. As my younger brother was living at Singapore and as I was desirous of paying a visit to him, I resigned the Vesharipoogar's post and went there. After a lapse of one year, I returned to my native land and was without employment. A native of Karrical of the Vellala caste was acquainted with me . . . He said he was going to Mauritius and desired me to follow him. I consented to it, and went along with him to Karrical.'

Manick, who stated that he was a former sepoy of the 'Indre ka pultun (52d N.I.)', decided to migrate in the belief that he was continuing in the service of the British *'sahib log ka kotee'* (government or company work). Having served his indenture overseas, he was philosophical about the experience: 'I am very willing to go back to Mauritius, it is a very beautiful country; but the Frenchmen are very bad. Give me food, and I am very willing to go.'

A Recruit

Il était de Tanjore,
Aventurier de l'or
Et tambour-major
> K Torabully, *Chair Corail, Fragments Coolies*, p. 85.

He was from Tanjore
An adventurer seeking gold
And a drummer.

The volume of migration overseas fluctuated according to rival opportunities at home. Thus in the early 1860s when the local tea companies launched a recruiting drive, the emigration agents for the overseas depots reported a slowing down in their admissions due to 'great demand for labourers for Assam and Cachar and the unsparing application of capital in procuring them'. By contrast, in 1865, when the tea planters had scaled down their recruiting operations, and this coincided with a partial failure of crops in some districts of Bengal, a renewed impetus was given to overseas emigration.[17]

A complex combination of local food production problems and labouring opportunities help to explain how and why coolies in some areas made the decision to migrate. Yamin's study of Ratnagiri district has revealed that the highest rates of migration occurred from the khoti or 'landlord-held' villages, which were characterized by 'greater poverty and intra-village inequality'. Moreover, she notes 'the power of the khoti landlords over their tenants increased between 1820 and 1880 as a result of the introduction of British concepts of property to India through the courts'. Thus she concludes that the structure of landholding is a crucial factor in the understanding of the volume of migration from particular regions.[18]

Escaping from Famine into Namelessness

J'étais d'Agamoudia de Cammalas de Pallys de Pallas
J'étais Sheikmoudine Sheikboudou
De Tottys de Vannias de Vellagas
J'ai fui la misère des paillotes de Fyzabad
De Cavares d'Ambalcacas

A la liste j'ajoute l'absence des pluies
A Rajpoutra Sourane
La raréfaction des grains ou disettes
D'Arcot de Tinnevely de Chinglepet
Et les archives des miettes
Qui me privèrent du combustible de mon nom.

K Torabully, *Chair Corail, Fragments Coolies*, p. 52.

I was from Agamoudia, Cammalas, of Pallys, of Pallas
I was Sheikmoudine Sheikboudou
Of Tottys of Vannias of Vellagas
I fled the misery of the straw-huts of Fyzabad
Of Cavares of Ambalcacas

To the list I can add the drought
In Rajpoutra Sourane
The rarefaction of grain and famine
In Arcot in Tinnevely in Chinglepet
And the archives of dust
Which deprived me of the fuel of my name.

The role of natural disaster in sponsoring emigration has been remarked upon by numerous studies of Indian economic history. In September 1849 French recruiters looking for coolies on the Coringhy coast found no difficulty in amassing recruits at a time when floods had ravaged the delta and starvation was stalking the countryside. Even when the local British Collector intercepted the French contingent and interrogated the migrants, most persisted in the wish to go overseas. In 1854 one of the colonial Emigration Agents at Madras noted that 'the failure of the North East monsoon rains of 1853 having been followed by a similar drought in June and July, the natives of the grain districts abandoned their lands in large numbers'.[19]

Ramalingum testified that problems occasioned by drought conditions in his home district precipitated his migration to Mauritius in the late 1830s:

'I am a pulley by caste and a cultivator of the village of
Tharannore, lying to the west of Trichinopoly, about the distance
of an Indian mile. About six years ago, there was a scarcity of rain
and I was obliged to quit my country in search of work . . . I went
to Trichinopoly where a Maistry of the name of Appavoo told me
that he was going to Pondicherry with a number of Coolies for
the Mauritius, and that if I wished to accompany him there, he
would give me five rupees per mensem beside one measure of

rice per day . . . my circumstances obliged me to agree to the terms, and to join the party of Appavoo, which consisted of thirty persons . . . Appavoo took us all to Pondicherry, whence we were shipped for the Mauritius thro' the means of one Curpayee, a rich female of that place.'

The notion that the Indian peasant preferred overseas indenture to life as a poverty-stricken labourer at home is articulated in this folk song from northwestern India:

Born in India, we are prepared to go to Fiji,
Or, if you please, to Natal to dig in the mines.
We are prepared to suffer there,
But brothers! Don't make us labourers here.

B V Lal, Girmitiyas: The Origins of the Fiji Indians,
Canberra, 1983, p. 88.

Whatever the causal factors, once a migratory stream was established, the steady trickle home of returnees, particularly those with savings, often sufficed to induce others to follow them. Juggon, who returned from Mauritius in 1860 to recruit his fellow villagers, was one of many men in the service of overseas planters who helped to maintain the momentum of indentured migration: 'I am a return Mauritius Cooly. About a month since I left Gyah with 17 coolies whom I had collected for the Mauritius Depot in Calcutta . . . I prefer Mauritius to Demerara or Trinidad because I am acquainted with the place and have a brother there'. Some returnee recruiters made several trips to different colonies. At Chittoor, the emigration inspector, Manley, came across a returnee named Chengleray Naidoo collecting more emigrants. The man had already been to Mauritius, Bourbon and Guadeloupe, accompanying his recruits. He held a recruiter's licence and lived in the Madras suburbs.[20]

Gill Yamin's study of labour migration from the district of Ratnagiri in Maharashtra notes that chain migration seems to be part of the explanation for the high rate of migration from the district: 'there is convincing, if scattered and anecdotal, evidence to suggest that a process of "chain migration" was developing in the district in the nineteenth century, with family and village members following each other in the same migration route.' She reveals that it was not the lowest, untouchable castes that migrated in the greatest numbers, but rather the main agricultural castes, Maratha and Kunbi, which is borne out by data from the immigration archives in Mauritius.[21] Under the influence of returnees, therefore, by the mid-nineteenth century a broad sweep of castes and classes was consenting to emigrate.[21]

The influence of relatives and returnees is apparent from the depositions of indentured labourers. Chummun was one of a band of twenty who set out for Mauritius on the advice of 'a relative of mine who had just returned from that Colony.' Moorzan had made several trips home to Calcutta and with her brother had recruited numbers of her countrymen and women. Jhurry declared that he was recruiting his villagers on behalf of the plantation owners where he had worked for ten years to repay their kindness to him. However, his brother who had left Arrah to join him had been 'enticed away by an Arkotty who took him to the Trinidad Depot. I endeavoured to communicate with my brother, but was prevented by the Arkotty who had charge of him. I have heard that my brother has been sent away to Trinidad'.[22]

The degree of effort which migrants, particularly returnees, were prepared to make to re-emigrate to a particular colony is exemplified by the story of Cassiram Juggurnath. Sent back from Mauritius with another nine men to recruit in Bombay, they arrived with their wives and families there only to find that the depot had been closed, and emigration from that port suspended. The recruiters and their bands remained for almost three months in Bombay waiting for a ship that might be able to take them to Mauritius. During this time, one of the ten recruiters died, and another declined to continue. With no passage to the island forthcoming, the eight remaining recruiters resolved to travel to Calcutta on foot. They set out in November 1855, but after a quarrel broke out amongst them at Nassick, Cassiram Juggurnath returned to Bombay. He was eventually embarked on the *Futtay Mobarak* in 1856.

The reverse scenario demonstrates the importance of returnees in sponsoring further chain migrations. After a series of severe epidemics had decimated the population of Mauritius combined with a decline in economic prospects resulting from falling sugar prices, the news of the colony's problems did not take long to circulate among would-be migrants in India. In 1871, the colony's Emigration Agent at Madras was reporting 'I am sorry to say that . . . there is a growing dislike towards the island, from malicious reports circulated by disaffected return emigrants.'[23]

Disaffected return coolies could thus effectively spike chain migration. Their information quickly spread rumours about adverse events in the colony – demonstrating the effectiveness of coolie information networks. Muthusamy, a sirdar from Natal who was sent back to India to recruit his countrymen ruefully reported that he had manage to collect only seven Indians:

'I would have done better if one Venkatachalam had not arrived in my village in the meantime from Natal. He was drawing there 4s. a month. He returned about two months ago. He told the villagers [about] the present agitation in Natal. He warned the villagers to take care of their children, chiefly young women. He made the people believe that some sirdars are purposely come to India to take away from their kith and kin some young women of fair complexion to get rich husbands in Natal, and thereby get some large amount. This was a talk all over.'[24]

Munusamy Naidu, another sirdar from Natal, who was one of several sent to India to recruit for the colony around 1911, provides a striking testimony of the filtering down of anti-indenture agitation to the Indian villages, and how through his simple honesty he sought to surmount such propaganda efforts:

'In India, everybody – young and old – did spit on sirdars. Sirdars are treated like pariah dogs – not as gentlemen . . . I am not a young man to stand all abuses, to receive kicks and blows from the public. I belong to a respectable family; I do not like to bring on my family any sort of disgrace. I knew fully well that I will be treated most disgracefully and mercilessly if I were to go into the interior villages and interfere with strangers. My master's advice was not to speak untruth, not to exaggerate Natal and its advantages, not to force Indians to emigrate, etc. I spoke to my own people. I told them the whole truth. I secured in April last

some Indians and sent them to my master. I patiently waited in
my village. All the time I was treated by the villagers very
respectably. They knew that I was one of the sirdars. They also
understood that I was not influencing by false statements and
pretences any Indian to emigrate. Of course, Tamil notices,
printed, warning the public not to emigrate to Natal were freely
distributed in my village. These notices did not interfere with my
work. I must admit that these notices contained some true
statements. I do not think I ever induced a stranger to emigrate to
Natal. When time came for my departure to Natal my people
about four quite willingly started with me. No one in the village
raised any sort of objection. I got a name for myself and my
estate.'

Even at times of anti-indenture agitation, returnees could influence close
relations to migrate. As V Sampson reported, on returning to India in
1911, in the midst of agitation against emigration: 'I thought that my stay
in India will be of no good at all. I asked my wife to go with me to Natal.
First she refused. Gradually by kind words I got round her and she came
my way. Through her I got her sister and two more Indians to emigrate.
I told my wife and her above relations that we are going to a place called
Natal, which is a paradise.'

Whatever their motivations, returnee and sirdar recruiters could only
take their recruits to the relevant depots – there was still bureaucracy to
be undergone and, it was alleged, foul play afoot and bribery and cor-
ruption galore. A Mauritian sirdar, Matadoo, complained in 1864 that,
having recruited seventeen men, he was obliged to pay a bribe to the
Madras contractor, Soobrayen, in order to get his men admitted to the
emigration depot at the port:

'All the coolies who wish to come to Mauritius have to apply to
Soobrayen or Barthe Sadoo, who are called contractors and
sometimes Perria Maistries (Great Recruiters). They divide and
engage the men as they like. Mr Burton (the Emigration Agent)
knows nothing about their doings. He employs them and pays
them; but he probably does not know how they ill-treat and
cheat the emigrants who pass through his office. They are
supreme masters in the office. Six of my men were put into other

gangs against my will. I consented because I was told that I would otherwise not be allowed to embark.'

If the destiny of the migrant was an uncertain one, the lot of the family left behind was in many cases even less enviable. The trauma of relatives left behind is articulated in the following letter received by Jaipal Chamar in Jamaica, from his son in India:

> 'Whenever your letter comes I wish I had wings
> And could fly away to see you.
> Your destitute sister has no one and
> I am looking after her.
> She has gone blind crying for you.
> She now lives only with the hope of
> Seeing her brother's face.
> And my mother after receiving your first letter cried for ten
>   days and died.'[25]

Family separations could last much longer than the initial envisaged period of migration. The five-year contract could become a ten-year renewal, and migrants frequently stayed on in the overseas colonies, re-indenturing or acquiring property and a profession. When Ramotar's brother finally caught up with him in Mauritius, after an absence of three decades, he was understandably anxious to claim him:

> 'Having heard that my brother has come to Mauritius as a Coolee,
> I have, most respectfully come to see you about his delivery. He is
> the only brother I have, and I have not seen him for upwards of
> thirty years. I have a great desire to take him with me;
>   I have therefore most humbly come to see you and beg to
> inform you that I will pay for his delivery, what a proprietor will
> pay to take him. I earnestly beg you to let me have him instead of
> a proprietor for he is the only brother I have.'

Folk songs are another rich source of anecdotal information of attitudes towards migration and the pain of those left behind. A folksong from Uttar Pradesh bemoans the poverty that was often the lot of those who lost a close relative to the emigrant ship:

'From the east came the rail, from the west came the ship,
And took my beloved one away . . .
The rail is not my enemy, nor the ship,
O! It is money which is the real enemy,
It takes my beloved one from place to place.'[26]

Another song recounts the anguished childlessness of a woman whose husband has migrated:

'All my friends have become mothers,
And I remain lonely and childless . . .
For twelve years you haven't written a word . . .'[27]

A third song depicts a woman toiling alone in the fields:

'Here, in these lonely fields,
I, the unfortunate, alone work,
My lord being in a distant land,
Who will tell me "Thy lord has come"
The day of my happiness has dawned.'[28]

With no ransom
We deploy clouds
At random:
The first words fell
On the pebbles
On the dust
On the storms.
And my dove lost in a flash of lightning
Anchored my dreams in ether's keel.
Anjali said the nave is a wrecker
Of our precipitated departures
Before the splayed handkerchief
Of a nail gobbler
Of a sabre swallower
Of an ember walker.

K Torabully, *Cale d'Etoiles.*

The Sea Voyage

For those migrants recruited fraudulently, hoping for work in India, the sea voyage was an object of fear. While some Hindus believed that crossing the *kala pani* or black waters would lead to a loss of caste, others, from inland villages, who had never before seen the sea, were simply terrified of boarding an ocean-going vessel. Abheeram's deposition, in 1843, provides an illustration of the depth of this fear. Like many caste Hindus, he refused to take cooked food while on the journey of several weeks, subsisting on a meagre diet of grain and uncooked rice. A native of Cuttack and a cultivator, Abheeram had accepted a job offer, which he believed to be in Calcutta. Discovering that he was bound for the Mauritius he recounted:

'. . . on my way to the ship I refused to go but the Duffadars told me that there was no fear as the Mauritius was only eight days' journey. I told the Duffadar Bulram Singh that I would never venture going on shipboard. He told me to keep quiet and to tell the Sahebs if questioned that I was going of my own free will and accord and to convince me that there was no fear. He the Duffadar said that he would go on the same ship with me to the Mauritius. As long as I remained on board I lived on the Chorah that I had got and occasionally a small quantity of dry rice.'

Radhamohun Das, of Tripura, steadfastly refused the temptation to eat food cooked on board by men who were not of his caste: 'while on board – I subsisted on the Choorah that I had, occasionally rice cooked by Musselmans was offered to me which I refused to take, being a hindoo I would not consent to lose my caste'. So traumatized by the experience was he that Das pleaded to be allowed to go home: 'I beg permission to be allowed to return to my country where I would prefer going door to door begging for my livelihood yet would not consent to go to the Mauritius.' Purtaub Singh of Orissa likewise stressed that he had had not intention of going 'to such a distance at the risk of losing my life and my caste'.

Mahadai Das recalls the notorious names of the first ships that transported the 'Gladstone' coolies in the mid-1830s to Guyana:

'From across the seas, they came.
Britain, colonising India, transporting her chains
From Chota Nagpur and the Ganges Plain.
Westwards came the Whitby,
The Hesperus,
The island-bound Fatel Rozack.
Wooden missions of imperialist design.
Human victims of her Majesty's victory.'[29]

Hands beat against water
Hands beat a rhythm against waves

Hands are hardly wet in water
They sweat – oil of body and skin

Pores, pores
Against crystal water

Etchings of waves
Register the crossing

'Atlantic Song' by Cyril Dabydeen in
India in the Caribbean, 1987, p. 295.

Arnold Itwaru has likened the voyage of coolies to the middle passage of slave journeys:

'Middle-passaged
Passing
Beneath the colouring of desire
In the enemy's eye
A scatter of worlds and broken wishes
In Shiva's unending dance.'

Even where migrants were aware that the journey on which they were embarking necessitated a sea voyage, the length of the trip, several weeks to the Indian Ocean colonies in the mid-nineteenth century, and longer for Pacific and West Indian islands, was a shock to many, and unaccustomed as they were to life on the ocean, spent in often miserable conditions. A song from Surinam remembers the difficult time of the voyage:

'Several months on the ship passed with great difficulty,
On the seven dark seas, we suffered unaccustomed
      problems.'[30]

Mon pays n'aura pas de statue
de l'homme d'orage aux pieds nus
J'ai brisé ma langue contre mémoire
quand la nuit trichait avec la mort
au jeu des bateaux et des ports.

K Torabully, *Cale d'Etoiles Coolitude*, p. 16.

My country will have no statue
Of the man of storm with bare feet
I broke my tongue against memory
When night cheated against death
At the toss of boats and ports.

It was not uncommon, in the early years of indenture, for migrants to hurl themselves off the ship while still in the Hughli river, and cases of men lost overboard feature regularly in ship logs. After a few weeks, the temptation to get off whenever the ship docked in a port proved overwhelming. In 1860, when the *Junon*, bound for Martinique, docked at Reunion, the Indians, suffering already from want of food on the lengthy voyage, understandably expressed a desire to disembark. They went on hunger strike, until the captain was obliged to intervene and put down the mutiny with vigorous measures.[31]

The Sea-Journey to the Antilles

Vos navires à voile lézardaient
La torpeur équatoriale. Saletés
Aux escales du Cap et Sainte Hélène;
Epidemies flanquaient rictus a la Mort émaciée.
Ma quarantaine aux îles des Saintes
Prolongea vos 100 jours de l'Inde aux Antilles –
Je dis voyage entre giraumons et salaisons
Poisson salé chutney carri de poisson.

K Torabully, *Chair Corail, Fragments Coolies*, p. 61.

Your sailboats crawled
Through the equatorial torpor. Grim
Stop-overs at the Cape and St Helena;
Epidemics engendering emaciated death
In quarantine at the isles of the Saints
Prolonging the 100-day passage from India to the Caribbean.
I say voyage between pumpkins and salted fish
Snoek chutney and fish curry.

The loss of caste and the discomfort of sea-sickness were not the only fears which preoccupied the nineteenth-century indentured migrants. Fire and wrecking on treacherous reefs or in heavy storms stalked the emigrant ships. In 1851 the *Kurramany*, carrying 354 migrants from Calcutta, caught fire while still in the Hughli river. Setting out in a steam ship, some hours later, searching for survivors, Dr McClelland described the west shore of Saugor island as 'literally strewed with dead bodies.' He counted 80 or 90 at that spot alone. Only 97 recruits escaped the conflagration.[32]

Shipwreck

Everything slackens in a wreck:
So many coal porters wash their necks
In dawn's smouldering specks.

K Torabully, *Cale d'Etoiles*.

In the following poem S Nandan harks back to a coolie voyage on the *Syria* in 1884 that ended in disaster when the ship was wrecked:

> 'O my children's children
> Listen to the voices from the Syria
> Drowning the silence of the sea!'[33]

A Death on the Voyage

Je veux parler pour le frère mort
Jeté par-dessus bord.
Il venait de Bengalore,
Rêvait d'un meilleur sort
Au pays de l'aurore.

K Torabully, *Chair Corail, Fragments Coolies*, p. 85.

I want to speak out for my dead brother
Thrown overboard.
He came from Bangalore
Dreamt of a better life
In the land of promises galore.

Totaram Sanadyha, who wrote a memoir of his indenture experiences in Fiji, described the voyage in the following terms: 'Twice a day we were given a bottle of water each to drink. Then no more, even if we died of thirst. It was the same about food. Fish and rice were both cooked there. Many people suffered from sea-sickness. Those who died were thrown overboard . . . After three months and twelve days we reached Fiji.'[34]

Migrant Epiphany

Shadows whisper when clouds flutter:
All comes to a halt to tell the heart of my trial.
When night was a tabla of flesh
I was made to see the staircase of shells.
I grasped the real reason of my voyages.

K Torabully, *Cale d'Etoiles.*

In 'Coolie Odyssey', Dabydeen vividly evokes the arrival of a boatload of coolies in the Caribbean, contrasting their high hopes with their wretched appearance:

> 'The first boat chugged to the muddy port
> Of King George's Town. Coolies come to rest
> In El Dorado,
> Their faces and best saries black with soot.
> The men smelt of saltwater mixed with rum. The odyssey was
>   plank between river and land,
> Mere yards but months of plotting
> In the packed bowel of a white man's boat
> The years of promise, years of expanse.'[35]

Whilst indentured migration differed from the slave diaspora in that the separation of families was the exception rather than the rule, there were cases where, often due to illness of one family member, spouses or parents and children were separated. When Narayanan was allotted to Umzimkulu estate in Natal around January 1907, his wife and young daughter were kept at the immigration depot on account of illness. By September of that year he was extremely anxious as to their whereabouts:

> 'To this day I am ignorant of the whereabouts of my wife and
> child, or as to whether they are living or dead.
>   I have often enquired, week after week, from my employers,
> and they have said they know nothing about her . . .'

He stressed that she was not a concubine, but 'my legal wife, married in my native village of Thenani, Thirunamallai, North Arcot, and I am therefore suffering day and night untold agony in thinking of my wife and little one.' No one had thought to tell Narayanan that his wife and child had been repatriated to India in April 1907 as 'invalids'. Whether he ever caught up with them again is not recorded.[36]

The Tears of Exile

For the commemoration of lost dreams
The ship is preceded by unseasoned tears.
It will deliver its cargo
Of bodies through a soft incision of the horizon.
Deep in the hold, which eyes
Can unload despair
Without leaking water everywhere?

K Torabully, Cale d'Etoiles.

Arriving single women were often kept at the depot until single men, looking for a wife, claimed and were accepted by them. In other cases women were assigned to specific plantations where indentured labourers would be expected to take up with them. Maharani, a Brahmin widow in Trinidad, described her reluctant 'courtship', arranged through the mediation of the plantation manager:

> 'Maharani you want de man
> I say no
> E say why
> I say
> I go go India
> Just so I tell him
> E say y fall sick an ting
> You have no body
> You have to take somebody . . .'[37]

In my ship's hold nudging the stars,
You knew waves would weave me
To the furthest instant of my destiny
Beyond you, me and myself.

In your eyes moistened by sea mist
You reclaimed a land – you shouted hell
Without many ports for my children,
For all of my kith and kin.

K Torabully, Cale d'Etoiles.

'My wife in saffron
hooked to the nautilus.
My fairy in mehendi
tied to the foams
my love in myrtle
stolen from the fish's wings.

My book of departure
is purer than death . . .'

K Torabully, Cale d'Etoiles.

'Coolie's dreams are pulley's rust
Scattered from ropes to rolling wreck'

K Torabully, Cale d'Etoiles.

2

Thrice Victimized:
Casting the Coolie

The coolie has always been negatively portrayed. Contemporaries dismissed labour migrants as the 'sweepings of Calcutta's slums'; the contracts they signed victimized them further, by identifying them as a societal 'other' – a prey to prison, pariahs amongst free men. As coolies settled in the countries which had imported them as plantation labourers, they began to feature in literary accounts, but were always redolent of exoticism, images of alienness, barbarism and fatalism casting them permanently in their lowly agricultural role. The hindsight of historians has served the coolies little better: they have been assigned the status of 'neo-slave', stripped of caste, culture, even of family in some accounts. This chapter deconstructs the changing stereotype of the coolie.

Contemporary Views of the Coolie

The overseas Indian labourer entered the perception of the colonial planter and administrator in the early decades of the nineteenth century as it became clear, from increasing agitation in Britain, that slavery as a system was doomed. Intellectuals of the period, however, were convinced that European men were constitutionally incapable of dealing with labour in tropical climates. Earl Grey's comments typify the thinking of the period on this matter:

'In all European countries, the necessity of supplying their daily wants is, to the labouring classes, a sufficient motive to exertion. But the case is very different in tropical climates, where the population is very scanty in proportion to the extent of territory; where the soil . . . readily yields a subsistence in return for very little labour; and where clothing, fuel, and lodging, such as are there required, are obtained very easily. In such circumstances there can be but little motive to exertion, to men satisfied with an abundant supply of their mere physical wants, and accordingly experience proves that it is the disposition of the races of men by which these countries are generally inhabited, to sink into an easy and listless mode of life, quite incompatible with the attainment of any high degree of civilization.'[1]

British Indian Official Perceptions of the Migrant Coolie

Colonial officials quickly adopted an attitude of 'laissez faire' with regard to the emigration of Indian labour. With the abolition of slavery in the British empire looming, Mauritius and British Guyana were the first of the sugar colonies to recruit Indian workers through agency houses in Calcutta. Some opposition was voiced by reformers within India, and by the Anti-Slavery Society in Britain, but the Indian Government maintained a staunchly neutral stance on the migration throughout most of the period of the operation of the indenture system.

Despite the increasing evidence of the existence of forms of slavery on the subcontinent itself, Indian migrants were invariably considered to be 'free' labour. This made their importation more attractive to colonial planters who thereby avoided the stigma associated with the recruitment of Africans who were generally suspected of being former or actual slaves. Even that most ardent defender of the rights of the slave, assiduous Colonial Office man James Stephen, considered that the matter of Indian migration could be left to proceed unregulated, although he disavowed the use of compulsion:

'If free labourers will come and work, no one can doubt that it would be a great advantage. But it seems that the difficulty is that when they come, they will not execute their agreement . . . Now to have recourse to any sort of compulsory labour in the persons of immigrants resorting to the island, would be so pregnant with danger, that I suppose it cannot be thought of . . . There is no law to prevent the introduction of free labourers into Mauritius; and thither they will assuredly resort, if wages sufficiently tempting, are to be earned. I see no room for legislation on the subject.'[2]

The Indian Government of the day by and large echoed the laissez-faire attitudes of the Colonial Office. The Indian Law Commissioners ruled in 1836:

'It does not appear that any complaint of ill-treatment has been
received from any of the natives of India who went to Mauritius,
or that there is any reason to believe that they have been ill-
treated. Besides ascertaining that such emigrants go voluntarily,
and with a knowledge of the conditions to which they subscribe,
measures have been taken, at the request of Government of
Mauritius to make known to them, before they quit India or even
their own districts the regulations to which they become subject
on their arrival in that island, the only colony under a British
Government to which it appears that any such emigration has
taken place. On the whole the Commissioners are of opinion that
with respect to emigrants to British or foreign settlements beyond
the sea no legislation is advisable except what may be required
for the purpose of supporting precautionary arrangements, such
as have been already made, to prevent undue advantage being
taken of the simplicity and ignorance of those persons.'[3]

This view was challenged in Calcutta, where reformers were numerous,
and where migration of Indians was denounced as a renewed slave trade.
An article in a Calcutta newspaper deprecated what it called 'The
Kidnapping Coolie Trade Revived': 'Young men and even women are
decoyed away and put out of their senses, and then either robbed, sold as
slaves or shipped.'[4]

The Calcutta Commission of Enquiry Report, published at the close
of a decade of merchant-organized labour migration, was effectively a
devastating critique of the entire system of shipping of coolies to
Mauritius and the West Indies. It challenged the Wakefieldian assumption that the impoverished, over-populated masses of a country, in this
case India, would automatically benefit by transposition to a colony
where labour was at a greater premium:

'We believe that a general persuasion exists in England, both in
Parliament and out of it, that there is a superabundance of labour
in British India. As far as this presidency is concerned (of which
alone we can speak with any knowledge of facts), we are by no
means convinced that such supposed superabundance exists, but
are rather persuaded that the contrary is the fact, and would soon
become apparent if any decided stimulus were given to

agricultural production, such as the late rise in the prices of sugar has temporarily created, and if such stimulus were continued for a sufficiently long period to make it extensively felt . . . We are convinced, in fine, that no laws or regulations likely to be passed . . . will suffice to prevent great misery and distress, even on this side of the Cape, and that if West Indian voyages be permitted, the waste of human life and misery that will fall on the Coolies exported under the name of free labourers will approach to those inflicted on the negro in the middle passage by the slave trade . . . It seems to us that the permission to renew this traffic would weaken the moral influence of the British Government throughout the world, and deaden or utterly destroy the effect of all future remonstrances and negotiations respecting the slave trade; and this effect would ensue, however stringent, minute or restrictive might be the regulations framed to check abuses. Regulations would be met by other regulations, specious and unobjectionable in form; the difference would be in the execution and in the good faith of the farmers.'[5]

The Bombay authorities, however, while recognizing the potential for trickery in the execution of contracts between agents and 'ignorant villagers', were inclined to accept the view that migration had been conducted by respectable parties and that abuses had been kept to a minimum. Pointing to the re-migration of individuals who had returned from periods of indentured labour in Mauritius to India, they effectively asserted that Indians were exercising free choice in indenturing:

'We have the satisfaction to report that there is no reason to believe the exportation of these people from this port to have hitherto been attended with the smallest abuse, or that the existing laws and regulations for their protection have not in every instance been fully acted up to. The highly respectable character indeed of the parties by whom, and for whom, all the labourers have been shipped from this port (to which their exportation from this side of India has as yet been entirely confined, as will be seen from the accompanying copies of the agreements and registers recorded in the police office) is in itself a strong assurance of such being the fact . . . As a striking corroboration too of the conclusion we have arrived at, we cannot omit to mention that several time-expired labourers who have recently returned from the Isle of France, would appear to have again embarked for that colony, under the same engagement as before . . . We cannot disguise from ourselves the apprehension that should the importation of these people increase so much as to lead to their being brought for that purpose from the interior, where they are of course more ignorant, or should it extend to the subordinate ports, or the business of engaging them pass into other hands at the port of Bombay, abuses are not unlikely to creep into it, which no regulation can wholly prevent, and under any circumstances, it is one which will always require to be very narrowly watched.'[6]

The reasoned opinions of the Bombay Committee, and the favourable impressions conveyed by those British Indian civil servants who had visited Mauritius and seen at first hand the living and working conditions of indentured labourers, helped to ensure that the watershed decision to permit Indian indentured migration with government blessing and under government control was facilitated in Britain. Major Archer was one of a number of British civil servants recruited by the planting and mercantile interests to support the scheme of Indian labour migration – viewed as crucial to maintaining the position of the sugar colonies, given the decline in the numbers of ex-slaves remaining in that sector after liberation. In his anxiety to bolster the prospects of business partners and friends, Major Archer depicted Mauritius as a veritable El Dorado for the impoverished Indian migrant:

'. . . long residence in India, and an intimate acquaintance with the natives of that country, together with adequate knowledge of the Mauritius (from frequent visits) and also of the nature and character of the husbandry in that island, have enabled me to form the opinion that, their condition as labourers at the Mauritius, would under fitting regulations, not only be materially improved, but would undoubtedly be as prosperous, as any belong to a labouring class . . . labour at the Mauritius offers to the native of India, an infinitely higher remuneration for his service than he can ever expect it to bear in his own country . . . a

sum large enough to arouse in the minds of their village friends
and neighbours, the notion of the travellers having visited the
fabled land of riches, the El Dorado probably of the Spaniards.'[7]

The Anti-Slavery Society made a last ditch attempt to prevent the
resumption of indentured migration, depicting the coolie villager as too
ignorant to be allowed into the clutches of the planters: 'The Coolie
knows as much – nay less – of this world, than any intelligent man does
of the moon . . . That the Coolie does not understand the nature of his
engagement is admitted by all . . . to commit men helpless and ignorant
into the hands of cunning and arbitrary men, the old slave proprietors of
the Mauritius, is [not] the way to improve their moral and physical
good, or to secure their liberty.' However, their protests were to no
avail. The momentous act of permitting indentured migration under
government control (first to Mauritius, in 1843, and successively to
other West Indian colonies from 1846 onwards, with the French colonies
and Fiji joining the scheme in the 1860s and 1870s respectively) was jus-
tified by senior British statesmen such as Lord John Russell in the
following terms:

> 'There seems no sufficient ground for prohibiting the Indian
> labourer in search of employment from seeking that employment
> in Mauritius. The climate is more healthy generally speaking than
> that from which the labourer is taken – the communication with
> India easy and frequent, the food adapted to the physical
> constitution of the Indian, and where a fair bargain is struck the
> comforts and mode of living of the immigrant are improved by
> the transfer of his labour.'[8]

Despite all evidence to the contrary, British Indian officials continued to
assert that the natives of India were not 'naturally migratory': 'the Hindu
has little of the migratory instinct, and all his prejudices tend to keep him
at home. As a resident member of a tribe, caste or village, he occupies a
definite social position, of which emigration is likely to deprive him.'
Crooke painted a picture of the Indian migrant dying in exile who would
be forced to 'wander through the ages a starving, suffering, malignant
ghost, because his obsequies have not been duly performed'.[9] The stereotype of the cupiditous recruiter and the helpless coolie was summarized

by the district magistrate of Ghazipur in 1871 when he described how migrants were ensnared:

> 'The *arkatias* entice the villagers with a wonderful account of their place for which the emigrants are wanted and bring their victims from long distances . . . On arrival at the sub depot, the intending emigrants are told the exact facts of their prospects, and on hearing them, decline to proceed . . . The wretched coolie may be a hundred miles from his home, and finding that he has the option of returning penniless . . . and of emigrating, chooses the latter alternative; but this is not voluntary emigration.'[10]

As the indenture system expanded and flourished over the nineteenth century, stereotypes of the 'helpless coolie as victim' gained a wide circulation. Transmuted to the sugar estates of the British Empire, the 'docility' of the Indian coolie, and his relative lack of ambition, became the official explanations for the seemingly smooth running of what was deemed an essentially coercive institution. How else could officials square the myth of 'kidnap' with the evidence of re-indenture and remigration? Writing in 1883, George Grierson contrasted the Indian with the Chinese character in this respect: 'A Chinaman's idea is to serve till he has saved sufficient to start himself as an independent rival to the planter. The Indian coolie's aspirations . . . seldom rise beyond his being a well-paid coolie servant, and nothing more.'[11]

On the sugar estates, the coolie was seen to have little free will, and to be trapped as effectively as if he were a prisoner. Edward Jenkins, who visited Guyana during the indenture period, described the Indian world on the sugar estate as one in which workers were kept in 'absolute heathen ignorance'. A British official in Guyana summarized the status of the indentured labourer as follows: 'Practically an immigrant is in the hands of the employer to whom he is bound. He cannot leave him; he cannot live without work; he can only get such work and on such terms as the employer chooses to set him; and all these necessities were enforced, not only by the inevitable influence of his isolated and dependent position, but by the terrors of imprisonment.'[12]

If Indian males under indenture were seen as drudges, content to toil for life on plantations, even to bear whippings with few visible signs of discontent, they were widely perceived to be volcanic and unrelenting in their personal relationships. The 'coolie wife murders' – cases in which allegedly 'jealous' husbands had killed their common-law spouses over infidelities – spread across the spectrum of colonial societies that received indentured labourers, and added much to European assumptions of the barbarism of Indian males and their treatment of women as their 'property'. Indian women, for their part, were not considered blameless in official eyes. It was frequently contended that one of the causes of the high ratio of wife murders was the 'low character' of migrant women. Respectable women would not cross the sea, it was believed, and coolie females were classed as starving widows, absconded or abandoned wives and prostitutes. The Protector of Emigrants at Madras dismissed the character of migrant women in the following terms, and his views may be seen as typical:

> 'There are few married men who take with them their wives and children, and I am certain that many of the women who say they are married to particular men are not their wives, as they very often take up with other men in the depot before their embarkation . . . As to the so-called single women, many of them are prostitutes, others are kept women, and the remainder after entering the depot in almost every case attach themselves to some man they meet there. No female of good character emigrates, except with her husband, father, mother or some very near relation.'[13]

The returning Indian, however, was, by some metamorphosis transformed from his customary docility and fatalism on his return to his homeland. Indian colonial officials viewed migration as a branch of the civilizing mission of the British in India and the overseas Indian was depicted as an individual liberated from a feudal relationship with the zamindar – presumably into the more 'modern' dependence on a capitalist producer – and from the 'prejudices' of native religion and customs. The returning indentured labourer was considered to have been trained out of customary indolence and backward ways of life by his exposure to western practices, and was praised for:

> '. . . the intelligence, freedom from prejudice, knowledge of improved modes of agriculture, and habits of industry brought

back by the return coolie to his benighted home . . . there was a shrewdness, spirit of independence, and worldly wisdom about the most intelligent of them, that would never permit them again to submit quietly to the crushing, heartless oppression, and utter selfishness of native zamindars, of whose tender mercies they had acquired a most correct and wholesome estimate.'[14]

Planters' Depictions of Indian Labourers

At the onset of the indenture period, planters extolled the virtues of the Indian immigrants whom they took such pains to encourage to migrate to their sugar estates. The advantages of emigration were painstakingly enumerated to convince the British that the establishment and maintenance of the indenture system were mutually advantageous to the employer, the labourer and the sending and receiving countries alike. Attempting to convince the British government to permit the resumption of Indian migration to Mauritius after its suspension in 1839, a group of Mauritian planters asserted that:

'. . . the introduction of Indian labourers into this island must be beneficial to India, by not only ridding her of her superabundant population, but by providing her with a future supply of workmen, who will have acquired here a competent skill and knowledge in the cultivation and manipulation of the sugar cane; as their emigration here is unquestionably advantageous to themselves, by their procuring higher wages, in a climate more healthy than their own, and by their removal from a country where, under Hindu and Mahommedan law, some degree of qualified slavery is still supposed to exist, to an island from whence its last vestige has for ever disappeared; as the supply of labour from India for this colony must benefit the empire at large, by the increase of the produce of sugar, and consequent augmentation to an immense amount in the custom dues on its importation to the ports of Great Britain, and, lastly, as the sudden suppression of the supply of manual labour from India, coming at the same critical moment with the equally sudden suppression of the Negro apprenticeship, must work the total ruin of your memorialists, striking a death blow to the commercial and agricultural prosperity of this important island, your petitioners therefore humbly pray, that Your Majesty will be graciously pleased to take this their humble representation into Your Majesty's royal consideration.'[15]

The Governor of Guadeloupe echoed sentiments of officials in other sugar colonies when he wrote back to the France that *'les Indiens se font remarquer par leur douceur et leur soumission* (The Indians are remarkable for their gentleness and submissiveness)'.[16.] However, as the numbers of arriving Indians increased, the concern of employers shifted from a desire to increase immigration to the perceived need to enforce 'discipline'. In this changed environment, the rhetoric and stereotype of the Indian also changed, and by the mid-nineteenth century, colonial newspapers were describing the indentured labourers as:

'Vagrants, people mostly without even a name (as their tickets carry those of others who sent them in their place), people without any education or principles . . . nomads, practically savages . . . a real invasion of barbarians . . . parias, the refuse of Indian society.'[17]

A traveller in mid-nineteenth century Reunion was struck by the anti-Indian sentiments revealed in the local press which declared that there had never been so many criminal incidents, even in the days of slavery, as were being committed after the arrival of Indians: *'A aucune époque, lit-on dans les journaux de la Colonie . . . même dans les plus mauvais temps de l'esclavage, le pays n'eut à gémir de forfaits si nombreux et si divers que depuis l'immigration indienne* (At no time, the colonial newspapers report, even in the worst time of slavery, has the country had to suffer incidents as numerous and as diverse, as have occurred since Indian immigration began.)'[18]

Along with the changed climate of opinion, there emerged a series of repressive laws across the sugar colonies, designed to stem the flood of ex-indentured Indians from staying on as free men, establishing themselves in petty commerce or as small planters. The 'docile coolie' who became an aspiring planter was not a welcome sight in the societies that had welcomed him as a labourer. At the same time, in colonies such as Mauritius, where by the 1860s an over-supply of labour was combined with a depression in the sugar industry, the slide into poverty of the indentured Indian, and the resulting rise in criminal convictions, produced a wave of hostility against men now perceived to be involved in 'thuggee'. Having resorted to a cheap immigration strategy, the resulting problems of urban overcrowding, immiseration and the spread of disease were blamed upon the very coolies planters had recruited in such vast numbers. The stereotype of the Indian as the bearer of disease, whose insanitary lifestyle was compounded by his unhealthy customs, became rampant:

'*Les habitudes des indiens rendent plus difficile l'exécution des lois et des mesures sanitaires. A Port Louis ils forment des agglomérations entassées dans des demeures insuffisantes, mal ventilées et malpropres. Dans les villages ils vivent souvent mêlés a leurs animaux et négligent les règles de l'hygiène.Ils contribuent à augmenter la mortalité générale et l'instrusité des épidémies qui sévissent de temps en temps parmi nous.* (The habits of Indians make the implementation of sanitary laws and measures more difficult. In Port Louis they are crowded in insufficiently large, poorly ventilated and dirty houses. In the villages they often share their dwellings with their animals and ignore basic rules of hygiene. They contribute to general mortality increases and to the occasional outbreaks of epidemics among us.)'[19]

In societies where the local legislators were generally also the representatives and often the relatives of planters, prospects for the coolie became bleak. Chief Justice Beaumont confessed in his memoirs that he was haunted by the malnourished indentured labourers he had seen in Demerara: 'creatures so worn by illness and starvation as to appear at first sight actual skeletons, every bone visible, perfectly fleshless, their legs appearing like long stilts, their very buttocks almost entirely exposed and worn to the bone, and the faces showing the terrible appearance of a skeleton's head, only lighted up in their great hollow orbits by eyes that yet reflected a dull glimmer.' A member of the Trinidad Legislative Council noted in 1910 that the planter was committed to maintaining the status quo in continuing to prefer bound rather than free labour: 'What he wants is an indentured labourer – not so much a labourer as an indentured labourer . . . somebody who is

bound to him for 5 years, and liable to be committed to prison for dis-
obeying orders.'[20]

Despite the pressure upon him to reindenture, the Indian in the
colonies was quietly buying himself out of his contract and establishing
himself on marginal lands in his new guise of gardener and small planter.
A member of the Mauritian plantocracy observed this process at the
close of the nineteenth century: '*Toutes les terres délaissées, soit qu'elles se
trouvent dans les quartiers secs, ou qu'elles sont placées dans des régions
généralement considérées comme impropres a la canne elle-même, sont,
aujourd'hui, dans les mains des Indiens.* (All of the abandoned lands,
whether they are in arid districts or in regions generally believed to be
unsuitable for cane cultivation, are, today, in the hands of Indians.)'

However, the coolie turned planter was still believed to be content
with his parcel of land, and unlikely to become a threat to the colony's
commercial interests: '*Il ne s'adressera pas à de grosses affaires, cela n'entre pas dans ses vues, et il n'achète et ne loue ces terres délaissées par le
Mauricien, que pour cette seule raison, qu'il les achète et les loue a bon
marché.* (He will not become involved in big business, that does not
enter his head, he only buys and rents land abandoned by Mauritians for
one reason, because he can buy and rent them cheaply.)'[21]

The notion that the coolie might one day aspire to be more than a
sugar worker, or small cultivator had been held back by the persistence
of stereotypes which denied him aspirations. Only partially redressed following Commissions of Enquiry in Mauritius and the West Indies, the
status of the coolie remained embedded in pauperization and victim-
hood until well into the twentieth century.

Contemporary Travellers' Accounts

A primordial characteristic of the overseas Indian was his cheapness. A
visitor to Mauritius in 1838 stated the case baldly:

'The great, but single superiority which Hindoostan possesses
over the Isle of France, is the exceedingly low price of labour in
the former country, though in a partial extent this benefit will be
neutralized by the introduction of labourers of the Danga caste,
whose wages are, at least, a third less than those of the (blacks).'[22]

However, the immigrant, cheap because over-common and underused in his own country, soon acquired a sense of his value in an overseas context where labour was at a premium. Within a few years of their migration, as this traveller writing in the mid-nineteenth century asserted, this transformation in conduct was all too apparent:

'A visitor from India, accustomed to the quiet demeanour and respectful behaviour of servants and labourers in that country, is apt to be surprised at their cool impudence and nonchalance in Mauritius. They do not hesitate openly to tell their masters that they dare not punish them, and to treat them with an amount of disrespect that would not be tolerated for a moment in their own country . . . The fact is that the coolie is too well treated in the Mauritius. He is well paid, pampered, and all his complaints are listened to, while his master appears to have little redress against the shortcomings of his immigrant labourers. It is nearly as much for the interest of India, as it is for that of the Mauritius, that a more extended immigration of a better class of tillers of the soil should be encouraged. By its means, much wealth is brought by the coolies to be expended in their own country. They come back more robust, manly, and less prejudiced than when they left their homes, and the influence of their acquired knowledge cannot fail to be useful to their own countrymen . . . Nothing can exceed the jealous, anxious, and scrupulous care with which the government of the Mauritius watches over the interests of, and protects the Indian immigrant. If anything, he is spoilt by the almost undue amount of consideration shown to him, and I have not the slightest hesitation in recording my conviction that he is better paid, clothed, fed, and treated in every way, than in any part of India with which I am personally acquainted.'[23]

It did not take much for the 'impudent coolie' to conform, in travellers' accounts, to the 'criminal' stereotype propounded by the planters. Indians in Reunion were depicted as barbarians, bringing with them the vices of an inferior civilization, and despoilers of an 'island Eden': '*les Indiens, en apportant avec eux tous les vices de leur civilisation décrépite, ont transformé, sous ce rapport, comme sous celui de*

la salubrité, ce beau pays que les anciens voyageurs appelaient Eden.
(bringing with them all the vices of their decrepit civilization, the Indians
have ruined this beautiful country which the early visitors likened to
Eden.)'

Even a sympathetic observer like C F Andrews succumbed to the
prevailing view that a significant proportion of coolies were escaped
convicts. He calculated that around ten per cent of migrating Indian
men were likely to be criminals on the run.[24]

The position of the ex-indentured Indian was also being observed, and
the rapidity with which an immigrant could better his position after his
contract had been completed was often remarked upon:

> 'The Indian labourer . . . is the tiller of the ground, and is
> everywhere to be met with. His lot . . . generally speaking, is an
> easy one, his temporal wants being well attended to, and his
> daily task, in general (when he pleases) soon accomplished. He
> seems quite to understand this; and on the expiry of his
> engagement with his employer, either sets an extravagant price
> on his services, if they be required; or cultivates land, and sells
> his produce on his own account; or, returns to his native
> country, with more money and healthier and better clad than
> when he left it.'[25]

The value to colonial societies of an indentured labourer transformed
into small planter and market gardener was not lost on contemporaries:
'*Sans eux, le prix des légumes, des fruits et du lait serait beaucoup plus élevé*
(Without them, the price of vegetables, fruit and milk would have been
much higher.)' commented Virgil Naz in Mauritius.

The 'freedom' of the ex-indentured immigrant, considered to be
greater even than in his native land, became a familiar refrain, despite
the fact that increasingly Indians in Mauritius and elsewhere were being
subjected to special restrictions, post-indenture, which required them to
carry passes, criminalized those without a job or a calling and effectively
limited their mobility. This notion of 'freedom' essentially implied a
liberation from the social oppression of native customs, in particular the
burden of being of low caste or an untouchable:

'. . . at the end of their engagements they become perfectly free, either to remain in the colony, or to return to their homes. If they choose to stay, they become free men, and in fact much freer than they are in the country of their birth . . . they are men and no longer parias.'[26]

An English Baptist missionary to Trinidad stated in 1866 that most coolies bettered their condition, and, more importantly, 'they have been delivered, to a great extent, from the intolerable yoke and curse of caste'. Oliver Warner measured the difference in a physical manner, noting that a coolie leaving India would touch his feet, while one returning home would shake his hand. The 'improvement' noticed in the coolie was not limited to his improved prospects and outlook on life. Nicholas Pike, the American Consul in Mauritius during the mid-nineteenth century, remarked a physical difference between new and old hands. He contrasted the 'thin frail form of the Malabar' arriving in Mauritius with the rounded and muscular physique of those who left. Above all, travellers remained impressed with the sober hard-working character of the Indian immigrant. In Reunion, a visitor observed: *L'Indien est sensible, impressionable, susceptible d'élan par cupidité ou par passion; il est sobre, excellent laboureur, intelligent, économe . . . sa cupidité même est le meilleur garant de son travail.* (The Indian is sensitive, impressionable, motivated by greed and by passion; he is sober, an excellent worker, intelligent and economical . . . his greed is itself the best guarantee of his work.)'[27]

Some observers saw a darker side to the indenture system, however, a feature that was to be increasingly remarked upon, as the century progressed. Arthur Gordon, governor of successive sugar colonies in the 1870s noted the potential for the sexual exploitation of Indian women within the hierarchical authority structures of the sugar plantation:

'. . . too generally, the planters had mistresses, usually half-castes, while the overseers and managers almost invariably lived with Indian women; and I was assured that the provision of pretty coolie girls was almost a recognised form of hospitality on a plantation when the visitors were young men.'[28]

Bronkhurst, a missionary in nineteenth-century Guyana, echoed official prejudices when he wrote that 'the great majority of women
imported from Calcutta are very loose in their habits: they were bad in
Calcutta and so they will continue to remain in Demerara.'[29] In
Réunion, Indian women were said to be frequently used as 'bait' to
lure men to an estate. However, having been 'sold' to him, it was
reported that the woman would often carry off her share of the profit
from the transaction and seek out another 'partner', leaving the man
who had sacrificed his freedom to obtain her to desert or commit suicide: '*emportant les avances sous une forme ou sous une autre, elle
abandonnait quelque temps après l'imprudent qui s'était fié à sa fidélité.
Celui-ci, n'ayant plus le gage pour lequel il avait aliéné sa liberté, le récla-
mait comme une des conditions du contrat, et quand la réalité de l'avenir
se montrait sans les douceurs qu'il avait espérées, il désertait ou se tuait.*
(. . . carrying off the goods advanced in one form or another, she would
abandon the foolhardy man who had trusted in her fidelity. He, no
longer possessing the sum for which he had renounced his freedom,
reclaimed the prize as a condition of the contract, and when the realities of the future intruded upon the dreams he had nurtured, he
would desert or kill himself.)'[30]

Walter Gill an Australian overseer who worked in Fiji in the early
twentieth century, described the Indian indentured woman as 'joyously
amoral as a doe rabbit. She took her lovers as a ship takes rough seas;
surging up to one who would smother her, then tossing him aside, thirst-
ing for the next. In the strong cruel light of the tropics, the elfin promise
of her said: "Stop me and buy one."'[31]

Towards the end of the nineteenth century, and in the early twentieth century, the rise of the nationalist movement in India brought a
further dimension to the debate over indentured labour. C F Andrews,
a well-known sympathizer with the nationalist cause, articulated their
sentiments when he described the conditions of labourers in Natal and
Fiji around 1920 as 'degrading the very name of "Indian" and making it
synonymous with the worst kind of sweated labour and hopeless illit-
eracy . . . No further emigration and no further repatriation!'[32]
However, the nationalist Indians and their supporters who called for
the abolition of indenture on the grounds that all of their compatriots
would be tarred with the 'coolie' brush were as guilty as colonial officials of stereotyping the overseas Indian in the most offensive and

unjustified terms. Andrews replicated prevailing prejudices when he described the Hindu woman in Fiji as 'a rudderless vessel . . . She passes from one man to another, and has lost even the sense of shame in doing so'.[33]

Gopal Krishna Gokhale, protesting against the continuation of indenture in 1912, was also reinforcing a stereotype – the characterization of the coolie as a victim, a dupe and a person of the lowest class: 'the victims of the system are generally simple, ignorant, illiterate, resourceless people belonging to the poorest classes of this country and . . . they are induced to enter . . . into these agreements by the unscrupulous representations of wily recruiters.' In a further, chilling replication of the nineteenth-century British view of Indian female migrants, he claimed that 'very few respectable women can be got to go these long distances', concluding that the system was 'degrading to the people of India from a national point of view . . . Wherever the system exists, there the Indians are only known as coolies, no matter what their position might be'.

Yet, further official enquiries instituted at the turn of the twentieth century refused to condemn indenture outright, and perhaps painted a more balanced picture of the actual conditions and prospects of the overseas Indian populations. When an Indian, Kunwar Maharaj Singh, was sent to report on his compatriots in Mauritius, he concluded: 'as a whole the Indians, most of whom or their forefathers came to this colony as indentured labourers, have prospered. In not a few cases they have amassed considerable wealth and in general, considering the classes from which they have come, they are more prosperous here than they would have been had they remained in India.'

The symbol of coolie as pariah was further entrenched as Indian nationalists alerted the attention of their compatriots and sympathizers to the existence of an outmoded and semi-free form of contact migration which had led to the settlement of thousands of indentured workers as far afield as Trinidad, Natal and Fiji. Indenture was decried as the cause of a rise in anti-Indian discrimination throughout the Empire. The stigma of the coolie was to haunt the overseas Indians for many years to come; in some respects it haunts them still.

The Coolie in Diaspora Literature

The pariah of the political stage was reinforced in the fiction and poetry that emerged from diaspora states in the first decades of the twentieth century. The nineteenth-century official stereotype which had posited a dualistic coolie character – yielding and bowed before the plantation manager, yet murderous and unflinchingly callous when facing his adulterous wife – was replicated and immortalized in literary works of the period. Even as the Indian sugar worker metamorphosed himself in the colonies to become an Indo-Guyanese rice farmer, or an Indo-Fijian shopkeeper, or an Indo-Mauritian planter, he continued to be fixed in the colonial novel, firmly attached to his hoe, eyes cast down, while his daughters increasingly peopled the fantasies of story-tellers who portrayed them in helpless, hopeless sexual bondage to the white salaried staff of the sugar estates. The casting of the coolie in diaspora literature has only recently been broken with the emergence of a new generation of novels which finally give diaspora Indians centre-stage, allowing them to act out a range of experiences which free them from the exoticism of ethnicity and posit them as the complex, universalist products of 'multicultural societies'.

Aliens in Creole Societies

Colonial societies hitherto composed of Creoles and Europeans, united, at least superficially, by language and religion, did not readily or quickly accept the presence of 'aliens' in their midst. Alix d'Unienville has expressed the hostility which initially greeted the arrival and settlement of non-Christian Indians and the exclusivist culture which subsequently developed as 'a kind of deep solidarity, a sort of moral cousinhood which excludes all the other ethnic groups'.[34]

The closing of ranks against the Indian intruder by the coloured and white inhabitants of the sugar colonies is expressed by a Creole character in Loys Masson's novel *L'Etoile et la Clef* (Gallimard, 1945) who remarks that 'between the whites and ourselves there is common ground, at least. We have the same character, more or less the same tastes. The Indian is a savage.'[35]

Hookoomsing has demonstrated how the emergence of a propertied class of bourgeois Indians, menacing white supremacy and the privileges of the coloured class, helped to foster a racist literature in which the alienness of the Indian was expressed:

'*L'émergence de l'Indien comme une nouvelle bourgeoisie terrienne et professionnelle réclamant une prise sur le cours de l'histoire bousculait les fondements du vieil ordre colonial, menaçait la pérennité de la suprématie blanche, seule garante des privilèges dont jouissait aussi le groupe de couleur. Le résultat dans le domaine de la production littéraire . . . a été une floraison de romans inspirés par une idéologie d'exorcisme, à base de race.* (The emergence of the Indian as a new bourgeois landowner and professional, claiming a share of history, upset the old colonial order, threatening the continuance of white supremacy, which in turn was seen as the guarantor of the privileges enjoyed by the coloured population. In the literary domain, the result was a flowering of novels inspired by an ideology of exorcism, based on race.)'[36]

The cultural inferiority of the Indian, which is posited as a self-evident if unarticulated truth in diaspora novels of the 1930s and 1940s is best expressed in the characterization of Indian women. Frequently the objects of sexual lust on the part of the white male narrators and fictional heroes of these works, Indian women are seen as immutably alien and 'other', incapable of civilization and integration into the cultural world of their European paramours. Examples of the genre include Savinien Mérédac's novel *Polyte*, published in 1926, about a Mauritian Creole fisherman who suspects that the child of his young wife is the product of her liaison with a 'Malabar', and Clément Charoux's novel *Ameenah* (1938), which describes the doomed relationship between a young white engineer and a beautiful Indian girl. The gulf between them is expressed by the author in the following terms: '*Elle était si loin de lui, la petite Indienne fruste et humble, si loin du Blanc créé pour commander, du Blanc qu'anime l'orgueil héréditaire, la fierté de la race qui depuis deux mille ans construit la civilisation et mène le progrès.* '(She was so far from him, the small, unpolished and humble Indian, so far from the White man who was created to lead, the White who was imbued with a hereditary pride, that of a race which for 2,000 years had constructed a civilisation and embodied progress.)'

One white tells another in the novel, 'those women can't improve, my dear, it is you who will descend to their level', and Charoux concludes 'On ne crée pas, un civilisé d'un jour à l'autre. (You can't create a civilised person from one day to the next.)'

In falling in love with Ameenah, Delettre seems initially to be questioning his own prejudices – 'Quel sens auront alors nos préjugés mesquins, de classe à classe, de race à race? (What meaning would our wicked prejudices then have, between one class and another, and between races?)' – but decides to 'raise' Ameenah to his level, to initiate her 'à nos goûts, à nos coutumes, à notre langage, à notre pensée (in our tastes, our customs, in our language and ways of thinking.)'[37]

Two stories from Reunion, *Moutousami* and *La Croix du Sud* by Leblond, feature Indian female characters whose corporal grossness, drunkenness and other negative characteristics: 'mettent en évidence la déchéance physique et morale des Indiennes des camps ainsi que leur vulgarité, leur mauvaise humeur et leur malpropreté. (demonstrate the physical and moral decadence of the Indian women in the camps, together with their vulgarity, their bad temper and their insalubrity.)'

In the Mauritian novels of Charoux and Mérédac, the terms 'malabar', 'Creole', 'coolie' and 'lascar' are used in a manner that implies their inferiority alongside the 'grand blanc'. The inter-ethnic barriers portrayed in the literature always evoke the difficulty of crossing them, of the gulf that separates them. Delettre renounces his aim of marrying Ameenah 'car l'atavisme se révèle trop puissant'. Joubert concludes that the novels of the 1920s and 1930s: 'véhiculent toutes sortes de préjugés, voire d'images dénigrantes sur telle ou telle composante de la population (convey all sorts of prejudices, for example denigrating images of one or other population group.)'[39]

The Dangerous Sensuality of the Indian Woman

The central characters in many colonial novels of the 1930s and 1940s are obsessed by a desire for Indian women whilst recognising the dangers inherent in the eventual liaisons. In *La Poupée de Chair* (1931) by Arthur Martial, the character of Jean Mariette is obsessed by a physical attraction towards Indian women: 'what he loved more than anything was the daily contact with these Indian village women, beautiful or ugly, young or old, but all attractive because of the tranquil sensuality of their jet-black eyes.'[40]

Together with *Sphinx de Bronze*, also by Arthur Martial, and Charoux's *Ameenah*, the theme of the risk to the white soul of assimilating the Oriental is paramount. According to Hookoomsing: '*l'assimilation de l'Oriental(e) est contre-nature, par conséquent, condamnée à l'échec; et que celui ou celle qui serait tenté(e) de l'entreprendre court le risque d'y perdre son âme* (assimilating with the Oriental is seen as against nature, and in consequence is condemned to failure, while whomever is tempted to transgress this rule risks losing his soul in the attempt.)'

In *La Poupée de Chair* the white-Indian relationship is at its most raw and brutal, where Liloa is dehumanized by her description as a '*petite souillon*', and a '*petit torchon*'. In Leblond's stories the notion of a *mésalliance* is rejected both by the Indian and white characters as inappropriate.

The sensuality of Indian women is also frequently associated with sorcery in the colonial novel. In *Ameenah*, the hero is bewitched by the sorcery of the Indian woman of the title. Indian women are seductive precisely because they represent an alien, 'other' culture, 'so different from our own, so opposed in habits, customs, traditions, and so perfumed by the picturesque, so curious with its multivarious Gods, veils, dances, joys'.[41]

An orientalist poem, written in 1806, is an early example of the double-edged sword which the beauty of the Indian woman represents for the European male:

> *Si quittant Brama pour l'Amour*
> *Et pleine du Dieu qui l'inspire,*
> *L'Indienne en peint tour à tour*
> *Les fureurs et le doux délire,*
> *De l'art malgré tout le pouvoir,*
> *Malgré sa danse mensongère,*
> *Le masque tombe et laisse voir*
> *Une stupide Balliadère.*[42]

> (Leaving Brama for Love
> And full of the God who inspires it
> The Indian woman depicts in turn
> Its furies and sweet furor

But in spite of Art's powerful lustre,
And of her dance of lies,
The mask falls and exposes
A stupid temple dancer.)

In *Le Feu*, which tells the story of fires attributed to the tormented soul of Foulmania, an Indian woman burned alive, Charoux is again depicting the cultural 'otherness' that renders the Indian woman dangerous.

Part of the mystery of the Indian woman is precisely the exoticism of the culture that she represents. A character in Ameenah notes that 'the eyes of a passing Indian girl reveal the depths of twenty elapsed civilizations',[43] while for Frédéric Delettre, the white lover of Ameenah, passing Indian women represent 'the laws and poetry of the ancient race, the Vedas and the Ramayana, religious and military pageants of primitive times, and the poetry of modern times, born of the contrasts exhaled from an earth where all is colour and magnificence; the fruits, the flowers, the women, the sky, the sun, the rain, riches and poverty'.[44]

La Malabare

A travers ta peau brune et fine
On voit ton âme étinceler;
Sous tes tissus de mousseline
L'oiseau dans l'air pourrait voler.

Mais le préjugé nous sépare;
Allons ailleurs pour aimer mieux,
Ici, sous tes voiles s'égare
Plus d'un œil tendre et curieux.

Through your brown and delicate skin
We see your soul shimmering,
Underneath your muslin clothing
A bird in the sky could fly.

But prejudice separates us,
Let's go elsewhere to love better.
Here, underneath your veils is lost
Many a tender and curious gaze.

Charles Castellan, (1812–51) *Beaux Jours et
Jours d'Orage*, Gosselin, Paris, 1837.

Writing about his poem, Castellan stated, '*Dans le morceau de la
Malabare je me suis attaché à reproduire la physionomie de ces
Indiennes que l'on rencontre dans un quartier spécial du Port-Louis, et
qui descendent directement de ces familles converties à la religion
catholique par les missionnaires, à l'époque de leur passage dans l'Inde.*
(In this text I have tried to reproduce the physiognomy of those
Indian women one meets in a particular part of Port Louis, and
who are descended from families converted to Catholicism by the
missionaries who passed through India.)'

Charles Baudelaire, the famous French poet, visited Mauritius in
1841, and wrote a poem about an Indian girl he saw there:

A Une Malabaraise

*Tes pieds sont aussi fins que tes mains, et ta hanche
Est large à faire envie à la plus belle blanche;
A l'artiste pensif ton corps est doux et cher;
Tes grands yeux de velours sont plus noirs que ta chair.
Aux pays chauds et bleus ou ton Dieu t'a fait naître,
Ta tâche est d'allumer la pipe de ton maître,
De pourvoir les flacons d'eaux fraîches et d'odeurs,
De chasser loin du lit les moustiques rodeurs,
Et, des que le matin fait chanter les platanes,
D'acheter au bazar ananas et bananes.*

Tout le jour, où tu veux, tu mènes tes pieds nus,
Et fredonnes tout bas de vieux airs inconnus;
Et quand descend le soir au manteau d'écarlate,
Tu poses doucement ton corps sur une natte,
Ou tes rêves flottants sont pleins de colibris,
Et toujours, comme toi, gracieux et fleuris.
Pourquoi, l'heureuse enfant, veux-tu voir notre France,
Ce pays trop peuplé que fauche la souffrance,
Et, confiant ta vie aux bras forts des marins,
Faire de grands adieux à tes chers tamarins?
Toi, vêtue à moitié de mousselines frêles,
Frissonnante là-bas sous la neige et les grêles,
Comme tu pleurerais tes loisirs doux et francs,
Si, le corset brutal emprisonnant tes flancs,
Il te fallait glaner ton souper dans nos fanges
Et vendre le parfum de tes charmes étranges,
L'oeil pensif, et suivant, dans nos sales brouillards,·
Des cocotiers absents les fantômes épars!

                                        Les Fleurs du Mal, p. 202.

Your feet are as delicate as your hands, and your hips
Are ample enough to make the most beautiful white woman
     envious.
To the thoughtful artist your body is sweet and precious.
Your large, velvet eyes are darker than your skin.
In the azure tropics where God gave you birth,
Your task is to light the pipe of your master
To provide draughts of cool water.
To chase lingering mosquitoes away from the bed,
To buy bananas and pineapples at the bazaar.
Everyday, there you go, treading on bare feet
Gently humming forgotten old tunes;
And as evening's scarlet mantle descends
You gently rest your body on a mat,
Where your dreams are peopled by humming-birds,

Always, like you, gracious and blooming.
Why, happy child, do you want to see our France,
This overcrowded country, full of suffering,
And confiding your life to the strong arms of sailors,
Say your goodbyes to your beloved tamarind trees?
You, half-clothed in fragile muslin,
Shivering over there in the snow and the hail,
How you will cry for your gentle, honest ways
A brutal corset imprisoning your curves,
As you beg for your supper in our gutters
And sell the perfume of your foreign charms,
Your thoughtful gaze, following, in our filthy fogs
The absent coconut palms, the disappearing ghosts!

Baudelaire came to Mauritius on 1 September 1841, aged 20. He stayed on the island for nineteen days and wrote several poems inspired by his visit including 'A Une Malabaraise'.

A Une Jeune Indienne

Sous les plis onduleux de ton pagne fidèle,
Pieds et bras nus, voilant à peine ta beauté,
Brune fille de l'Inde, aux regards de gazelle
Inconsciente volupté;

J'aime à te voir passer d'un pas tranquille et libre,
Souriante, les bras arrondis à ton flanc,
Et portant sur ton front, – prodige d'équilibre –
Ton pot de cuivre ou de fer-blanc.

Under the undulating folds of your faithful robe
Arms and feet bare, scarcely veiling your beauty,

> Brown Indian girl, with the look of a gazelle
> Unconsciously voluptuous.
>
> I like to watch you go by, calm and free
> Smiling, your arms curved around your hips,
> And carrying, on your head, – a feat of balance –
> Your copper or tin pot.
>
> > Mauritian poet Charles Gueuvin (1834–1905),
> > author of *Les Savanaises* (1856–66).

In the poetry of Raymonde de Kervern, *La Danseuse Malabar* and *Apsara la Danseuse*, the sensuality of India is once again at the forefront:

> *Tu danses le péché*
> *Sous tes voiles intimes*
> *Tes longs yeux mordorés*
> *Mènent vers les abîmes.*
>
> (Your dance reveals the sin
> Under your intimate veils
> Your wide bronze eyes
> Lead towards the abyss.)

But the image of India presented has little to do with the realities of the Indians in Mauritius, it is a sanskritized, idealized ancient Indian civilization that is evoked through the dancers, and cannot be considered to be more than an abstract intellectualized evocation of India.

The Impossibility of Inter-Racial Relationships

It is no surprise that it is usually the Indian woman who is required to do penance for her transgression in falling in love across racial lines, rather than the white lover. In *La Poupée de Chair*, the young Indian girl, Liloa, who has a love affair with a young white on a sugar estate, tries to kill herself when she is supplanted in his affections, and is saved only through religious penance, prayers and walking on fire. A young leprous Indian with a limp is the only person willing to marry her. The Indian woman as a sexual plaything of whites faces a double burden: she is inevitably rejected as too alien, too 'other', but is now tainted goods; the Indian who is willing to save Liloa is not himself whole.

Novels and short stories of this period portray Indians as fatally attracted to whites, frequently at the cost of their own happiness. *Saheytra*, published in Paris in 1929, tells the similar story of a young Indian girl invited to live with a white, but whose parents quickly marry her off to an old Bombay Indian. She runs away from her husband but finds that the white man already has another girl living with him. In *Sphinx de Bronze*, published in 1935, A Martial portrays the opposite side of the coin – a young Indo-Mauritian doctor brings his white French wife home to Mauritius. He is a converted Protestant who is ashamed of his Hindu origins, and is unable to confess to his wife that he is the son of an Indian immigrant. When the husband faces a conflict of interest – he needs to look after his elderly mother, but does not want to bring her to live under the same roof as his wife – the French woman sacrifices herself by returning to Paris. The inference again is that inter-racial relationships are well-nigh impossible to sustain.

The hero of *Mutins* (1951) deals with the story of a man who is sacked from his job on a sugar estate because he has fallen in love with an Indian girl, which displeases his wealthy employers, who also happen to be his cousins. In the first issue of *L'Essor*, a literary magazine, Pierre Raymond Philogéne published a story entitled 'Sitalia', in which a young, beautiful seventeen-year-old Indian girl drowns herself in a river over an unhappy love affair. The object of her affections, a white chemist on the sugar estate, is cynically unmoved by her death: '*A aucun moment ne crut-il devoir se reprocher d'avoir été le bourreau de sa brune maîtresse.* (At no time did he consider reproaching himself for having been the executioner of his brown mistress.)'

The colonial novel was moving away from stories in which the Indian woman was seen as the seductress to those in which she had become the victim.

André Masson, brother of Loys, published *Le Chemin de Pierre Ponce* (Calmann Lévy, 1963) in Paris. In this novel Valee, a young and pretty Indian girl married against her will, falls in love, and commits adultery with a young white, Ashley, in yet another example of an illustration of the social oppression of Indian customs, and the fascination which Indian women are deemed to hold for white men. As Joubert has noted, Ashley's romances with the daughter of a fisherman and Valee are equally doomed: behind each of these love stories '*se dresse, implacable, le milieu, avec ses barrières infranchissables, ses tabous et ses préjugés.* (arises, implacable, the social milieu, with its impregnable barriers, its taboos, and its prejudices.)'

The novel is a further expression of the unhappiness which is often attributed to Indian women, they are always '*mal dans leur peau*', seen as unable to profit from their beauty and youth, tempted into amorous liaisons which inevitably run counter to their social and familial situations.

Early stereotypes of the Indian woman on overseas sugar plantations in the Caribbean context can be found in a series of short stories published in issues of the *Guyana Daily Chronicle* in 1899. Entitled 'Tales of the Tropics', they relate stories of Indian female labourers who seduce their white overseers and are subsequently murdered by their jealous husbands. Caribbean novels and stories which depict East Indian women in relationships with Creoles include 'Boodhoo' (1932) by A Mendez and *Corentyne Thunder* (1941). Bibi in *Those That Be In Bondage* (1917) is described as a 'smooth-skinned, bare-toed East Indian'. Poynting has defined her characterization in the novel as adhering to the 'prurient estate stereotype' typical of the period.[45]

Stereotypes of the Male Coolie

The clearest evocation of the replication of the official discourse in early colonial novels is the theme of the coolie wife murders. In a story entitled 'Le Possédé', a young indentured labourer, Jaypal, courts Rookmine, the wife of Jankee, and is murdered by the latter. In another evocation of this potent symbol of the 'otherness' of the coolie, Yves Ravat published a story in 1954 entitled 'En Forêt' in which a young Indian girl, Soumitra, is murdered by her jealous husband.

Colonial stereotypes abound: in the novel *Polyte*, the fatalism of Indians makes them 'fearful of everything'. Among Arthur Martial's early stories is the tragi-comic tale of Ramkissoon who is more overcome by the death of his cow than that of his wife. The Indian is frequently depicted in the colonial novel as an invader, stealing the land of the Creoles, and dedicated to profit. Polyte expresses: '*la vieille haine de toujours, la rancune du Noir contre l'Indien plus industrieux, plus économe et moins jouisseur.* (The old ever-present hatred, the resentment of the black towards the Indian seen as more industrious, more economical and less pleasure-loving.)'

The struggle between the descendants of slaves and the descendants of coolies also figures as a strong theme of *Lal Pasina* by A Unnuth, a novel written in 1975 in Bhojpuri, in Mauritius. Similarly, in *Le Nègre et L'Amiral* of Raphaël Confiant, flashes of this rivalry are evident. Also from a Caribbean perspective, more recently, David Dabydeen's *Terres Maudites* describes the competition between an ex-slave mistress and a coolie's wife to win the favours of the master of a sugar-cane plantation.

In 1945, Loys Masson's description of a working sugar estate in the novel *L'Etoile et la Clef* (Gallimard, 1945) is, again, based on his own experiences as an employee. However, Masson details the struggle of a young, marginalized white man leading the workers to revolt. He was inspired by a struggle which he had himself witnessed – the sugar-workers' strikes of 1935–6. Despite writing at around the same time as the novels of Charoux and Martial, Masson portrays the relationship between white and Indian in a much less stereotyped way, informed, as it is, by broader ideals of class struggle and fraternity. Ramdour, an Indian character in the book, dreams of a Mauritius which would be '*une vaste confraternité, blancs, Créoles et Indiens, épaule contre épaule.* (a vast brotherhood with Whites Creoles and Indians rubbing shoulders.)' (p. 68).

Yet, even as Masson used his writing to denounce discrimination, the sense of the superiority of the white is still evident in his novel. The character of Ramdour in the novel, a high-caste Hindu whose parents are not labourers but merchants from Patna, expresses his appreciation of certain characteristics of the white colonists: '*leur propreté, leur distinction, quelque chose qui en faisait des seigneurs, si haissables fussent-ils.* (their cleanliness, their distinctive class, something which made them noblemen, even though they were despisable.)' Further, in the novels of Loys Masson coolies are still seen as stoic victims who 'have no time to think, no time to witness life's passage, nothing but the hoe, the hole that they dig'.[46] Indians are still only a supporting cast.

When Clément Charoux was writing about Indians, he drew his inspiration from his years working on a sugar estate, and he could not see beyond the agricultural role of the 'coolie'. Indeed he was articulating the opinion of the colonists for whom: '*Un coolie, c'est peu de chose: une paire de bras qui s'emploie avec des milliers d'autres à faire fructifier le bien d'autrui*. (A coolie is insignificant: a pair of hands along with a thousand others, labouring for the benefit of others.)'[47]

Colonial writers like Charoux extolled the worker virtues of the Indian, whilst being unable to see beyond his labouring status. Watching the Indian labourer bent over his hoe, Charoux wrote:

> '*Avec cette pioche-là, l'humble Malabar a conquis une notable partie de notre île Maurice. Il s'est d'abord lentement constitué un maigre pécule, puis il a tenté de réaliser son plus beau rêve: posséder en propre un lopin de terrain qui s'agrandirait jusqu'à former de petites propriétés de quelques arpents où l'on vit à l'aise parmi ses cannes, ses vaches, et ses chèvres, et même, qui sait, par la suite, des domaines d'importance. L'Indien type, je me le représente toujours courbé sur cette terre qu'il aime et qu'il veut, perpétuellement besognant car il sait que le travail seul, incessant, continuel, en donne la possession.*
> (With his *pioche*, the humble Malabar has conquered a notable portion of our island of Mauritius. First gathering a meagre sum, then attempting to realise his dearest dream: to possess a strip of land which he would enlarge until he had acquired a establishment of some arpents where he could live at ease among his canes, his cows and his goats, and even, who knows, later, on his sizeable estate. The typical Indian, is always seen, bent over this land that he loves and wants, always needy, because he knows that only work, incessant, continuous, will ensure his possession of it.)'[48]

Arthur Martial also paid homage to the agricultural labour of Indo-Mauritians: '*Oui, ami, l'Indien, c'est l'âme de la propriété, que dis-je, c'est l'âme de l'industrie sucrière elle-même . . . il est travailleur infatigable et se montre reconnaissant quand on le traite avec équité.* (Yes, my friend, the Indian is the soul of the estate, what am I saying, he is the soul of the sugar industry itself . . . he is a tireless worker who is grateful when treated fairly.)'

Replicating the deep-seated antagonism between Indian and Creole, he contrasted the spendthrift habits of the latter with the parsimonious Indian: '*Tandis que l'Africain, vivotant au jour le jour, frondeur et jouisseur, va au cinéma . . . les mains dans les poches vides, dans chaque taudis indien, hommes, femmes, enfants, vieillards triment et s'esquintent à l'épargne.*

(While the African, living from day to day, riotous and pleasure-loving, goes to the cinema with his pockets empty, in every Indian hut, men, women, children and the elderly scrimp and toil.)'

Régis Fanchette's homage to the Indian labourer in 1958 who had: '*épousé la terre, la rude terre paysanne, qu'il a cultivée avec amour, en préparant ses fils lentement, patiemment comme on mûrit un grand rêve, aux leviers de commande* (married the earth, the crude soil of the peasant, which he cultivated with lover, while slowly and patiently preparing his sons, as one nurtures a great dream, on the food of his orders)' demonstrates how long the stereotype of the docile, laborious coolie persisted.

Callikan-Proag notes, however, the evolution of attitudes as the novels of the 1950s onwards began to laud 'the typical characteristics of the Indo-Mauritian such as the spirit of thrift, the austere life-style and the work ethic, which were generally objects of derision on the part of other ethnic groups' but which now began to elicit admiration.[49] Mauritian novelist Marcel Cabon, in particular, turned his attention to village life, as evoked in his *Contes de Brunepaille* (1953–5), *Namasté* (1961) and *Contes de l'Enfant Bihari* (1966). Cabon introduced the concept of the earth as salvation, as opposed to the earth as: '*la terre-salut opposée à la terre-malédiction.*'[50] As the author himself observed: '*J'ai dans* Namasté *et* l'Enfant Bihari *dit ce travail qui jette hommes et femmes hors des cases dès le premier chant du coq, que les conduit au bois et au champ par tous les temps, de ce mépris des obstacles, de ce goût de l'épargne.* (In *Namasté* and *l'Enfant Bihari* I have described the nature of the work which drives men and women out of their huts at the cry of the cockerel, carrying them to the woods and the fields in all weathers, contemptuous of obstacles, for the love of saving.)'[51]

Cabon's novels also provided a more realistic portrayal of the overseas Indian woman. In his writings, rather than appearing as objects of lust, and unhappy adventuresses, Indian women are always seen at work – grinding 'masala', fetching water from the well, rubbing coconut oil into their children's hair, cleaning the stables, washing their clothes in the river and so on. Cabon details some of the more realistic dramas that could occur in a woman's life. In *Namasté*, for example, a serious problem is detailed in the inability of Oumaouti to bear children, and her very real sense of shame in front of the other villagers: 'in her daily comings and goings she felt the weight of glances at her stomach, it was like a challenge'.[52] As Callikan-Proag has noted, 'He touches on one of the most important preoccupations of women, and even of men, in Indian civilization: women who are not pregnant some time after their marriage, are almost the parias of society. They are despised by others, and themselves feel a sense of guilt which makes their life unbearable.'[53]

However, Cabon tends to present an idyllic, idealized portrait of romantic life between the couple at the centre of his novel *Namasté* – Ram and Oumaouti – which does not accord well with the social realities of the Indian village overseas. He describes them holding hands, playing hide and seek, and in other romantic scenes which would be inconceivable within the mores of the time. Moreover, a large part of the novelist's fascination with the Indian remains linked to an orientalist perspective: he is imbued with nostalgia for the grandeur of the Indian past. Cabon extols the virtues of past customs and manners of dress. In *Le Marchand* (1955) he criticizes the adoption of western dress by a seller of Indian cakes, the '*marchand de poutous*', and describes a village artisan in *Epousailles*, 'so tall, so strong – with such a demeanour – that I like to imagine him in the uniform of one of Shah Jahan's generals, or in the clothes of a Prince of Punjab or Kashmi', in a way which indicates that the exoticism of the overseas Indian remained a very real element in the appraisal.[54]

Cabon is seen as one of the first Mauritian novelists to capture the soul of the Indo-Mauritian labourer, '*l'âme du paysan mauricien*'. He expresses the closeness of the Indian to agriculture, with descriptions of Ram's long hours spent working his land.

Significantly, Cabon does not regard Indians as belonging to an alien or inferior culture. *Namasté* represents the contribution of Indians to Creole society by demonstrating the linguistic infiltration of the Indian, bringing into play many expressions in bhojpuri, the lingua franca of the villages. Ram dies towards the end of the novel but leaves behind him a son who is destined to completed his monumental work, '*le mauricienisme – la construction d'une vraie nation mauricienne*'.

The Emergence of the Indian as a Positive Element in Diaspora Societies

In recent decades, the diaspora literature has moved from depicting Indians as manifestations of the exotic, the mysterious, the sensual, or of fixing them as downtrodden coolies forever tied to the land, to a recognition of the cultural permeability of Creole society and of the pervasive influence of Indians within those societies. This acknowledgement has taken many forms.

The richness of multi-cultural society has been portrayed by writers such as Robert Edward Hart in Mauritius whose poetry distils the pleasures of watching his compatriots of different faiths going about their daily rituals:

> '*Un hadje vénéré qui revient de la Mecque*
> *Médite avec ferveur tel verset du Koran . . .*
>
> (A venerated Hadji returning from Mecca
> Fervently meditating on a verse of the Quran.)'

With wry and self-deprecatory humour, writers like Hart have restored to the descendants of the coolies the beauty and profundity of their cultural heritage. He describes a young boy unable to master an Indian musical instrument: '*Comment parvient-il à dessiner une mélodie, ce petit Malabare, alors que toi, enfant de Blancs, tu ne peux tirer de sa flûte que des sons rauques qu'étranglent davantage tes impatiences?* (How could he produce a melody, this little Malabar, while you, offspring of Whites, could not coax from his flute anything but raucous sounds, further strangled by your impatience?)'

Moissonnez, beaux enfants de l'Inde aux mille dieux!
Malgré l'accablement du jour trop radieux,
Amassez, courageux toujours aux tâches dures,
La richesse des cannes mûres.

Les Voix Intimes, 1923.

Reap, India's beauteous children of a thousand Gods!
Despite the ardour of the too radiant day
Gather, forever courageous in the face of difficult tasks,
The riches of the ripe canes.

Malcolm de Chazal – a white Mauritian 'Hindu'

'*Je reste occidental par mes hérédités, par ma langue, par ma manière de manger et de m'exprimer. Mais mon âme est sur le Gange et à Benarès. Je respire l'Inde.*

Quoted in *The Triveni*, June 1970.

(I remain western through heredity, and through my language, by my way of eating and my manner of expression. But my soul is on the Ganges at Benares. I breathe India.)'

'*Je me considère plus hindou qu'européen parce que pour moi l'hindouisme n'est pas une nationalité, mais l'hindouisme est surtout une manière de vivre. Dans ce sens, parmi les Hindous de Maurice, je suis peut-être le le plus grand Hindou.*

Indian Cultural Review, July 1966.

(I consider myself more Hindu than European because for me, Hinduism is not a nationality, but is above all a way of life. In this sense, among the Hindus of Mauritius, I am perhaps the greatest Hindu.)'

Malcolm de Chazal's notion of a lost continent of which Mauritius formed a part drew him to the conclusion of a 'coexistence' with India. He rediscovered the flora and fauna of Southern India in Mauritius and considered that the island belonged, geographically, to India rather than to Africa. In some respects, however, Chazal's homage to Indians in Mauritius, his idealization of the overseas Indian, is still based on the notion of the Indian as gentle, submissive – a subject race, in effect: '*Les Hindous à l'île Maurice font le charme de l'île Maurice par leur tolérance, leur absence d'orgueil, leur douceur.* (The Hindus of Mauritius give the island its charm, with their tolerance, their lack of pride, their gentleness.)'[55]

Nonetheless, the writing of Malcolm de Chazal prefigures coolitude, because it has as a fundamental tenet the influence of Indian culture and language beyond the confines of the overseas Indians, and across the societies where they have settled. The universality and the inclusiveness of coolitude was already understood and acted upon by Malcolm de Chazal.

Gaston Malherbe's detective novels, which began appearing in 1969, deal with typically Mauritian social situations, and in this way, treat ethnic issues in a factual rather than judgemental manner. In the novel *Soir de Divali* (1970) an Indo-Mauritian, who has a child from his religious marriage to an Indo-Mauritian woman, leaves for his studies and while in Ireland falls in love with and marries an Irish woman in a civic ceremony. After his return to Mauritius with his wife, the former spouse makes a great effort to win him back.

Edgar Janson (1861–1927) wrote a poem about an Indian cake seller.

Le Marchand de Moutailles

De chauds gateaux rangés sur les tables en ligne
Le miel coule à flots d'ambre, et l'on voit tout autour
Les abeilles vibrer dans l'or léger du jour,
Le Madras est assis, tel un dieu grave et digne.
La flamme fait chanter la noire lèchefrite
Ou tournoie en festons, et lentement crépite
Le moutaille doré, bon en toutes saisons.
Et comme dédaigneux des douceurs qu'il prépare
Le vieil Indien bronzé sur ses jarrets se carre,
Très fier de sa science, il éteint ses tisons.

Le XXe Siecle, (1885–7).

The mithai seller

Hot cakes arranged in line on the tables –
Honey flows in amber pools, and all around one sees
Bees humming in the light golden glow of the day.
The Tamil is seated, like a solemn and dignified god.
The flames make the old black pot sizzle

Where the golden moutaille, good in all seasons,
Is slowly taking shape.
And as if disdainful of the delights he prepares,
The old Indian, with bronzed knees, sits in state,
Very proud of his science, he puts out his embers.

In 1972, Alain Le Breton won an international prize for his story entitled *La Terre et l'Amour*, which tells the tale of Bharati, a twenty-year-old Indian girl, who becomes a widow while pregnant. She acquires some measure of tranquillity after the birth of her baby, by relocating to the Montagne Bleue valley where she: '*travaillerait la terre, comme faisaient son père, ses ancêtres.* (Working the land, like her father, and his ancestors did before him.)'

While this may be seen as continuing the stereotype of the Indian's attachment to the soil, the author makes a break with the traditional depiction of relationships in Mauritian literature by recounting the mutual love story of Bharati with an Afro-Creole, Lindsay. Even more significantly, the couple's marriage is not seen as implausible by the author, who, on the contrary, castigates as 'stupid' those who would oppose it. The old topic of inter-racial marriage thus acquires a new significance, and perhaps a greater relevance. Similarly, in Gilbert Ahnee's novel *Exils* (Edition du CRI, 1989), among social problems treated are: '*le douloureux problème du castéisme (les amours impossibles de Satish et d'Anju).* (The painful problem of casteism (the impossible love of Satish and Anju).)'

In one of his poems, Alain Le Breton reveals the continuing idealization of the rural tranquillity of the Indo-Mauritian through his reproach to those of his compatriots of Indian origin who allowed themselves to become 'alienated' from their ancestral culture through westernization:

Jeunes ruraux, jeunes Hindous,
Pourquoi faites-vous comme nous?
Vous regardez vers l'Occident
Qui tend les bras vers l'Orient.
De grâce, ne quittez vos champs.
L'Europe sent le carburant.
N'échangez pas votre douceur
Contre la violence et la peur.

(Young countrymen, young Hindus
Why do you want to be like us?
You look towards the West
Which holds out its arms towards the East.
For heaven's sake, don't leave your fields.
Europe smells of motor fuel.
Don't exchange your gentle ways
For violence and fear.)

In so doing, Le Breton conforms to the powerful current in Mauritian lit-erature that exhorted the Indian to stay in his fields, praising him for his 'gentleness', a euphemism for docility. Does this not therefore imply that Le Breton and his ilk were unwilling to see the Indo-Mauritian rise to usurp the position of the urbanized, westernized coloured and white populations? Furthermore, this stance was still to some extent guilty of positing the Indo-Mauritian as the 'other', not an integral component of the social mélange celebrated in créolité that has the merit of equalizing the ethnic groups.

By contrast, the Indian has been strangely absent from French Caribbean writing, which has tended to emphasize *créolité* at the expense of *indeanité*. Where the coolie appears, it is often in situations of confrontation with the Creole. In *L'Echappée-coolie* (1958) Gilbert Gratiant pits an Indian woman against an Afro-Creole in a comparison of physical charms. In Alfred Parepou's *Atipa* (1885) coolies are mentioned briefly and even in the first novel of Confiant, *Le Nègre et l'Amiral*, the Indian is still relegated to a marginal role.[56] Confiant's later novel, *Le Retour de la Vierge*, has a stronger characterization of the coolie cultural element. By contrast, Maryse Condé's novel *La Traversée de la Mangrove* effectively portrays the kaleidoscopic identity of Guadeloupe. The Ramsarans and the complex character of Francis Sancher, who is of mixed origin, effectively incorporate the Indo-Guadeloupean.

In recent years the diaspora Indians have been placed firmly at centre stage by the works of descendants of the coolies themselves. Ananda Devi Nirsimloo, in *Le Voile de Draupadi* (l'Harmattan, 1993) recounts the torment of a woman whose son is dangerously ill; Abhimanyu Unuth's *Les Empereurs de la Nuit* (EOI, 1983) identifies frustration of many kinds, emotional and sexual – men in love with prostitutes, old maids dreaming of marriage, neglected spouses – among overseas Indian populations. Following on from V S Naipaul, David Dabydeen and other Caribbean writers have used dark humour to depict the trivia and the trauma of lives lived in diaspora. Diasporic writing, such as Balachandra Rajan's *The Dark Dancer*, frequently tackles the theme of cultural conflict between the modern world and the perceived traditional culture of Indian forebears. In *Coolie Odyssey* Dabydeen recalls the Caliban figure, demonstrating how in the white world the coolie descendants are still considered exotic: 'like a Hindu corpse I burn and shrink/To be reborn to your desire!'[57]

A recent novel from Mauritius, *L'histoire d'Ashok et d'Autres Personnages de Moindre Importance*, by Sewtohul, may be considered to be one of the finest prose expressions of coolitude. Whereas Unnuth's earlier novel of the Indo-Mauritian experience, *Lal Pasina*, portrays Indians as the continuing victims of trickery in migration, Sewtohul's reality is more diverse and complex, and unfolds into a vision of a composite universe. Sewtohul's work also echoes the linguistic diversity which is a characteristic of coolitude, mixing French, English, Creole, Hindi and Bhojpuri.

Sewtohul's novel takes us into a mysterious world of dreams and beliefs in which his character Vassou overcomes the constraints of time and space to become the ultimate 'maroon'. In an extraordinary passage, Sewtohul engages the reader in a spiritual and historic voyage through slavery and indentured labour, which may be considered one of the strongest literary manifestations of coolitude in which '*Vassou sentait affluer des souvenirs qui ne lui appartenaient pas.* (Vassou was overwhelmed by memories that were not his.)' He meets a white man '*style edwardien*', a '*soldat chinois . . . habillé à l'indienne* (Edwardian style, a Chinese soldier, dressed like an Indian)', a '*corsaire*', an African boy, while '*des travailleurs indiens au visage rude les regardaient passer et il entendait des phrases en bhojpuri . . . Rouvrant les yeux, il se sentit à l'étroit, étouffant de chaleur. Mais il comprit qu'il ne devait pas quitter la pièce. Il était planqué ici, échoué dans une petite île de l'océan Indien après un long voyage, déguisé en coolie . . . Et ainsi, Vassou vogua d'esprit rebelle en esprit rebelle, butinant chez chacun un trait, un regard particulier.* (Indian workers with coarse faces watched them go by, and he heard phrases in bhojpuri . . . opening his eyes again, he felt trapped by stifling heat. But he understood that he could not leave the room. He was fixed here, stranded on a small Indian Ocean island after a long voyage, disguised as a coolie . . . and thus Vassou moving from one rebellious spirit to another, reaping from each a characteristic, a particular trait.)'[58]

Changing character, Vassou at one stage becomes a sepoy fleeing the Indian Mutiny: '*un Gurkha en fuite de l'Inde après l'échec de la mutinerie de 1857 qui, ravalant sa fierté, acceptait docilement un métier de laboureurs subissant les insultes des sirdars.* (A Gurkha fleeing India after the failure of the 1857 mutiny, who swallowing his pride, accepted with docility the work of a labourer at the receiving end of the insults of the sirdars.)' Finally Vassou understands: '*Etre marron, c'était fuir. Mais il vient un moment où on ne peut plus fuir et où il devient nécessaire de se révolter.* (To be a maroon, was to flee. But there comes a moment when one can no longer flee and it becomes necessary to revolt.)'

Vassou's *marronage* is a universal one, in which the descendant of a coolie is able to reconstitute his identity and his place in the world:

'*Comprends bien que ce n'est pas seulement parmi les créoles qu'on devenait marron. Il y avait des Indiens marrons, aussi. Des Blancs marrons, des Chinois marrons, toutes sortes de marrons, qu'il y a. Tu verras toi-même.* (You should understand that it is not only Creoles who went maroon. There were Indian runaways also. White runaways, Chinese runaways, all kinds of maroons. You will see for yourself.)'

Historians and the Appraisal of the Coolie

Hugh Tinker's pioneering work entitled *A New System of Slavery* was the first to recast the overseas Indian labourer as a subject of academic study in the early 1970s. His title alone revealed his sentiments, and sparked numerous other studies that, like Tinker, emphasized deception in recruitment and slave-like working conditions.

Many of these works were characterized by uncritical acceptance of official sources that in turn led to parodies of the stereotypes of Indian female migrants in the historical literature. Thus, writing about conditions in nineteenth-century British Guiana, Brian Moore wrote:

'Women shifted their allegiance with consummate ease to whichever male was prepared to make them the best offer. It was reportedly not uncommon for a woman to desert a man with whom she had cohabited for another, then for a third and perhaps a fourth, and sometimes even return to one of those whom she had previously left – and with apparent impunity.'[59]

The notion that family life was albeit impossible on estates has proved persistent. Of Reunion Indian estate life, Michèle Marimoutou has written '*Une polyandrie forcée s'établit dans le camp, parallèlement au commerce des femmes: ce sont les signes de la détresse morale de ces engagés isolés dans les camps et séparés de la population locale par la langue et les coutumes.* (A forced polyandry was set up in the camp, parallel to the commerce of women: these are signs of the moral distress of the indentured labourers isolated in the camps and separated from the local population by language and customs.)'[60]

Parekh has recently reasserted the difficulties of family life under indenture:

'When the indentured Hindus began to settle down and reconstitute their family life on the expiry of their contracted period, they ran into great difficulties. Women had got used to sexual, social and financial independence; men saw them as little more than sex objects; the tradition of sexual loyalty had considerably weakened; and illegitimate children carried little social stigma . . . they set about rehabilitating the traditional patriarchal family in a most determined manner.'[61]

Nationalist writing about indenture in the context of the Indian fight for independence and the removal of discrimination in the Empire has tended to crystallize such stereotypes. Turn-of-the-century accounts of indenture by participants in the system, such as Totaram Sanadhya and later interviews with the last surviving ex-indentureds, in Fiji, place great stress on the labourers as the dupes of unscrupulous recruiters.

R Mishra notes that such works which represent the *girmitiyas* as apologists: 'is symptomatic of a severe guilt-complex, and . . . explain why the Fiji Indian has always confused historical processes and facts and has relied on a "mythic transformation of reality" to keep his basic faith intact.'[62]

Brij Lal is one of several revisionist historians who have cast doubt on the generalized kidnap theme, arguing that: 'the recruiters and arkatis did not play the major role that is normally ascribed to them in inducing Indian peasants to migrate.'[63] Statistical studies have also gone some way to reassessing the imputed chaos of diasporic personal lives under indenture. Other stereotypes about overseas Indians have proved remarkably resilient. Writing about Trinidad, Brereton has commented: 'Indians were considered to be deceitful, prone to perjury and fond of litigation. Their thrift was considered to be almost a vice.'[64]

Walter Rodney has provided a more realistic reappraisal of the legacy of indenture throughout the ex-sugar colonies without recourse to stereotypical accounts of coolie 'thrift' as opposed to Creole profligacy: 'external supplies of labour guaranteed the survival of the sugar industry in British Guiana during its most difficult years. However, it is also true to say that the availability of subsidised external sources of labour simultaneously guaranteed the persistence of backward hand-husbandry and of heavily supervised work routines associated with the plantation as a unit of production. Above all, immigration rapidly created a labour surplus that made unemployment and underemployment endemic in the late nineteenth century.'[65] The over-population and marginalization of the labour force, which was one of the lasting consequences of indenture, created the conditions for remigrations of Indian diaspora communities from the territories of settlement well into the twentieth century.

The cultural legacy of indenture has proved more problematic. Whilst some studies have over-stressed the social conservatism of the Hindu migrant, others have subscribed to a wholly unrealistic depiction of overseas Indians as casteless and rootless. In describing indentured labourers as 'reluctant migrants', Parekh runs dangerously close to a replication of the nineteenth-century official discourse of the coolie as immobile peasant, asserting that they left 'India not in a mood of alienation or a spirit of adventure and curiosity but out of economic necessity. Not surprisingly they saw their migration as a semi-voluntary exile very like that of Rama'.[66]

In the 1990s, a more balanced appraisal of the 'coolie' has emerged from the postcolonial literature. Northrup's overview of indentured labour is unemotional and treads a sensible middle ground:

'Perhaps one person in ten who left a natal village in search of
new opportunities ventured abroad. Of those who did, only about
one in ten became an indentured migrant to a distant overseas
colony. In examining those who became overseas indentured
migrants, it is thus necessary to consider both how they reflected
the larger patterns of migration and how the complex process of
self-selection and official selection limited their
representativeness . . .'

Northrup notes that there is no clear-cut distinction between those
recruited by deception and those who volunteered to go overseas:

'. . . since few first-time recruits had a realistic image of what they
were getting into, partly because of misinformation but mostly
due to their own inability to imagine the geography and
conditions they would encounter at their destinations. In
addition, once overseas, most migrants seem to have adopted a
fatalistic attitude toward what they had to endure, which further
blurred the differences between their forms of recruitment.
Instead, recruits' reactions were more likely to be formed by the
actual conditions at their destinations and by their individual
abilities to cope with unfamiliar circumstances . . .'

Whilst he remarks that only around 25 per cent of Indians migrated
with their spouses, he breaks with other revisionist historians like Tinker
who stressed the incompatibility of indenture with family stability to
assert that 'couples were able to form agreeable temporary or permanent
relationships overseas. However, in the competition for women, richer
and stronger men, especially foremen and overseers, had distinct advantages, a fact that drove other men to despair.'

Dealing with the notion that indentured labourers effectively
became international proletarians, unable to return home, Northrup
points out that the decision to return home 'was not irrevocable and
many subsequently signed up for another indenture overseas . . . it is
worth noting that oscillation between place of origin and overseas settlement area was also typical of migrating Europeans in this period.
Indeed, a high degree of alienation has long been an intrinsic part of
every migrant's lot.'

Northrup concludes that, whilst migrants who survived the indenture experience tended to be better off physically and financially, the system itself found it difficult to escape 'from its origins as a marriage of high moral expectations with the grim practical realities of plantation labour'.

Indentured labour is ultimately defined by Northrup as 'a distinct historical phenomenon'. Not a continuation of slavery, it was nevertheless concerned with sugar production, remained largely confined to non-Europeans, and was abolished in a campaign that stressed its incompatibility with humane standards of free labour. He concludes: 'Indentured labour was also distinct from the larger European migration of the nineteenth century in its composition, in its destinations, and in its legal circumstances. Yet indentured migrants' motives in emigrating, the voyages that carried them and their struggles to establish a new life once their contract was over do resemble those of "free" migrants and deserve to be included in that larger story.'[67]

Madhavi Kale's recent book on Indians in the Caribbean, reflects this careful modern appraisal of indenture as somehow occupying a middle ground between victims and opportunists:

> 'Represented both as victims and as rational maximizers of opportunity throughout the history of indentured emigration, Indian indentured emigrants probably included fair shares of both . . . Implicit in the 'new system of slavery narratives is the assumption that traditionally people in the recruiting regions were largely stationary, and that indentured emigration was just another facet of the ongoing displacement and immiseration precipitated by colonialism . . . Neither alternative seems satisfactory on its own. While a continuous history of massive deception seems implausible, there is also evidence that cases of abduction and entrapment continued . . .'[68]

In essence, historians are still struggling with a system which was uncompromising in its unpalatability and harshness, and yet which produced, after decades of poverty, thriving, prosperous communities around the British Empire.

3

Surviving Indenture

Coolies 'knew' where they were going. They would think about their
separation, devise a strategy for survival and settling down, and work out
their place in the new existential structure that would take them in.

K Torabully, 1996, p. 14.

Disembarking coolies usually passed through an immigration depot from
where they would be registered and distributed to employers. The depot
enclosure prefigured the confinement of the estate to which new arrivals
would be indentured for up to five years. This chapter explores the serf-like
conditions that prevailed on plantations in the ex-slave sugar colonies and
the strategies adopted by Indians to circumvent and recast the inferior status
imposed upon them.

The lengthy, cramped voyage was succeeded, for new immigrants, by the
procedures of disembarkation and allocation to employers. In some cases
indentured labourers were engaged to a specific plantation in India and
would be sent directly, usually on foot or in carts, to the estate-owner
who had requisitioned them. In other cases, new arrivals would be placed
in an immigration depot, to be viewed and engaged by local planters.
Women who arrived without a male partner were often also 'looked
over' by prospective spouses. The new arrivals would be taken before a
magistrate to sign indenture contracts, which varied in length between
one and five years. As the nineteenth century progressed, the five-year
indenture became the norm. This effectively placed the labourer under
a requirement to work continuously for the entire period, time off only
allowed for the rare annual designated holidays, and where special permission could be obtained from the owner. Sickness or absenteeism was
punishable by imprisonment, and in addition to a loss of pay, unsched-
uled leave had to be made up before the contract terminated. In some
colonies, such as Mauritius, a so-called 'double-cut' was in force, which

required labourers who were absent through sickness, absence or prison to make up double the time lost. The penal clauses were onerous, particularly for those immigrants who succumbed to unfamiliar tropical diseases, or who were unaccustomed to unremitting manual labour.

Une paille, deux pailles
Sipaye
et pour tout entrailles
un coulis d'hommes bleus
détaille
les champs caillots.
Nous sommes bagasse, nous sommes mélasse,
mon frère cafre,
notre peau notre trace,
comme toi de la même sale race.

K Torabully, *Cale d'Étoiles*, p. 76.

One strays, two straws
Sepoys
For entrails
A coulis of blue men
Pick through
The stone-strewn fields
We are bagasse, we are molasses
My African friend
Our skin is our mark
Like yours, of the same dirty race.

Life and Work on the Estate

Totaram Sanadhya is one of the few indentured labourers to have recounted his experiences in a published memoir. He served in Fiji for 21 years before returning to India in 1914. His book *Fiji Men Mere Ikkis Varsh*, published in 1919, contains striking testimony to the loneliness and alienation experienced by new immigrants:

'I haven't had food for three days, my body is weak, my throat is parched, and I won't be able to go to work tomorrow. Every ounce of strength has deserted my body. What type of human beings will understand my plight? Only the poor people of the villages who have experienced hardship; it would be useless to relate my suffering to self-seeking and degraded slaves. Oh Lord, how will I live through five years of girmit (hell). You are the friend of the poor and helpless, but it seems You have neglected me. Perhaps I am paying for the misdeeds of my previous life. At the moment, I am completely helpless. I see everyone here suffering, but my plight is unbearable.'[1]

Returning coolies provided revealing insights into the common lot of the overseas indentured labourer. Mooneswawmy recalled his ten years in Natal with this short account: 'I served on Mr Lister's estate . . . Mr Lister was a very bad gentleman. He would sometimes put a rope around my neck, and send me to the police. He often beat me with a chambuck, tying my hands, and pouring salt water on my back.'

In Guadeloupe, a group of Indian immigrants drafted a petition to the Governor of Madras in 1885 in which they complained of being imprisoned in dark cells, placed and rolled in barrels full of needles, and beaten with rattans. In 1866, the Natal Mercury received a letter from 'a Calcutta coolie' complaining of ill treatment, which they summarized as follows:

'Some planters give half Rice half Mealie Meal, because they say there is not Rice enough in the market; what has the coolie to do with that . . . when they hire coolies they knew they must feed them . . . Then again if a coolie be sick, a shilling a day is stopped, hence if sick for a month, 3 months' pay is gone. Who made this law, the Government or the planter? . . . Noone protects the coolie.'[2]

Hausildar, an ex-indentured immigrant, interviewed about his experiences, remembered of his working life on the Fiji cane plantations:

'We were whipped for small mistakes. If you woke up late, i.e. later than 3 am, you got whipped. No matter what happened, whether there was rain or thunder you had to work – we were here to work and work we had to do, otherwise we were abused and beaten up.'[3]

That Indians frequently equated their conditions with slavery is evident from this Surinami folksong:

'Like the fly trapped in honey, we became slaves.
We toiled in the fields day and night, without sleep.'[4]

je suis la bannie l'exclue l'exilée
décidée à me perdre dans l'anonymat de l'engagée
entre agent recruteur et agent consulaire
Entre Protecteur d'émigrants et colons tortionnaires
j'avais déjà perdu mon chemin dans la sécheresse
du coeur des cannaies
K Torabully, *Chair Corail, Fragments Coolies*, p. 53.

I am the banished, excluded, exiled
Who decided to lose myself in the anonymity of indenture
Between the recruiter and the consular agent
Between Protector of Emigrants and torturing settlers
I had already lost my way amid droughts
In the heart of the canefields.

Available information about deficiencies in the living and working arrangements of indentured labourers, and of ill-treatment meted out to them, is principally gleaned from petitions which Indians addressed to the immigration authorities in the colonies. In the territories to which they migrated, an office was set up to administer the indenture scheme and a 'Protector' appointed to look after their interests. Whilst this office degenerated in most circumstances to being merely an administrative arm of the policing of the coolie, the individual responsible for the Indians became a figurehead to the labourers, as a symbol which was neither planter nor policeman, nor colonial magistrate, to whom they could protest about infringements of their contracts, to complain of poor living conditions and of unfair treatment at the hands of estate personnel.

Petitions commonly addressed the Protector as 'our father and mother' to indicate the responsibility he had towards the immigrants. When Urjoon and Hari found themselves unexpectedly in Mauritius while trying to join family members in Natal, it was natural to address themselves to the Protector. Their petition stated:

> 'One Urjoon and his brother Hari paid their passages from Calcutta to Natal. But instead of landing to Natal they were landed to Mauritius. As they were quite strangers in this island and they don't know what to do here. And they desired to return back to their native country but they have no means to do so. Wherefore Urjoon most respectfully pray your Protectorship to grant them a free passage to proceed to their own country. They have landed to Mauritius by the Colombo mail SS *Hultala* on the 19th June 1908. The annexed is the license of Urjoon which will give you full particulars. Hoping that his request will be granted and feeling assured with a favourable speedy reply.'[5]

Mahadai Das' poem 'They Came In Ships' evokes the massed presence of indentured labourers before the door of the Protector's office in Guyana and the visits of Royal Commissions to investigate labourers' working and living conditions in the sugar colonies:

The cry of coolies echoed round the land.
They came, in droves, at his office door
Beseeching him to ease their yoke . . .

Commissioners came,
Capital spectacles in British frames
Consulting managers about costs of immigration.

Mahadai Das, in Dabydeen & Samaroo (eds),
India in the Caribbean, p. 289.

In other cases, coolies would address their petitions directly to the Governor of a colony, or to various authorities concerned with their grievances. In 1872 a group of coolies employed in Durban petitioned the municipal authorities asking for higher wages:

'. . . we the undersigned Coolies have got large family and the wages that we get at present is not enough to maintain our poor distressed family and we have left all our nearest relations from India, and we came to this Colony in order to work hard, and give every satisfaction to the employers. Considering to our great regret we have left our relations from India and we have no one to look for protection.'[6]

The petition underscores the sense of isolation the migrants felt and details the crucial motivation for migration – to support families that were in 'distress'.

Rughoonath, an estate marker, and Coopen, estate guardian, both positions of responsibility, addressed a letter, marked 'Confidential' to Mr O'Connor, one of the few Inspectors of Immigrants who actively investigated grievances of labourers in Mauritius, on behalf of their indentured comrades. The letter, signed in their native languages, is indicative of the increasing sophistication of written complaints and the astuteness of the estate populations of immigrant Indians:

'We, the undersigned, respectfully beg to bring to your notice the following facts which, we hope, will meet with your early and favourable consideration.

1. That our wives and ourselves are exposed to the greatest trouble when the rain falls in the camp of the estate owing to its incessant leaky condition and the filthy matters which are daily accumulating around it and the bad smell emanating thereof.
2. That although, true it is, the proprietor has at last ordered new camps to be erected, yet, we are, in the meantime, unable to sleep without being inconvenienced by the rain almost every night, and the result is that most of the men, after having laboured all night long, under insomnia and

feeling unwell the following day, are, naturally obliged to absent themselves from their work.

3. That, I (Rughoonauth) marker on the estate think it my duty to inform you that all the labourers are bound, contrary to the Labour Law (according to what I am given to understand), to go to the cane field to receive their pay on the Sundays whereas the proprietor is only entitled to the corvee. In order to detect what I put forward I strongly advise you to come there on a Sunday early in the morning (that is, at 4.30 am).

4. That the proprietor of the La Laura estate is in the habit of speaking to us in such a bluntly rude manner that we are obliged willy-nilly to do what we are ordered, whether wrong or right, without any comment or representation, even, when we are to appear before the magistrate in any case against him Mr Hewetson, we are compelled to say (contrary to our conscience and feeling) what we are directed by him to say and not what we known of the case.

5. Under such circumstances and in presence of the above allegations, we have no other alternative than to lay our case before you firmly convinced that you will do your utmost to better our painful position, thereby sparing us the trouble of writing to His Excellency the Governor.

Kindly keep all these facts secret otherwise we shall be ill treated and dismissed from our respective places.'[7]

Owen O'Connor, the Inspector to whom the letter was addressed, noted that the missive had been forwarded to the Protector instead of himself, but reported that he had already addressed the matters mentioned, in his report on the state of the camp, after a visit on 30 May 1883.

> *Loi*
> *ce mot du sceau défait nos pétitions*
> *Loi sa Majesté roi-reine-son-altesse*
> *mots levés en plaie de silences respectueux*

Objection Votre Honneur!
Ces yeux incapables de nos juges d'être juges
d'eux-mêmes
leurs mots de mauvaise pénitence pour sanctionner
nos vagabondages de pure destinée
Loi
quelle scrofule démange la peau de leurs raisons
Loi
ta hauteur plus haute que la tour de l'usine
K Torabully, *Chair Corail, Fragments Coolies*, p. 77.

Law
This scything word undoes our petitions
Law His Majesty Your Royal Highness
Words raised from the wound of our respectful silences
Objection Your Honour!
Those incapable eyes of our judges, incapable of judging
Themselves
Their words of penitence serving to sanction
The vagabondage of our destiny
Law
What scrofula irritates the skin of their reasoning
Law
Your honour higher than the chimney of the sugar estate

The popularity of conscientious officials like O'Connor in Mauritius and Crosby in the Caribbean stemmed from the generalized distrust of magistrates evinced by Indians who quickly realized the close ties which connected the local judiciary and plantation owners. This was articulated by a group of Indians who complained to Des Voeux:

'O massa, no good go mahitee. Mahitee know manahee – go manahee's house – eat um breakfast – come court – no good coolie go court – mahitee friend manahee: always for manahee, no for Coolie.'[8]

This general climate of united opposition to the coolie, which spread from the overseer on the plantation to the local magistrate, impeded their recourse to justice, creating fear and suspicion on estates. This explains the desire for secrecy expressed by Rughoonauth and Coopen in their petition, and was articulated by Bechu, whose evidence to the West India Royal Commission included the perception that, because of 'the fear of their drivers, who keep indentured coolies so under subjection by abuses and threats, outspoken complaints are rare'.[9]

Protest at the poor working conditions which was so much at variance with expectations was articulated through folk songs:

Hearing the name of the island Mauritius
We arrived hoping to find gold
Instead we were beaten with bamboo sticks
That peeled the skin off the labourers' backs
We became the bullocks of the cane crushing machine
Oh! We have left India only to become coolies

A Unnuth, *Lal Pasina*, p. 226.

Women had particular subjects of grievance. Vellach, employed in Pietermaritzburg around 1880 complained to the Deputy Protector:

'About ten days ago whilst in my master's bedroom regulating it, he came in, striking his pocket and saying that he would give me three pounds if I were to lie with him, as the mistress and her family had gone to town. I refused saying that my husband would beat me. He said he would not tell him.'[10]

Some women expressed their vulnerability in the overseas labour context as a form of disgrace that prevented them from reintegrating in their former lives. Parbatier, who stated that she had been kidnapped in India, declared that she could not return home after her five-year contract in Trinidad had expired, 'because, according to Indian tradition, when a woman left her house – especially having spent the night out – she was not accepted back'. She accordingly married and settled in Trinidad.[11]

We have Survived

Uprooted
We have survived
The piercing morning
We have survived
Death in the backdams and hovels of hope
We have survived
We are the surviving
We who know the snake's fangs
The tides' and the seasons' treachery
The boot the fist the spit of the British Empire

A Itwaru, in Dabydeen & Samaroo (eds),
India in the Caribbean, 1987, p. 292.

Survival through Resistance

When the grievance procedure failed, or where complaining was perceived to be fruitless and even pernicious, indentured labourers had recourse to the age-old methods of resisting – desertion, arson and various forms of escapism. Ramasawmy, who returned from a five-year overseas contract in 1842, described the typical denouement of the unwilling indentured migrant:

'I was not accustomed to such work, and finding it too laborious
and painful, I left the plantation without leave, and absented
myself for two days . . . I was tried and sentenced to break black
stones for one month, after which I was sent back to my Master. I
remained at work in the Garden a few days when finding an
opportunity I deserted again, – I was apprehended and again
sentenced to break stones for a month which work I preferred to
that in the sugar cane plantation, consequently I committed some
offence continually . . . I was continually watched by police
officers, and frequently taken and treated as a vagrant and
sentenced to break stones.'[12]

Veeran ran away from his employer in Natal after a particularly vicious assault: 'I was 5 years in the service of Mr Greig as a field labourer and cook. He beat me on the head one day with an iron rod and cut my forehead because I would not make up the fire. I then ran into the bush for 3 days. When I came back I worked for 3 months for him, but never got any pay.'[13]

Boodhoo Khan, who described himself as a Pathan from Gya, had been working as a sepoy in the service of the British when he became one of the first indentured labourers to go to Mauritius in the mid-1830s. He was appointed a sirdar, or foreman of a band of estate workers, but after being demoted, refused to work as an ordinary fieldhand. His story of desertion and imprisonment ending in deportation was shared by many migrants who refused to work as common 'coolies':

> 'I was degraded from my sirdarship, and it was given to a
> Khalashee of the name of Buxoo who understood French. I was
> desired to do Coolie work; I refused, and was put in the stocks; I
> ran to the police sahib, who saw the marks of the stocks, and sent
> me back again, telling me I would get my sirdarship back . . . I
> was desired to do carpenter's work, I said 'Give me a musket and
> I will stand sentry; but I do not know carpenter's work', upon this
> I was beaten and again put into the stocks; I broke the stocks and
> again ran to the police; I was again sent back; and after being
> beaten, stocked and confined, I tried my hand at carpenter's
> work . . . I should not like to return, why should I? I went as a
> sirdar, was degraded and put in the stocks, and have left the
> country – why should I return?'[14]

Desertion was often only a short and unsatisfactory means of escaping estate labour. It inevitably ended in capture, jail, and an extended contract. Others reacted to ill-treatment by lashing out at their tormentors. On some occasions they collectively plotted to attack an overseer or a planter, or spontaneously turned on a brutal sirdar when they saw a workmate beaten. Indians resorted to violence against the oppression of the plantation in every country to which they migrated under indenture. In Reunion, 27 Indians turned on their overseer, Maunier, in 1851, striking him with their hoes. When a group of Indians in Mauritius killed the planter for whom they worked, their stark confessions to the police made chilling reading. Jhugroo pleaded guilty, explaining: 'Having assembled my friends, I assisted in killing my Master, because having been a shopkeeper in my own country, I had to learn field-labour and before knowing it I was much beaten. The treatment I received from my Master is what would not be done to an animal.' Bhowanee, who also pleaded guilty, stated:

'My master ill-treated me and my friends, gave small quantity of rations and kept us in a very miserable state. I told him once, to his face, I don't know whether he understood: kill me at once, and not to keep me without food. He was a very severe man, and did much harm to me and my friends. We claimed no wages on account of his ill treatment to us. I sold my clothes for food. Therefore we all assembled and killed him.'[15]

Arson was a means of striking against the oppression of the plantation while remaining anonymous and, generally, unpunished. Some migrants even committed such acts so as to be classified 'incorrigible vagabonds' and obtain cancellation of their contracts and ultimately a deportation order back to India. In 1896 Thayimansami rapidly succeeded, by his disorderly behaviour, in having himself sent back to Madras in 1896. The Mauritian Protector accordingly addressed a letter to the Emigration Agent at that port in the following terms:

'Thayimansami is a man of bad character, he will not work himself and incites his comrades to refuse work also, and his last escapade was to burn down a range of huts on the Mount Estate to which he had been engaged on arrival here. In consequence of this the Manager handed Thayimansami back to me, and as the man was willing to return to Madras I have given him a free passage in the Warora. I enclose Thayimansami's photo. Please do not send him back to this colony. He is young and strong and might have done very well here had he chosen to do so.'

In 1908, Mahadeo and Raghoo, both new immigrants engaged on Rosalie–Constance estate in Mauritius confessed to the harbour police that they had set fire to a range of huts. The Protector subsequently minuted:

'The two men Raghoo and Mahadeo seem to be of the type that
will do nothing to maintain themselves and prefer an easy life in
prison to working for their living. Raghoo is evidently the worst
of the two as he would not work at all. Both were deserters from
the estate and it is possible that owing to their vagrant habits they
had become unfit to work. There are only two methods of dealing
with men of this class – One is to return them to this home in
India, which is impossible now as they have committed a serious
crime for which they must be punished, the other is to send them
to a place where they will have to work such as the prison . . . I
went to see Raghoo and Mahadeo at the Port Louis prison
yesterday and can see no reason why they should not have
worked for their living on Rosalie–Constance estate. Raghoo who
is evidently a lazy man says the only work he ever did in India
was to act as a guardian, Mahadeo says he was a silversmith in
India and was consequently not able to work in the fields here.
Both of the men could have worked had they chosen to do so.
They say the object they had in view in setting fire to the range of
huts was to have their engagements cancelled.'[16]

For numerous indentured men and women, the ultimate escape from the
drabness and brutality of estate life was through suicide. Some hung
themselves because they were unable or unwilling to submit to the
degrading or severe manual labour expected of them. The vulnerability
of women placed many tensions on indentured families and were
another cause of suicides much discussed by officials. Ammakarina
explained her husband's suicide in the following words, in 1917:

'We were married five years ago. We had quarreled constantly. He
had complained constantly of my shortcomings as a housekeeper.
He placed a rope on the beam of our room a fortnight ago when I
expostulated with him.'[17]

All too often, the sexual exploitation of indentured women provoked
violence on the estates, and the phenomenon of the coolie 'wife murders'
was noted throughout the colonies to which Indian workers migrated.
The following account of Mulwa, a labourer in Natal, was replicated
across the sugar plantations of the British Empire. Mulwa murdered his

common-law wife, Nootini, in April 1890. The couple had been living with another Indian, Sahabdeen, who had offered money and food to both Mulwa and Nootini in return for the latter's sexual favours. Nootini was found one morning with Sahabdeen at a time when Mulwa's illness had threatened to leave them without food. After her death Mulwa stated 'I killed her because she went with other men.'[18]

A common form of escape from the drudgery and daily humiliations of life in the coolie lines was through addiction to rum and narcotics. Rum was a lucrative by-product of sugar estates, and its consumption was all too often facilitated by sugar planters looking to recoup wages paid through purchases made in the estate shop of alcohol. This was another example of the short-term profiteering which characterized some plantation owners, and which were to aggravate depressed socio-economic conditions in the late nineteenth century sugar colonies.

Indenture Escapism

je dormis sur la roue du désespoir
immigrant incendiaire suicidaire

K Torabully, *Chair Corail, Fragments Coolies*, p. 66.

I slept on the wheel of despair
Immigrant fire-hydrant heading for suicide.

O, my beloved,
I cannot leave yagona.
I have left my country, and my caste,
I have left my parents behind also,
But I cannot leave yagona.
Yagona is the Bhang [drug] of this island,
Which we drink to pass our nights.
I cannot leave yagona.

Quoted in B V Lal, 'Approaches to the Study of
Indian Indentured Emigration with Special
Reference to Fiji', *Journal of Pacific History*, p. 70.

For those indentured labourers whose thrift, contractual terms or disorderly conduct had not procured them a return passage, there was a final
option: the slim colonial fund which provided ship places to the old, the
diseased and the pauperized. Despatching the frail and elderly was one
means of shifting the burden of supporting the socially marginal back to
India. It was scant gratitude for decades of work provided by such
Indians, but in many cases, Indians themselves were desperate to return,
at the end of their working lives, or when ill health beset them, to the
care of long-absent family members.

Petitions begging for a return passage were common. Gopaul, who
wanted to go back to his family in India, wrote a heartfelt letter to the
District Magistrate of Pamplemousses, in Mauritius:

> *Monsieur Courtois,*
> *Désirant retourner dans mon pays natal, étant malheureux, je viens*
> *solliciter de vous, de votre coeur compatissant la faveur d'aller*
> *rejoinder mes père et mère. Ayez pitié de ma position, je suis sans feu*
> *ni lieu,l'idée de retrouver mes parents me chagrine. A vos genoux*
> *Monsieur j'implore votre bonté. Admettez moi, je vous en supplie,*
> *jusqu'à ce que j'ai passage gratis, laissez-moi, Monsieur, allez*
> *retrouver les auteurs de mes jours. Ici, dans ce pays, je suis*
> *malheureux.* (Monsieur Courtois, Wishing to return to my native
> country, being unhappy, I come to solicit your compassionate
> heart for the favour of rejoining my father and mother. Take pity
> on my position, I am without hearth or home, the idea of seeing
> my family again grips me. At your feet, Sir, I plead for your good
> grace. Let me in, I beg you, until I have free passage; allow me,
> Sir, to go and find those who gave me birth. Here, in this country,
> I am unhappy.)'[19]

Once disembarked, returning Indians who had been offered free passages – as opposed to those who were paying their own way – were
often penniless. Gajadhar, a 34-year old Thakur, returned from Suriname
with just one rupee in savings, and addressed a petition to the Protector
of Emigrants at Calcutta, explaining that having worked there for 15
years he had no money, and begged 'do me such favour as I get to my
native place, Banda, by railway, as I have none here to help me with a
copper'.[20]

Les cannes fleurissaient parce qu'ils avaient défriché, pioché, sarclé, dépaillé, – comme l'esclave, jadis – parce qu'ils avaient donné leur sueur à cette terre qui n'était pas à eux, dont pas une parcelle ne serait peut-être à eux, malgré les rigueurs auxquelles ils s'astreignaient, malgré ces travaux de chaque heure et ce riz qu'ils se refusaient pour que le fils eût une case à lui . . .

Oui, combien de ces hommes n'avaient eu de terre (eux qui aimaient tant la terre!) que la fosse où on les avait couchés dans le langouti de tous les jours!

M Cabon, *Namasté.*

These canes flourished because they had cleared the land, hoed, weeded, like the slave, heretofore – because they had given their sweat to this land which was not theirs, of which not even a small plot would belong to them, in spite of the hardships which they had suffered, despite the work at all hours, and the rice of which they deprived themselves so that the son could have a house of his own . . .

Yes, how many of these men did not have land (they who loved the earth so much!) only the ditch where they lay down to sleep in their langoutis, day in, day out.

Coolie Survival Strategies

Land and Liberty

Unlike the slave who envisaged liberation *from* the land which had for generations tied him to the whim of the estate owner, the coolie, frequently dispossessed in his own country, saw a path to prosperity and status *through* the land, firstly as a wage labourer under indenture, and ultimately through its cultivation on his own account and acquisition in his own right. In Mauritius, as soon as they had acquired some capital through wages, Indians rapidly investigated the means of purchasing land. Juggoo, on of the first wave of migrants to Mauritius in the 1830s, and a native of Lucknow, addressed a petition to the Mauritian

Governor, requesting to be allowed to purchase land in his own name. Whilst Chinese traders on the island, as aliens, were not accorded the right to own immoveable assets, the Indians, as British subjects suffered no such restrictions. In reply to his petition, therefore, Juggoo was told: '[T]here can exist no objection to your holding landed property in your own name in this island.'[21]

A class of Indian landholders rapidly grew in Mauritius, to such an extent, that from the 1860s onwards a series of laws were implemented designed to hold the indentured and ex-indentured labourers on the estates, and to obstruct their freedom to work the land on their own account. A letter addressed by an old immigrant to the Aborigines Protection Society in London, sought to reveal the extent of discriminatory practices put in place:

'I beg leave to call your attention to Ordinance no 13 of 1875, which has just been enacted by the Legislative Council of the Mauritius.

This Ordinance, under pretence of preserving the woods and forests of the Colony, contrives to eject from their lands hundreds of petty landowners whose sole means of livelihood and fortune consist in those very lands. Among the sacrificed tribe are a vast number of old immigrants who have acquired their land by purchase: in conformity with instruments and deeds of ownership which have hitherto been reputed sacred and inviolable by the laws and customs of this island.

In pursuance of the newly enacted law they are threatened with complete ruin, and their families and children doomed to poverty and misery, since not a farthing is to be paid to them in the shape of indemnity or compensation for the injury they are to sustain . . .

As the matter is a very serious one for the old immigrants, I venture to hope, Sir, that it will meet with the earliest consideration of your Association.'[22]

As a consequence of the rapid development of a property-owning and entrepreneurial class of ex-indentured Indians in Mauritius, other colonial administrations sought to prevent a similar situation developing in their own territories. Various means were put in place to ensure this: Natal repatriated ex-indentured Indians, while Fiji instituted restrictions on acquisition of land by immigrants.

Another avenue of mobility for the Indian was through entrepreneurial activities. An example of the socio-economic progress of an overseas Indian is demonstrated in the career of Somnath Maharaj, a nineteenth century Indian migrant to Natal. He had 'served the Colony for five years under indenture, had been resident in the Colony for 13 years as a free Indian, had by dint of perseverance raised himself to the position of a trader, had held a licence in Mooi River in the Colony over six years, had a cash capital of £50, held a piece of freehold land in the borough.'[23]

Wherever schemes were put in place to restrict the mobility of the ex-indentured Indian, he devised means to circumvent them. In Natal, Gandhi soon found that indentured Indians were among his most reliable supporters in anti-discrimination agitation. And in Mauritius, where an elaborate pass system of tickets with photographs was put in place to identify and control ex-indentured labourers, or so-called 'old immigrants', a thriving industry of fraud and duplication was soon in place. The case of Maree, who obtained and used the ticket of a deceased 'passenger' or free Indian, is one of many. He was found in possession of Ramsamy Pandien's ticket, after its real owner had hanged himself. Maree's explanation of how he came to have the ticket revealed a traffic in tickets originating within the Immigration Department itself:

'My name is Maree and I was born in Madras, my father's name is Chinaven. I am 6 years in the colony of Mauritius. I was engaged to Mr Lervile of Riviere des Creoles estate in the district of Grand Port, but I have been discharged from the estate. I have lost my immigration ticket and certificate of discharge. The ticket now in my possession was given to me in Port Louis by a peon of the Immigration Office by paying Rs 12 to the Peon . . . this Peon had been speaking to me on several occasions, and said it is not good to go about without any papers, give me Rs 12 and I will give you a ticket which I have got, I went and worked as Porter at the bazaar of P Louis carrying small parcels for persons at Bazaar, and it was by way of working he gathered the sum of Rs 12 which was the sum asked for by the Peon of the

Immigration Office . . . one day I met the Peon the street . . . the
peon gave me the ticket and I gave him the Rs 12 . . . the peon
warned me not to inform anyone that he had given me the
ticket.'[24]

With indentured immigration bringing thousands of new labourers to the
colonies every year in the mid-nineteenth century, when high prices
produced a flurry of activity among sugar capitalists, ethnic entrepre-
neurs also began to migrate, seeing the huge profits to be made from
providing services to the new communities springing up overseas.
Barbers, jewellers, priests, many making their own passages, or reverting
to these service occupations after completing indenture contracts, could
make a good living from restoring some semblance of the familiar to
overseas Indians. Men with some learning, who could translate for police
and court officials, or who could write letters home for their comrades
and petitions to the authorities, were in great demand. In Reunion
Antoine Rayen carved a lucrative career out of interpreting for Indian
merchants in the late nineteenth century.[25]

Indians set themselves up as traders and market gardeners, predom-
inantly serving their own community. In Mauritius, within a few years
of their arrival, Indians were already petitioning the authorities for
licences to establish small businesses. For example, in 1848, Ramsamy,
who had arrived from Madras in 1843, and had just completed his
obligatory period of work on the estates, known as 'industrial
residence', was already requesting permission to open a grocery
shop.[26]

In St Lucia, Comins, a British Indian official, came across Umeer, an
ex-indentured Indian who, he reported 'now does no work, but owns
12 cows, two ponies and some goats, and is worth about Rs 1,000.'[27]
Mahadai Das, in this succinct couplet, evokes the ambitions of those
indentured labourers for whom economic gain seemed a far away
hope:

> 'Dreams of a cow and endless calves,
> And endless reality in chains.'[28]

> Indentured labourers adapted as best they could, recreating some home comforts even in the drab 'coolie lines' as this song from Fiji indicates:
>
> The six foot by eight foot room
> Is the source of all comfort for us.
> In it we keep our tools and hoe,
> And also the grinding stove and the hearth.
> In it is also kept the firewood.
> It is our single and double-storey palace,
> In which is made our golden parapet.
>
> > Quoted in BV Lal, 'Approaches to the Study of Indian
> > Indentured Emigration with Special Reference to Fiji',
> > *Journal of Pacific History*, p. 68.

Culture and Religion

Migration entailed a temporary release from traditional sanctions and disciplines that were exercised in the natal villages through customary structures such as the *panchayat*, or meetings of community elders. In the overseas setting, Indians found themselves subject to new pressures – the initial scarcity of women made their partners vulnerable to exploitation and abduction, for example – and many turned to a substitute authority: the immigration departments, and the Protector of Immigrants appointed in British colonies where they settled, to resolve their disputes and redress their grievances. In seeking to restore their authority over their wives, indentured men were adopting one of several strategies designed to reinstate some semblance of the cultural values of their homeland. The letter Moothen sent to the Protector in South Africa in 1875 is typical. In it he complained that his wife of 24 years, Chinnamah, had left him, with their four children to look after, while she was:

'. . . living with another Indian named Theracumny. Thay are both living together about a mile and a half from Pietermaritzburg and my wife is conceived of a child by this Theracumny . . . I humbly leave it for your judgement and trust that my wife may be sent back to me.'[29]

From the earliest years of migration, Indians sought, in the overseas context, to reaffirm customary values and principles, as a means of protection against exploitation and intrusion. Djooram, who went to Mauritius as an ayah in the 1830s, described how her affirmation of her 'caste' and status as a Muslim was invoked to resist the sexual aggression of her employer:

> '. . . went to Mr Boileau; I served him for two and a half years; he treated me very ill, gave me no pay, beat me, and said he would give me much money if I would let him have connexion with me; I told him he ought to be ashamed, that he had a wife in his bosom; that I was a Mussulmanee, and would lose my caste among my fellows, and refused, and he beat me; I was made to sweep the rooms and do mehtranee's work, and I complained to the police and they said as my master so spoke to me, and I did not wish to serve him, I might go back to my own country.'

Heemgun, from Bihar, was one of many Indians who refused, overseas, to undertake work that was associated with an inferior caste. He reported that having worked as a 'khitmudgar' in India, he left his first employer, in Mauritius 'because my master's relatives insisted upon my cleaning the floor of the house'. These sources give the lie to official stereotypes of the overseas Indians as having lost 'their respect for the caste and religion of their fathers which they neglect'.[30]

In fact, indentured labourers used such notions of self-worth to prevent themselves from being reduced to servile status in the ex-slave sugar colonies. The creation of an intermediary class of overseers and foremen was one of the important means through which Indians began to recreate their own structures of hierarchy and authority. The recognition of the superior role of the sirdar was articulated by Ismael who had come to Mauritius as a child and worked for many years as a sirdar on the estate of Beauchamp in Flacq, but was reindentured as an ordinary labourer after having returned to India to recruit new immigrants for his employer:

> 'How can you think that I, knowing the hardship of a laborer's position, having been already a sirdar on the estate, with my

people in good circumstances on the estate, would engage as a common laborer on that estate. I was deceived and it has been the cause of much misery to me and my mother.'[31]

The importance of the sirdar's role in the recreation of 'traditional' cultural values is indicated by their prominence in the reconstruction of a religious life on the estates and in the new villages that grew up around them. They frequently took the lead in raising funds for the construction of places of worship and organizing religious celebrations. When the Coolie Commission came to investigate the conditions of Indians in Natal in 1872, an ex-sirdar turned hotelier, named Rangassamy, took the opportunity to inform his interlocuters of the religious and social aspirations of the indentured labourers:

'We want temples wherein to worship. We should like the government to establish a Coolie location, and let us build a shrine there . . . among the coolies we first imported, too many males were single, and the scarcity of females caused many debauches, and in many cases they committed suicide . . . if a woman commits adultery, she should be punished by cutting off her hair, and 10 days imprisonment, and cautioned that if she goes to another man, she must pay the first husband 10 pounds . . . schools should be built, because the white children will not take Coolie children in to their schools.'[32]

The anxiety of these new 'cultural leaders' of the Indians overseas to legitimize their cultural and religious traditions is revealed by the letter of Marimouthou, an Indian sirdar on the French island of Reunion, who carefully described a religious procession which the Indians wished to organize in 1872, in terms synonymous with Catholic rituals:

'Nous sortons, en grande pompe, en procession, de l'Etablissement de Sucrerie Laprade à Saint Paul, ou se trouve le siège de notre autel, à deux heures de l'après-midi; nous faisons un tour en ville et nous sommes toujours rentrés à cinq heures. Ce n'est seulement trois heures de procession pendant lesquelles évidemment, les tambours et nos chants se font entendre. Chez les catholiques, c'est identiquement semblable.

(We leave, with great ceremony, in a procession, from the
Lamprade Sugar Estate at Saint Paul, where our church has
its base ; at 2 in the afternoon we make a procession round
the town, and we are always back by 5 pm. The drums
and the singing are only heard for the three hours during
which the procession lasts. It is exactly the same as the
Catholics.)'[33]

Bone Sculpture
A mourner in the Mohurrum
Procession, mixing blood with
Mud, memory with memory.

A S Ali, *Bone-Sculpture*, p. 1–5.

The importance of the recreation of religious and cultural traditions
overseas was also articulated by a group of Indians in Guadeloupe who
in 1884 addressed a petition to the Governor of Madras in which they
detailed their sufferings. Among their grievances, they noted:

'*Pour les gens de notre classe qui émigrent dans d'autres contrées, il
n'y a ni temples, ni fêtes, ni adorateurs, ni bons ni mauvais jours; pas
d'écoles pour nos enfants; ils ne reçoivent aucune education. Il nous
semble que les bêtes et les bestiaux soient mieux traités que nous
dans cette colonie* (For people of our class who emigrate to other
lands, there are no temples, no festivals, no idols, no good or bad
days, no schools for our children, who receive no education of any
kind. It seems to us that animals are better treated than us in this
colony).'[34]

Thus wherever Indians settled, small temples sprang up, and at various
times of the year, processions and festivities could be seen, which replicated the seasonal and spiritual rites and rituals of the mother country.
Lifestyle customs were also recreated where possible overseas, with
Indians seeking permission to cremate their dead, and instituting complicated matrimonial arrangements. When old immigrant Bahooram's
marriage plans for his son fell through, due to the withdrawal of the

intended bride, he informed the Protector of the 'elders' of the community who could give evidence in his favour: he named several Hindu shopkeepers who could speak on his behalf.[35]

> *Au village coolie, c'est fête ce soir,*
> *le divali sème ses lumières*
> *dans nos yeux constellés d'espoirs*
> *Malini brule l'encens de myrrhe*
> *danse au rythme saccadé du navire.*
>
> *. . . Soudain, je revois Malini*
> *quand elle quitta le dépôt de la quarantaine.*
> *Ses yeux vides erraient sa vie en peine,*
> *lourde de leur mépris.*
>
> *La foule se lève au son du dholok*
> *Malini danse . . .*
> *Et le village coolie célèbre la ferveur retrouvée.*
>
> *. . . le camp coolie exalte l'incendie des vaisseaux*
> *. . . les coupeurs de cannes brûlent*
> *leurs songes carniphages*
> *dans un littoral hésitant entre départ et amarrage.*
>
> K Torabully, *Chair Corail, Fragments Coolies*, pp. 115–19.

In the coolie village there is rejoicing tonight
Diwali is sewing its lights
In our eyes with their constellations of hope
Malini is burning incense of myrrh
Dancing to the jerky rhythm of the ship

Suddenly I see Malini as she was
When she left the quarantine depot
Her empty eyes wandering as in pain
Heavy with contempt

> The crowd rises to the sound of the dholok
> Malini dances
> And the coolie villages celebrates a regained fervour
>
> . . . The coolie camp exalts in the burning of the ships
> The cane cutters burn
> Their meat-eating dreams
> Veer between arrival and departure in the hesitant littoral.

The indenturing, or verbal engagement, of children as young as ten on estates entailed a loss of control on the part of parents, who could not protect their offspring from penal sanctions instituted by employers for acts of desertion or neglect, which they also sought to redress. When the ten-year-old son of Bhagoo, who had been given charge of 50 sheep, ran off one evening, on his return the estate owner 'tied the boy's hands together with a strap and hung him naked to a rafter in the dining room and thrashed him with a hunting crop'. Bhagoo addressed a letter to the Protector complaining of this act and of his own treatment on the estate, ending 'The other coolies on the estate witnessed my son being beaten. I refuse to return to the estate'.[36]

Clinging fiercely onto their status as parents, spouses and as fellow human beings was an important means by which indentured workers, who replicated slave labour in the fields, sought to avoid having servility thrust upon them off the canefields. That immigrants resented the status of coolie is indicated by this folk song from British Guiana:

> 'Why should we be called coolies,
> We who were born in the clans and families of seers and
>   saints?'[37]

In seeking redress for the seizure of his papers, Narayanin Gangapanaiken, a Tamil labourer in Reunion, addressed the authorities in 1870, insisting on his rights as a French citizen in that colony:

> *'Je suis, Monsieur, par ma position et par ma famille, Français quoique*
> *né dans l'Inde, et d'ailleurs il y a 22 ans que je suis dans la Colonie.*

(I am, Sir, by my position and by my family, French, despite being born in India, and furthermore I have been in this colony for 22 years.)'[38]

The spirit of dignity with which the indentured labourers bore their exile, and the long years of their subjection to the sugar estate under their indenture contracts is captured in this couplet from 'We have Survived' by Arnold Itwaru:

> 'Our men are proud: they bear handsomely
> The garments of their imprisonment.'[39]

In the poem 'Illegitimacy', Sheila Ramdass has also described the humiliation of the designation 'coolie' and its inappropriateness to the indentured labourer:

> 'christened coolie
> by French Creole and slavery
> a derogatory label
> for a stalwart people'[40]

Je suis
l'indien de Saint Alary
blessé de la dénomination de coolie
D'Aubéro à Port Louis
rapatrié aussi
re-engagé sans terre ni pays
> K Torabully, *Chair Corail, Fragments Coolies*, p. 95.

I am
The Indian from Saint Alary
Wounded by the designation of coolie
From Aubero to Port Louis
Repatriated eternally
Re-engaged without land nor country

The theme of dignity in adversity as characterizing the indentured Indian is strongly conveyed in Chandran Nair's poem 'Grandfather':

> 'he grew with age, aged to ripened toughness
> to resist anger, misfortune of stricken years
> with dignity unpersuaded.'[41]

In similar vein, Rajkumari Singh pays homage to the Indo-Guyanese woman, in her poem 'Per-Ajie':

> 'I can see
> How in stature
> Thou didst grow
> Shoulders up
> Head held high
> The challenge
> In thine eye.'[42]

The refusal to accept an inferior 'coolie' status and the consequent aspirations of Indian immigrants for a better life continued in their hopes and ambitions for their colonial-born offspring. David Dabydeen captures brilliantly the determined drive for their children's betterment, in his poem 'Coolie Mother':

> 'Beat clothes, weed yard, chop wood, feed fowl
> For this body and that body and every blasted body . . .
> Because Jasmattie heart hard, she mind set hard
> To hustle save she one-one slow penny
> Because one-one duty make dam cross the Canje
> And she son Harilall got to go school in Georgetown . . .
> Learn talk proper, take exam, go to England university,
> Not turn out like he rum-sucker chamar dadee.'[43]

The veneration of indentured ancestors by diaspora Indians has, paradoxically, occurred alongside the dramatization of their experiences of oppression. In 'Slave Song', David Dabydeen portrays the cane cutter as a symbol of exploitation and endurance. The brokenness of the Creole language employed in the poem is designed to evoke the broken desires

of the cane cutter.[44] While it seems difficult to equate this with the dignified bearing and high aspirations of Indian labourers, it is an extension
of coolies' own remembrances of their days in 'narak' or hell, as the Fiji
Indians described indenture. Guyanese-born Indian writer Cyril
Dabydeen has turned the cane labour of his father into a symbolic battle:

> 'gone
> To battle canes, and to return
> Flailed.'[45]

One of the last colonies to import indentured labour, Fiji also was one of
the few to record detailed interviews with survivors of 'girmit'. In their
statements the ex-indentured Indians tended to stress the harshness of
the estate regime. An Indian who arrived in 1911 later described his
arrival in Fiji: 'we were herded into a punt like pigs and taken to Nukulau
where we stayed for a fortnight. We were given rice . . . full of worms
[and] kept and fed like animals.'[46]

Migrant testimonies which recall the bitter days of indenture and which
emphasize the deceit employed in recruitment, may be counterbalanced
by songs from the colonies of settlement which indicate that migration was
equally seen as an avenue of escape from social oppression. A Hindi folksong from Surinam pokes fun at the 'high castes' in India and implies that
emigration was a means of flight for the underdogs of the caste system:

> 'I call India blessed, and the Brahmans and Kshatriayas too,
> Who attach untouchability to their subjects.
> They rule by the power of these very subjects,
> While keeping the company of prostitutes.
> The subjects escaped and came to the islands
> And, yes, India turned on her side.'[47]

Recreating A Homeland Overseas

Derek Walcott describes how the overseas Indian recreated images
of his homeland in his adopted country. The Hindu in Trinidad of
his poem does not miss India because it is everywhere around him.

From the fireflies 'making every dusk Divali' to the very cane-fields of his Caribbean home:

Once the sacred monkeys multiplied like branches
In the ancient temples; I did not miss them,
Because these fields sang of Bengal,
Behind Ramlochan Repairs there was Uttar Pradesh . . .

> D Walcott, *The Star-Apple Kingdom*, p. 33.

For others, the sense of nostalgia for India is never satisfied and only finds articulation in rum-sodden fantasies. In 'Coolie Odyssey', we are told about Old Dabydeen's fate:

Dreaming of India
He drank rum
Till he dropped dead

> D Dabydeen, 'Coolie Odyssey', in Dabydeen & Samaroo
> (eds), *India in the Caribbean*, p. 281.

'To the Indians who died in Africa'

A man's destination is not his destiny,
Each country is home to one man
And exile to another. Where a man dies bravely
At one with his destiny, that soil is his.

> T S Eliot, quoted in Northrup, p. 31.

4

Reclaiming the 'Other':
Diaspora Indians and
the Coolie Heritage

*Coolies had a culture of the written word, and they set off on their voyage
with books: the Qur'an, the Bhagavad Gita and the Ramayana. These
sacred texts were part and parcel of their journey . . . a struggle against
deculturation took place. Coolies clung to their founding texts.*

K Torabully, 1996, p. 15.

*The coolie was never the passive instrument of the colonialist imagination or
the historian's pen. The coolie was not forever condemned to be famine
victim, dully toiling with the hoe, helpless to eradicate the burden of a
momentary hunger. The indenture experience was not static and the coolie's
adjustments and aspirations carried a first-generation of migrants forward,
beyond the indenture contract, towards the hopes of prosperity, ownership
and return. For many years, however, 'coolie' was a symbol of economic
degradation and social submissiveness, and the descendants of coolies felt
themselves to be equally stigmatized, exoticized and ostracized. The
reclamation of the 'coolie' and the transformation of the indenture heritage is
an ongoing process.*

In most of the colonies to which indentured Indians migrated, and where
subsequent or pre-existing mercantile communities from India also settled, the latter made strenuous efforts to disassociate themselves from
the negatively stereotyped 'coolie'. For example, in 1888 a group of
Indian merchants in Johannesburg urged the government to resist agita-
tors who sought 'to class your petitioners with Arabs, Coolies, or Chinese
not suitable to do business in this State . . . your petitioners assure your
Excellencies that they are none of these people and have nothing in

common with them.'[1] In 1894 the Natal Indian Congress clarified the distinction between trader and indentured Indians: 'The better-class Indians feel and see there is a difference between the raw coolie and themselves.' Gandhi himself, in his early years in South Africa, persistently agitated on behalf of the Indian merchants, to distance them from the coolies. In 1899 he requested the British Agent on behalf of the Indians of Johannesburg that the official 'Coolie Location' change its name to 'Indian Location.'[2] In 1905 Gandhi reproached Lord Selborne, the British High Commissioner, over his employment of the word 'coolie':

'The use of the word "coolie" has caused a great deal of mischief in Natal. At one time it became so serious that the then Justice Sir Walter Wragg had to intervene, and to put down the use of that expression in with any but indentured Indians, it having been even imported into the court of justice. As Your Excellency may be aware, it means 'labourer' or 'porter'. Used, therefore, in connection with traders, it is not only offensive but a contradiction in terms.'[3]

While one negative construct in the overseas context identified the coolie with a downtrodden labourer, another, particularly prevalent in the sugar-producing islands, viewed the Indian as the usurper of the indigenous worker's rightful, negotiated place in the socio-economic hierarchy. A British Indian civil servant who visited Mauritius in the first decade of indentured immigration reported a case: 'where the old slaves of an estate had come to their master and begged him to send for no more Indians to take the bread out of their mouths'. The Anti-Slavery Society in Britain, for its part, lost no time in driving home the message that 'the real object for which this host of Indians has been imported into Mauritius has been to lower the price of wage, by compelling the Negroes to accept such terms as their masters choose to give them, or to starve . . . whilst the planters are allowed to import any amount of adult labourers they please to cultivate their estates, they never will care for rearing a Creole peasantry.'[4]

> *Je ne suis pas d'ici comme on est commis de seconde classe.*
> *Je suis père des métamorphoses*
> *après avoir longtemps courbé ma langue*
> *devant le saccage des cervelles.*
> *On ne dira plus c'etait un bon coolie . . .*
> *On ne dira plus que la gale de sa misère*
> *le ravale a l'insignifiance de sa présence*
> *. . . on dira qu'il a retrouve l'appétit des mots*
> *au cri puissant de son humanité*
>   K Torabully, *Chair Corail, Fragments Coolies*, p. 101.
>
> I am the father of metamorphoses
> After having for so long held my tongue
> Before the looting of minds
> They will no longer say 'he was a good coolie' . . .
> They will no longer say that the scab of his misery
> Reduces him to the insignificance of his *physionomy* . . .
> They will say that he has rediscovered an appetite for words
> At the powerful cry of his humanity.

Indian indentured workers and their descendants were thus stigmatized as 'scab' labour. The Royal Commissioners who visited Guyana in 1870 remarked on the antagonism which still persisted between Creoles and Indians there, although they imbued this with their own orientalist perceptions: 'The coolie despises the negro because he considers him . . . not so highly civilised as himself, while the negro despises the coolie because he is so immensely inferior to himself in physical strength.' However, when Kesaddat, a 'passenger' or free Indian who arrived in Mauritius in 1879 to visit his son, found the latter unable to support him, he was obliged to ask to be considered as a 'coolie' in order to obtain a free return passage:

'. . . having no means to support himself he wishes to return to
Calcutta, where he has family, but has not the means of doing
so . . . Therefore he humbly prays that you may be pleased to take
his poor situation into your serious consideration and allow him a

free passage as coolie in order that he may return to Calcutta and join his family or otherwise, he will be in a very sad position here.'[5]

Faced with cultural and economic fixing, indentured immigrants sought to mitigate hostility and climb off the bottom of the heap through acquisition of linguistic skills and material assets. Coolies were well aware that they suffered through inability to comprehend their new employers. One indentured Indian women in Natal complained that she was beaten after failing to understand the instructions given to her: 'because they do not speak to me in my language.'[6] When Jubboo, in Mauritius, sought to prosecute his employer for non-payment of wages, he found that his insufficient knowledge of the language of the court prejudiced his hearing: 'your Petitioner regrets to state that owing to his being totally unacquainted with the English language (and . . . having not given sufficient evidence to support your Petitioner's claim) – the Stipendiary Magistrate dismissed the case.'[7]

Je suis braconnier
j'écris l'histoire d'arracheurs de pages
de courtiers marrons apposant le codicille
de ma reddition . . .

K Torabully, *Chair Corail, Fragments Coolies*, p. 39.

I am a poacher
I write the history of those who tore its pages
Of runaway clerks fixing the seal
On my surrender . . .

Indentured workers quickly learnt that acquisition of the colonial language was a prerequisite for socio-economic mobility, while their very status and situation depended on the correct formulation of the written word. The indenture contracts and later their old immigrant tickets effectively wrote them into colonial social and economic relationships. A misleading clause in the former, or a mistaken spelling in the latter, could spell economic hardship or even prison. The importance of comprehending the language of the colonists and of its verbal variants was soon addressed by indentured Indians.

Etrange miroir
Qui me nomma
Sans savoir parler
Tel ce scribe etrange
Qui assassina mes ombres
En arrachant le parchemin
De mon grand registre de corps.

K Torabully, *Cale d'Étoiles*, p. 27.

Strange mirror
Which named me,
Unable to speak –
Like that strange scribe
Who murdered my shadows,
By tearing the page
From the large logbook of my body.

The 'Coolie Code':
Colonial Languages and Legalities

The lives of indentured labourers were regulated by pieces of paper, generally written in unfamiliar languages. Their signature (or, more usually, thumb print) on an indenture contract signed in India or overseas was therefore an act of trust. Believing in the terms and conditions offered by officials acting in the name of the Indian government, migrants were understandably upset when the realities of life under indenture did not tally with the promises made by recruiters and emigration agents. When Boyjoo wrote to the Mauritian authorities to complain that he was not in receipt of rations, clothes and wages as stipulated in his contract, his sense of injustice is apparent: 'what thing is wrote I could not get. I am injure. I am not get the Calcutta paper. Told you go to there your paper is crodit by company. I come to the Moritious I could not get . . . not give fish not give tobacoo not give oil . . . I am eat my own pokit.'

The senior police officer in Mauritius noted that Boyjoo had been in Mauritius for three years, and that he 'complains that he is not victualled according to his engagement and that he has several months wages due to him'. It was decided that Boyjoo should be sent to the local magistrate of his district, to ascertain the correct terms of his engagement.[8]

The raison d'être of migration, for the vast majority, was economic. Thus the sending back of money assumed a huge importance both for migrants and those left at home, for whom the official slip indicating a money order might be the only contact with a relative and could also represent the difference between a year of poverty and one of plenty. However, the difficulties of ascertaining the correct details of would-be recipients often necessitated much confusion as complicated bureaucratic procedures were carried out. When Pethuyee Themalarajinpattanam received a money order sent by his son Cooppan from Natal, he was obliged to make several trips to the Post Offices of Negapatam and Tanjore in South India in an effort to cash the order. At one point, having asked his daughter to look after the order, 'she slipped it into a gooseberry-pickle pot and pickled it up', as he later ruefully reported to the authorities![9]

Pour ses premières racines
comme des rois inconnus
coolie naquit sous un multipliant:
son tatouage est ma seule marque d'oubli
ultime vésanie, mon ultime habit.

> K Torabully, *Cale d'Étoiles*, p. 24.

Came the first roots
Like so many anonymous kings.
Coolie was born under the banyan-tree . . .
His tattoo was my oblivious signature,
My ultimate attire, my private folly.

Despite their initial unfamiliarity with the omnipotence which their contracts and tickets represented, Indians overseas quickly adapted to the legal and linguistic norms of their countries of adoption, drafting petitions which asked for redress and pleaded for favours in elaborately stylized phrases. Gopaul's heartfelt letter in French to Monsieur Courtois is a good illustration of this.

For those Indians who could not afford to pay a letter-writer who would couch their plaints in a style designed to appeal to colonial officials, petitions in their own broken English or that of their slightly more literate peers, provide examples of the process through which the unfamiliar language was painfully acquired. In 1841 Porunsing drew the attention of the authorities to his unhappiness at being transferred to work on an estate in the district of Savanne, far from Moka where he was employed. He had been on hunger strike for seven days when he sent the following letter, which conveys, through the stumbling, broken phrases, the drama of his predicament and the steadfastness of his resolve:

'I am able to duty but my massa not give try of us. Tell if you go to Lasabad I will give your duty, I am not give duty in Moco. We are not give try in Lasabad. We are able to give the duty in Moco. I am past four years. Four days is past not take duty not give rice not give place. You are god and father and mother you do sufficient other tell yourselves where you are please you may go there. I am not money not food one month 9 days not give gee and gram. We are go to his house. He come and flog us. Where you are please you may go that way. I am no place you go to Company Road. I got witness Aunut, Jock. You are father and mother of this particular if you want to try in Moco. We are able neither you give the paper. We are duty in other place. Neither you send in my place at Calcutta other we will get much pains, if you understand neither we are . . . in the water you have carried from my house. If you please to injure you cut of my throat of you own hand neither we are not go to Lasaboo. Quickly you do concede. We are died for food. I am not able to steal of any one. What is concede you may concede. We are go to want us . . . that not give we come to flog. Say you may go to hell done come to my house, if you want to duty in Lasaboo you come to my house neither I am not want.'[11]

An enquiry into the case revealed that Porunsing and nine others had declared that they were ready to forfeit their lives rather than go to

Savanne. In the event, three guards conducted them by force to the far-flung district.

Arnold Itwaru conveys the sense of isolation caused by the exile from the mother-tongue country:

We have survived the breakage of speech
Language which formulates us
In its curse
>   A Itwaru, 'We have Survived', in Dabydeen & Samaroo (eds),
>   *India in the Caribbean*, p. 292.

When Mr Pillay sought to reveal his plight to the colonial authorities, he stressed his proficiency in English, but apologized in advance for his poor writing:

'Honoured Sir I educated in Tamil Telegu and English can speak and write well beside I can draw plans tracing survey in Engineer Department. I were employed in Madras Irrigation Canal Company as a masonary on the salary of 45 rupees since 7 1/2 years. After receiving the notice I applied in the D-P-W as a surveyor since 5 years in the Balampully Chanks, by the Hills water. I resigned my post from Cuddapah District came to Nellore District in that place I engaged through the Immigration Maistries. I do not know how I came to Mauritius. Up to this time I did work the hard work, at present I too sick and I cannot work in sugar garden – honoured Sir please give me any official work or in the Engineer Department – . . . my forearm is lame I cannot work . . . or else I can take my life front of your honour.

For such act of kindness I shall pray for your long life and I am bad sick I cannot sit or stand and therefore I cannot write well.'[12]

The combination of the obsequious – 'honoured Sir' – and the dramatic – threatening to take his life in front of the Protector – was a notable feature of the petitions of indentured Indians. On enquiring into his case, the Immigration Department discovered that Pillay had been offered hospital treatment by his employer, and initially recommended that he be sent back to the estate. Ultimately, however, the authorities and his employer relented, and a final report on the case noted: 'He was employed in India as a surveyor and has received a certain education – this circumstance also unfits him to a certain extent for working as a labourer. Ask the Manager to consider these circumstances and to see whether, for humanity's sake, he cannot find some employment in the estate for him more compatible with his previous training and physical strength which will permit of his completing his industrial residence on the estate.'

As more and more Indians migrated, their identification and control became a time-consuming task. Immigration Departments, headed by Protectors of Immigrants, increasingly became the depositories of registers, and the headquarters of a bureaucracy that policed the indentured and time-expired labourers, rather than the nerve-centre where grievances could be investigated and redressed. The identification of Indians according to an immigration number, which was reproduced on all official documents, assumed a huge importance in their lives. A spouse might lose all claim over his or her partner if the documents did not tally, and a number on a ticket could make the difference between a continuation of servitude or the acquisition of 'old immigrant' status. As the petition of Peerally reveals, knowing the immigration number and acquiring an 'order' might be the only means of proving a claim to an inheritance:

'. . . *je désire Honorable d'obtenir de vous le numéro de Moosaheb et mon numéro et vous demander un ordre . . . je suis un des héritiers à Moosaheb mon Cousin; Honorable je vous demande un ordre afin que je puis réclamer mes droits.* (Honourable Sir, I desire to obtain from you the number of Moosaheb and my number, and ask you to order . . . I am one of the legatees of Moosaheb, my cousin; Honourable Sir I ask an order from you in order to reclaim my rights.)'[13]

The drafting of a letter was a serious undertaking for those less well-educated indentured labourers who had to enlist the services of a writer, or take a permission to leave the estate in order to complete the necessary formalities for the despatch of a remittance home. For those returning to India, the written testimonial of the colonial authority or of the employer was an equally crucial symbol of their induction into overseas service. It differentiated them from their less well-travelled countrymen, indicated that they could be trusted with money, and that they had, by dint of hard work or good leadership qualities, been wholly absorbed into the labour requirements of the plantation system. Within a decade of the commencement of indentured migration, such Indians were being sent back to recruit their compatriots. They carried with them written guarantees as to their status and reliability. Thus when Dhibby Deen, an early recruit to Mauritius, returned to collect fellow countrymen for service overseas, he was provided with the following note:

> 'The bearer of this, Dhibby Deen, is a man of good character, who
> returns to his native country with a sum of money. His intention
> being to come back to the Mauritius, we authorise you, should he
> apply to you for the cost of his passage, to pay the same at a rate
> not exceeding [company rupees] 30 besides the cost of food, as
> well as to any able-bodied men who may wish to accompany
> him, not exceeding 50 in number, forwarding us their receipt in
> duplicate for the sum paid.'

Ramasawmy was promised the handsome sum of two rupees for every labourer he was able to recruit in India and was given 'a letter to the address of Messrs Hall and Bainbridge at Madras, with direction to draw on these gentlemen as much as I may require to hire labourers'. Munnoo Missir, a bramin, who was appointed a sirdar, or foreman in Mauritius, was so much appreciated by his employers, that when he left for India they gave him 'a present of 120 rupees, as well as a silver watch of the value of 30 rupees and a written testimonial of good conduct and then procured me a passage on board a ship'.[14]

Such men had a vested interest in the acquisition of colonial languages as they represented a bridge between new immigrants and the plantation societies in which they had flourished. However, the class of sirdars that emerged from the ranks of indentured labourers came to be as much defined by their role as purveyors of Indian culture and religion as by their mediating function in plantation labour relations.

j'ai planté vos rejetons de canne
et vous ai laissé la pyramide volcanique

J'ai perdu ourdou hindi tamil
langue créole aux veillées funèbres

. . . je pousse mon patronyme dans la masse
de signes neutres

K Torabully, *Chair Corail, Fragments Coolies*, p. 68.

I have planted your cast-off canes
And left you the volcanic pyramid

I have lost Urdu, Hindi, Tamil
The Creole language at the funeral rites

. . . I push my patronym into the mass
Of neutral signs.

The Indian Identity Overseas

Bilingualism became a key advantage to those Indians who settled overseas during the indenture period. They could be gainfully employed by the courts and other public departments, as interpreters, and they were much in demand on the estates and embryonic Indian villages as intermediaries, writers and translators. Furthermore, in alien societies, the continuing use of Indian languages, both orally and scripturally, came to represent a cultural bulwark, a means of retrenchment, of self-justification and an important marker of identity.

Communicating in a language that could not be understood by employers of Creole or European origin had distinct advantages. When Laligadoo's daughter was asked to accompany a Miss Calamel to Rodrigues (an island dependency of Mauritius) as her companion, he was able to discover his daughter's true feelings about her situation as a result of a letter she wrote to him in the Tamil language. He accordingly addressed the Governor as follows:

> '. . . last month, your peititioner received two letters from his daughter, one written in the French Language in which it is stated that she is well and is well cared for by Miss Calamel and that she will come back to Mauritius at the end of the year; in the second letter written in Tamil, your Petitioner's daughter complains of being subjected to bad treatment on the part of Miss Calamel, and expresses the desire of returning at once to Mauritius . . . Under these circumstances, your petitioner humbly begs to approach your Excellency with a prayer that the Magistrate of Rodrigues be suggested to ask Miss Calamel to send back his daughter to Mauritius.'[15]

A knowledge of the vernacular language could help Indians to overcome deficiencies in their knowledge of English and French, in the courts and offices of the colonies to which they migrated. Rambhujun used a letter in Hindi to clarify his position in a case brought against him by eighty-three Indians who worked on land he had purchased in Moka, Mauritius.[16]

> I, Rambhujun, hereby consent that the judgment of the Stipendiary Court at Moka of 10th ultimo, declaring itself incompetent to try the case of Dowlut and 82 other men against me for want of jurisdiction, be set aside; and the case by heard and tried by the Stipendiary Magistrate of Moka. I am ready to answer any guilt that may be found against me. I know that I am not in the least guilty in this case. I am ignorant of the fact alleged.
>
> Rambhujun

If their mother-tongues functioned as a means of more perfect expression for overseas Indians, their native languages could also be a source of comfort and cultural sustenance. It was not uncommon for migrants to carry with them manuscript copies of their sacred texts; the literate amongst them would read aloud stories from the Ramayana and other religious epics to their fellow labourers. As Parekh has argued, 'of all the religious books, the Ramayana has come closest to becoming the central text of overseas Hinduism. It was immensely popular among the contract and especially the indentured labourers in places as far apart as Fiji, Trinidad, South Africa, Surinam, Guyana and Malaysia . . . its central theme of exile, suffering, struggle and eventual return resonated with the experiences of the Hindu migrants, especially but not exclusively those of the indentured labourers. The Ramayana gave them conceptual tools to make sense of their predicament, articulated their fears, and showed them how to cope with these.'[17]

Tapasa besa bisesi udasi
Caudaha barisa Ramu banabasi

Tulsidas, *Ramacaratimanasa.*

Bereft of goods, as mendicant, as beggar
Rama to spend fourteen years in the woods.

Increasingly, as overseas Indians became permanent settlers, they recreated the sacred topography of their homelands, constructing sites of worship and places where gatherings of their co-religionists could be held. Moving off the estates and into towns and villages, status was defined less by a superior position in the plantation hierarchy than by one's attendance at spiritual and cultural functions of one's peers. Thus, when Moonsamy Pillay, an old immigrant, working as a butler, reported a grievance to the Protector, he was chiefly concerned with a perceived affront to his dignity and social status. Having purchased a small monkey, Pillay had taken it with him to a religious ceremony at his local Tamil temple in Mauritius when he was arrested for being in possession of stolen property. He complained:

'I merely bring to your knowledge the manner in which I was treated by the Constable who arrested me. I told him to take and catch me by the collar but still he dragged me. I told him that I was in the Pagoda not to hold me by the Collar and still he continued to drag me, I again asked the constable to let me walk on, he would not allow me to do so . . . and in presence of the great crowd of people who had assembled on the 2nd of January last, whilst there was a great Indian Ceremony called "The Fire Walking", I at the same time was prevented to accomplish my vows to our Goddess at the Pagoda. Both socially and religiously I was so humiliated, therefore I humbly appeal to your Honour's help where alone I insist my grievance will be favourably dealt with by making or ordering an enquiry to be made in this case and then to mete out the just censure to the Constable in question who had abused the authority in such a vulgar manner and at a place of Public Worship.'[18]

The Protector was inclined to agree with Moonsamy that the constable had probably not taken any trouble to enquire as to his respectability after having arrested him, but the Inspector of Immigrants, noting that Pillay had indeed been in possession of stolen property, felt that it was not reasonable to prosecute PC Brown for assault. In addressing Pillay, however, the Protector tacitly recognised the justice of the man's plaint, while advising him to carry it no further: 'the constable was needlessly rough in the manner in which he arrested you, and that this was probably owing to ignorance and too much zeal on his part. I advise you to let the matter rest now where it is.'

Minorities in Creole societies, overseas Indians took refuge in the language and culture of a homeland, which became more and more mythical as the notion of return faded. Paradoxically, as fast as Indians became part of a Caribbean or Pacific or African landscape, they sought to distinguish themselves. In *Coolie Odyssey*, Old Dabydeen sees Creole as an 'impure' language which is 'Babbled by low-caste infected coolies'. His virgin daughters need the protection of his Hindi prayers, 'from the Negroes'.[19] This depiction of an elderly Indo-Caribbean man reveals an innate conservatism, as well as recalling the old rivalries between the two communities.

> . . . *partir est s'enraciner*
> *dans une autre terre*
>
> *Parler pour ne pas oublier*
> *qu'est-ce sinon le vrai don des langues?*
>   K Torabully, *Cale d'Étoiles*, p. 70.

. . . to leave is to embed oneself
In another land

Speak so as not to forget
Is this not the real gift of language?

Images of a Continuing Exile –
Mobility in Time and Space

Once overseas, the indentured labourer plunged ever further into diaspora, wandering further and further afield. From Reunion, Tamil workers
re-migrated to Mauritius; from Mauritius, labourers were engaged for
Natal, and there was cross-migration between the Indian Ocean,
Caribbean and even the later Pacific Ocean Indian diasporas.

When Seeniwasa Padayachi charged her husband with bigamy in
Durban in 1895, her deposition revealed an extraordinary story of migration and re-migration. She had originally married her husband seventeen
years earlier in the French Indian Ocean colony of Reunion (then known
as Bourbon). Ten years into the marriage, he left her, taking two of their
sons with him. As she later recounted:

'About nine months after my husband deserted me, I went to
India and searched for them at Pondichery and other places but
could not find them. Then I started for Mauritius, stayed there 15
days and searched for them, but could not find them. I then went
to Bourbon and stayed there for a year, went back to India, stayed
there for 7 months, returned again to Bourbon and remained
there 3 years, when I received a letter from my eldest son
Sawapathy giving me the full particulars of my husband and
himself. At once I started for Madras and then made enquiries at
the Indian Emigration Office there. They informed me that my
husband emigrated for Natal with a woman named Valliammal as
his wife . . . I then started for Natal with my youngest son
Gurusamy and arrived here per SS *Congella* in December
1894.'[20]

The intrepid Seeniwasa was eventually reunited with her sons and with her wayward husband, but finding him unwilling to leave his new companion, decided to charge him with bigamy.

In 1879, 145 Indo-Mauritians were reported to have migrated for work as far away as Rio de Janeiro, Brazil, while Valiama, the daughter of indentured immigrants in Martinique, migrated to Trinidad with her daughter after her own marriage failed.[21]

Such remigrations left relatives in India with a problem of tracing their departed ones. Pakeria Poulle was reputed to have migrated from Mauritius to Algoa Bay and was believed to have died in Johannesburg. His wife contacted the immigration authorities in Mauritius, asking them to trace his whereabouts and confirm his current status.[22]

Dabydeen's poetry evokes the thwarted ambitions of the diaspora Indians in their remigration efforts; their attempts to better themselves as hopeless as those of their migratory forebears. In 'Coolie Son' a toilet attendant writes a letter home in which he gives a positive gloss to his 'achievements':

Taana boy, how you do?
How Shanti stay? And Sukhoo?
Mosquito still a-bite all-you?
Juncha dead true-true?
Mala bruk-foot set?
Food deh foh eat yet?

England nice, snow and dem ting,
A land dey say fit for a king,
Iceapple plenty on de tree and bird a-sing –
Is de beginning of what dey call 'The Spring'.

And I eating enough for all a-we
And reading book bad bad.

. . . Soon, I go turn lawya or dacta,
But just now, passage money run out
So I tek lil wuk –

I is a Deputy Sanitary Inspecta,
Big-big office boy! Tie round me neck!
Brand new uniform, one big bunch keys!
If Ma can see me now how she go please . . .
  David Dabydeen, 'Coolie Son', in Dabydeen & Samaroo (eds),
                    India in the Caribbean, p. 285.

Re-migration was one outlet for the continuing quest of the overseas Indian – a better life. Dabydeen evokes the ironic continuation of the migration fantasy in the minds of the descendants of the coolie diaspora who have themselves left the sugar islands to seek their fortunes in new metropoli, such as England:

> 'Still we persist before the grave
> Seeking fables.
> We plunder for the maps of El Dorado
> To make bountiful our minds in an England
> Starved of gold.'[23]

Another avenue of mobility was seen to be through the acquisition of knowledge. Parekh has stressed the importance of education as an avenue of socio-economic mobility for the indentured labourers: 'Almost from the early days of indentured labour, Hindus stressed the importance of education for their male children. Education was the only way out of their wretched condition, described by many of them as narak (hell) . . . Preoccupation with making money is also a common and persistent feature of the Hindu diaspora. This is not unique to it, for every community that migrates for economic reasons seeks in wealth both a vindication of its decision to migrate and a compensation for the humiliations and privations suffered in the process.'[24]

The London taxi driver in the poem of the same name is shown to have exchanged the slow life of rural Guyana for one which cannot be said to be much of improvement:

He has come far and paid much for the journey
From some village in Berbice where mule carts laze
And stumble over broken paths . . .
Now he knows more the drama of amber red and green,
Mutinees against double-yellow lines
His aggression is horned like ancient clarions,
He grunts rebellion
In back seat discount sex
With the night's last whore.
David Dabydeen, 'London Taxi Driver', in Dabydeen & Samaroo
(eds), *India in the Caribbean*, p. 286.

In *Coolie Odyssey* David Dabydeen dramatically conveys the drive of the overseas Indians to lift their children out of the drudgery of plantation labour:

'There are no headstones, epitaphs, dates.
The ancestors curl and dry to scrolls of parchment.
They lie like texts
Waiting to be written by the children
For whom they hacked and ploughed and saved
To send to faraway schools.'[25]

His poem also provides an eloquent testimony of the work of remembrance, recovery and recasting of the 'coolie' being conducted by the descendants of the indentured labourers.

However, as Mahadai Das has observed, the indebtedness of the diaspora youngster, contemplating the sacrifices made by parents to educate them, often culminated in a rejection of the values of the elders:

'Your bleeding hands grasp the roots of rice
In my fields
And the seed of life you delved into the earth
Has sprung up to mock me.'[26]

The process of acquiring a western education, by its very nature, inevitably leads to estrangement from the ancestral culture. The descendants of the Indian indentured labourers, distancing themselves from their forebears, have at times echoed the colonial discourse, depicting their own parents and grandparents as forever bound in servitude to the white estate owner:

> 'You were always back home, forever
> As canefield and whiplash, unchanging.'[27]

The difficulties experienced by diaspora Indians in seeking to shake off the 'stigma' of being of coolie descent is sharply outlined in *Le Petit Coolie Noir*. The narrator is walking along a street on an island of the French Antilles, wearing French military uniform, when a man calls out to him '*Coolie a tire chapeau a en le tete ou* (Coolie, take off that hat.)' Despite his extensive voyaging, his experience of the metropolis and numerous adventures, the descendant of the coolie is still cast as such, in some parts of the world, and the implication is that he is not fit to wear a French uniform.[28]

They've given you the name 'coolie'
You've come to Natal, give thanks in song, brother
With a mess-tin in your hand, and a hoe on your shoulder
Let the foreigners go home.

> R Mesthrie, 'New Lights from Old Languages:
> Indian Languages and the Experience of
> Indentureship in South Africa', in Bhana (ed.), p. 204.

The clerks and other officials who recorded the names of migrating Indians were frequently of a different ethnic background and invested them with their own curious spellings. The resulting distortions have produced a set of unique names which are common to diaspora Indians descended from the nineteenth century indentured labourers whether they are Indo-Trinidadian, Indo-Mauritian or Indo-Guyanese. They are part of a continuing 'coolie' heritage. In the poem 'Illegitimacy' Sheila Ramdass refers to this process of naming the coolies that occurred at the ports of departure and arrival when coolies would be 'registered'. She refers to 'conspirators games . . . distorted names.'[29]

j'affute tout ce que nos noms pirates annoncent
pleinement

K Torabully, *Chair Corail, Fragments Coolies*, p. 40.

I reinforce all that our pirated names cry
Aloud.

Un coup de mer
me fit tort
aboli par hasard
dans un pire nom.

K Torabully, *Cale d'Étoiles*, p. 30.

A sea storm
Me tore
Abolished by chance
In a worse name.

Mais hurle enfin ce cri du bateau
pour te libérer au plus profond du commentaire
de ton histoire!

K Torabully, *Chair Corail, Fragments Coolies*, p. 61.

Shout aloud at last this cry from the ship
To free yourself fully from the commentary
Of your history!

Shana Yardan, of Indo-Guyanese descent, writes about the difficulties of being visibly Indian in a society where racial antagonisms had become prevalent:

'Oh grandfather, my grandfather,
Your dhoti is become a shroud
Your straight hair a curse
In this land where
Rice no longer fills the belly
Or the empty placelessness
Of your soul.'[30]

Rejection of the discrimination and humiliation of their forebears in the British Empire was one means of destroying the negative legacy of the 'coolie':

'But my eyes shall burn again,
A resurrection of brown pride
For I see you now, my father,
Fling the Victoria Cross
Into the dung-heap of the British Empire.'[31]

Cyril Dabydeen has turned the attack upon the legacy of history into a metaphor in his poem 'Atlantic Song':

'They raise
Machetes in a virulent sun
Assault upon history

Pauper thin echoes
Loss and separation

Words criss-crossing
Galley after galley.'[32]

Aly Remtulla, 'Of Emerald's Bubble' is an example of how Indians in diaspora generally continue to feel that they are considered as the 'exotic' other even when native to the countries where they are in a minority. This feeling is expressed by a poem in which the Indian in the USA is likened to:

'. . . an exotic fox running through your green pastures
I am trapped inside a bubble which cannot be collapsed.'[33]

This theme is further picked up by Sherazad Jamal who paints a vivid picture of the isolation of the Asian woman in the USA, and the continuing representation of herself as the 'other':

> '. . . they do not want to see past my face . . .
> men look at me like
> I have leprosy, untouchable.'

She vividly continues the theme of sexual exploitation outlined by earlier diaspora writers when she reports on the experiences of her brothers: 'My brothers fare differently . . . They are exotica for some.'[34]

The desire to shake off the traditional values and garb of the 'coolie', alongside the recognition that Indianness was an undeniable aspect of their identity, was a dilemma which confronted Indo-Caribbeans and which is echoed in their writings. Walcott's poem makes an ironic reference to those Indo-Caribbeans who no longer follow the Hindu gods of their ancestors:

> 'Suppose all the gods too old,
> Suppose they dead and they burying them,
> Supposing when some cane cutter
> Start chopping up snakes with a cutlass
> He is severing the snake-armed god.'[35]

Indenture lives in dates and distances
Not in the antic dance we dance
Speech which peaks our death
In postures of greed and denial,
Pain which strikes in the striking of each stricken hour
      A Itwaru, 'We have Survived', in Dabydeen & Samaroo (eds),
                            India in the Caribbean, p. 293

Emmanuel Nelson has noted that Indo-Caribbean diasporic writing is characterized by a central tension, that between 'the desire for cultural separation and the opposing urge toward creolization, both of which are different psychosocial responses to the same historical event: the loss of

India and, consequently, the absence of home. Often unable to negotiate the dilemma, the diasporic Indians in the Caribbean remain perpetual travellers.' The writing of Indians in the USA shares this common theme – the 'aesthetics of loss'.[36]

A folk song evokes the westernization of diaspora women. A husband bemoans the modern habits his wife has picked up overseas:

You go out walking down the roads
I shall do the dishes myself
You dab powder on your face
And wear your sari back-to-front
You've abandoned family traditions.

Mesthrie, p. 205.

Cyril Dabydeen has described the delocalization of identities and cultures among diasporic peoples in the memorable phrase 'mud bound in memory'.[37] In 'Poem to your Own', Cyril Dabydeen, addresses the notion of cultural loss, in his description of the overseas Indians as:

'You who dream perpetually
Of meaning beyond the ocean . . .
Hungering for the lost pride . . .
Of past people and culture . . .
Your pride of country.'[38]

Terre natale accrochée au fil
de mes rêves tissés et retissés,
réticents?

K Torabully, *Chair Corail, Fragments Coolies*, p. 84.

Natal land attached to the thread
Of my cited and recited
(reticent) dreams?

Fragments coolies pour réveiller
les épaves émiettées,
les couronnes d'étoiles exposées
au premier matin des confidences.
Fragments d'histoire niée
que l'insulte a éparpillés
sur deux siècles de regards
en chiens de faïence.

K Torabully, *Chair Corail, Fragments Coolies*, p. 97.

Coolie fragments to awaken
The shattered wrecks
The crowns of stars exposed
To early morning confidences
Fragments of a history denied
Which insults have scattered
Like porcelain chippings
Onto two centuries of neglect

As Emmanuel Nelson has noted, the literature of the Indian diaspora is characterized by 'cultural anxiety' in which 'desperate attempts at cultural self-perpetuation' appear frequently. A good example of this is the Tulsi family in *A House for Mr Biswas* by V S Naipaul. The isolation of the Indo-Caribbean is perhaps most famously illustrated in the impregnable, windowless house of the Tulsis. Nevertheless, Walcott's poem contains an upbeat note; he demonstrates how the Indo-Caribbean can invest something of the sacred even in the image of his taxi-driver friend singing Bollywood hits:

'Sacred even to Ramlochan,
Singing Indian hits from his jute hammock
While evening strokes the flanks
And silver horns of his maroon taxi.'[39]

Many Indo-Caribbean novels deal with conflicts between assimilationists and traditionalists – and tend to sympathize with the former. For example,

A House for Mr Biswas by V S Naipaul (London, 1961); *A Brighter Sun* by S Selvon (London, 1952), *Laddoo's Yesterdays* (Toronto, 1974) and *A Casual Brutality* by N Bissoondath (Toronto, 1988). Ultimately, however, diaspora Indians are replacing the aesthetics of loss with the recognition that a new identity is in the process of being created. Mena Abdullah obliquely represents this in one of her short stories, by focusing on a garden shown to relatives:

> '"It is not India", said Father.
> "And it is not the Punjab", said Uncle Syed.
> "It is just us", said Ama.'[40]

> *mieux qu'endurer*
> *exprimer*
> *ces phrases en nous enfouies*
> *depuis grand-papa*
>
> *. . . ne plus être intouchable des mots*
> *ne plus prendre caste*
> *en langage*
>
> *les mots détonnent enfin en nous*
> *de la majestueuse force*
>
> *. . . lèvres crispées sur le pays englouti*
> *a l'estuaire des salives ravalées*
> *nous voici nous voici!*
> > K Torabully, *Chair Corail, Fragments Coolies*, p. 57.
>
> Better than enduring
> Expressing
> These phrases buried within us
> For two generations
>
> To no longer be untouchable through words
> To no longer derive caste
> From language

Words finally burst forth from us
With majestic strength

Frozen lips on a devoured country
At the estuary of our checked speech
Here we are here we are!

5

Some Theoretical
Premises of Coolitude

This chapter reproduces the text of a lengthy interview conducted between Marina Carter (MC) and Khal Torabully (KT) in which the poet and author outlines his evolution and definition of the concept of Coolitude, particularly within the framework of négritude *and* créolité, *and elaborates on key facets of Coolitude, such as the coolie memory and the role of aesthetics and literature. Khal Torabully draws attention to writers whose work may be placed within the literary definition of Coolitude, among them Naipaul and Rushdie.*

1. Césaire, Négritude and Coolitude

MC: You had a very interesting encounter with Aimé Césaire, the great poet from Martinique who coined the word *négritude*, in December 1997. What is the link between *négritude* and coolitude?

KT: Aimé Césaire invented the word *négritude* in the 1920s, in the midst of colonial turmoil. Coolitude was framed in 1992. There are two principal similarities between *négritude* and coolitude:

– The recollection of a common phase of history and the need to redress the state of oblivion and neglect attached to the condition of the Negro, and to that of the Coolie. The descendants of indentured labourers, like those of slaves, often knew very little of their past history. They were ignorant of the cultural implications of the Voyage. One of the aims of coolitude is also to foster a larger community of vision encompassing the experiences of people of African descent and fostering interaction with the later immigrant groups in those colonial societies, to which coolies migrated in the period immediately following the abolition of slavery, even though Indian labour was already present during slavery.

– Like *négritude*, coolitude originates from a debased and pejorative word – coolie. Césaire appropriated the term *negro* to give it new dignity and value and attached to it a system of thought which enabled the 'negro' to conquer his own place in the world. The term *coolie* like that of *negro*, has been used in the past, and continues even today to be used as an insult to the descendants of the overseas indentured labourers. I chose this word because the coolie was essentially the one who replaced the slave in the plantocratic society. The coolie's life-history, albeit in somewhat modified historical circumstances, resembled, in many aspects, that of the slave. The word dignifies this condition and aims to illuminate the plight of, to quote *Cale d'Etoiles-Coolitude*, '*les oubliés du voyage, ceux qui n'ont pas eu le livre de leur traversée* (the forgotten travellers; those who have no logbook to record their voyage). However, Coolitude is not *négritude à l'indienne* (or a kind of Indian version of *négritude*). It is not essentialist, i.e. referring to one people, or race, or religion. It springs in fact, from a word (coolie/indentured), which at the beginning, designated an economic status, and has been broadened to encompass a human situation. Before resorting massively to coolies from India, there were experiments to bring coolies from China, Ethiopia, Brittany, even, from Africa . . . The coolie symbolizes, in its broader definition, the possibility of building a composite identity to ease the pain and enrich culturally the lands in which he/she settled. As the vast majority of those described as coolies and who settled in ex-slave societies of the Caribbean, Pacific and Indian Ocean, from the mid-nineteenth century onwards, originated in India, it would have been unwise to overlook this historical and human fact.

MC: Was Césaire receptive to the term 'coolitude'?

KT: When I met Césaire at Fort de France in 1997, I offered him a copy of *Cale d'Etoiles-Coolitude*. He was immediately struck by the word *Coolitude*. He asked me to explain the concept, which I did, and he responded to me with the following words: 'Now I can die in peace. Coolitude is the poetic force I was waiting for . . .' These words are extremely important, and will have to be weighed against the proper situation of the 'Indian' in the West Indies. I remember having told him that coolitude comprises two main facets: a '*remise en perspective*' (recollection) of the cultural elements of the coolie which were *mis à mal* (stifled) by colonial history, and, the interplay between cultures, mainly African and European, in the embryonic Creole society, often in a hostile environment, but which ultimately led towards the perception of a composite identity. Césaire explained how Creole society in the French Caribbean was in close interaction with, in his words, the 'Indian element'. He gave several examples, ranging from cooking (Colombo, a form of curry, is the national dish of Guadeloupe and Martinique) to religion (Marie-Aimée, one of the saints of the population, is a deformation of the Tamil cult of Mariamen).

It was a moving moment for me to have this exchange with the celebrated poet who, in his legendary *Cahier d'un Retour au Pays Natal*, mentioned the coolie as *'l'homme hindou de Calcutta'* (the Hindu man from Calcutta), words which proponents of *Créolité* criticized as a form of ostracism for the coolie descendants, indicating that the Indo-Caribbean was still seen as a foreigner – an Indian, rather than as a part of the population of the *Antilles*. Raphaël Confiant, one of the principal advocates of the *créolité* movement, went even further – declaring that he could not understand how Césaire could omit the coolie element in his poetry, especially given that Césaire himself had a coolie '*da*' (nanny) when he was a child, as did Alexis Saint Léger, better known as the Nobel Prize winner, Saint John Perse. But whereas the latter refers to the cultural component of coolitude in his writings, Césaire is silent about it. I remember having been told about this influence of coolitude in the works of Saint John Perse by poet and psychoanalyst Joël Des Rosiers, a fine reader of the writer of *Amers*, while visiting the birthplace of the Martinican-born poet. Whatever the polemics, in relation to the 'Indian element' during our conversation, Césaire expressed pride in the cultural fusion between his ancestral Africa and India. And he was sincere about it.

MC: Do you share with Césaire the same definition of India and Africa?

KT: Césaire and I discussed the misunderstanding attached to geographical terms. I spoke of *les Indes*, not the mythical Indies of Columbus, but the generic name of plural India, and stressed the fact that India is not such a monolithic nation as one would sometimes think it is, being in fact a mosaic of Indias. From Bihar to Tamil Naidu, from

Gujarat to Maharashtra, there are so many different cultures and languages, religions and creeds, so many poetics or visions of the world, that one may described the subcontinent as itself the epitome of diversity. Césaire agreed and added that the same applied to Africa, which in fact should be referred to as the Africas, given the plurality within individual countries (Mali, for example with its Peuls, Bozos, Dogons, Tuaregs and its linguistic variety).

I thought then that Césaire had often been misquoted as a poet or a visionary whose scope was said to be limited to the plight of the Black man only, and who was moreover thought of as a Negro devoid of a diverse cultural background. *Négritude*, to quote another theorist and poet, Léopold Sedar Senghor, refers to the values of the Black man, and represented an attempt to give him his dignity in a colonial world in which the Negro seemed to be almost devoid of humanity. When Césaire speaks of his '*négritude universelle*', he points to the plural connections of African cultures and their ability to recognize their own varied roots, together with the possibility of proposing those values to other cultures, and, of being open to other cultural references. This seems quite far removed from the essentialist theory and practice often attached to *Négritude*, as founded exclusively on a monolithic negro *être* (being), excluding other cultures, in its extremely militant definition, and as limited or defined by the historical violence suffered by persons of African origin, whether as slaves or second class citizens in the USA and elsewhere during the decolonization period. Maybe, at that time Césaire had no choice. Given the context he had to bring out the more militant definition of his poetics.

MC: Nowadays, what is the perception attached to *négritude*?

KT: Generally speaking, *négritude* has kept this essentialism, (others would say 'fixist attitude', opposed to the hybrid nature of creoleness), and is usually understood as an ideology to restore to the Black his pride and place in a colonial and post-colonial world built on the assumption that the Black was inferior. I would underline one fact, however. Senghor, the other great *négritude* thinker, gave a potent definition to the term *métissage*: '*Notre vocation de colonisé est de surmonter les contradictions de la conjoncture, l'antinomie artificiellement dressée entre l'Afrique et l'Europe, notre hérédité et notre éducation. C'est de la greffe de celle-ci que doit naître* *notre liberté* (Our vocation as the colonized has been to overcome the contradictions inherent in the dichotomy artificially erected between Africa and Europe, our heritage and our education. It is from the grafting of the one onto the other that our freedom will be born.)'[1]

History has rather negated the development of this poetics, as the proponents were entrenched in this binary opposition and desired exchanges between the Black and the White civilizations. Many have criticized Senghor for this bipolarization. Moreover, Black Power or Afrocentrism, to quote two movements which have had a long and durable influence in the Americas, have contributed to the entrenchment of an exclusivist view of *négritude* within the racist American context prevalent at that time. When I met Césaire however, he seemed very concerned with the possibilities of convergence with coolitude.

MC: You seem to be suggesting that Césaire did not see in coolitude the Indian alter ego of *négritude*, but rather that he was open to its dynamic, hybrid character?

KT: The enthusiasm with which Césaire welcomed the poetics of coolitude reveals one central idea in his vision of Caribbean society: the meeting between its different components, especially that of two peoples brought together by the abolition of slavery, the slave and the indentured labourer. As a man and as a poet of human encounters and human generosity, he readily understood that *Négritude* and Coolitude sprang from the same tragedy.

MC: Therefore, you would argue that you and Césaire were inspired by a similar vision in devising your concepts?

KT: When I left him, Césaire told me, 'you will do for India what I did for Africa'. These words suddenly brought home to me a difference in our poetics and in the foundations of our approach, anchored as they have been in different historical contexts, a generation gap indeed. In fact, if Césaire designated Africa as the reference from which his theory sprang and towards which it pointed, mine, despite having a basis in India, did not point to India as the nucleus, the apex of my vision or the 'Ultimate Referent'. It is certainly one of the starting points, but definitely not the final goal of coolitude, in an ontological perspective. I doubt even that

Africa had ever been the homeland dreamt of in the mythical return approach of Césaire and of the West Indians. Perhaps Césaire thought that the coolie descendant was not, even in present times, recognised enough in the West Indian context, and certainly his openness is not to be questioned.

However, we have a different approach. I would not say that coolitude would do something for India, but for the people of the West Indies, and eleswhere, indeed, for the 'Indians' born or living abroad. Depending on the social and historical circumstances, some of them are keen to remember and to retrieve whatever they can of a disappearing or evanescent culyure. But at the heart of coolitude, there is a view that the 'Indian migrant' should become part and parcel of an identity open to the dynamics of cultural interplay. This does not mean doing away necessarily with India, as every cultural element is worth scrutiny and interplay . . . The views of Césaire can be explained by the fact that, at that time, he was engaged in a struggle to bring out a voice which was muffled, a culture which was in tatters, an identity which, in the context of the time, could be framed only by opposing the 'Dominant White', in a binary configuration of the 'Oppressor' and the 'Victim'. When he made the comparison between what he did for Africa and what I would do for India, he meant probably that a literary, a cultural voice was still to emerge to represent the 'Indian element' of Martinique, of the French West Indies, and that an identity which was bruised in History had to be restored. The reference to India as a cultural source to rejuvenate a fading culture was important to him, just as the fact of recovering the rhythm, the primitive force of Africa, had been important in his own poetic revolt. Coolitude, in any case, is imbued with the notion that this 'Indian element', which is to be taken into account, is already engaged in the interaction of the 'Diverse', and is an identity wrapped in *altérité* (Otherness).

MC: Can you, then, define the relation to India more precisely in your poetics of coolitude?

KT: For coolitude, India is a reference, just as Africa is present within the very weave of creoleness or creolization. It is the essence, or the essences, from which the 'self', the cultural perception and complex identity of the coolie originate. Where the original culture has been erased, tortured, threatened, or in its most positive configuration, partially, or more fully preserved – as in Mauritius – the human suffering and the yearning for recognition which this obliteration or mutilation has created, cannot be ignored, and the reference to India is more than understandable as one cannot frame his relation to himself and the world *ex nihilo*.

Just as creoleness or creolization, sooner or later, is doomed to revert back to Africa as the first point of reference, so does coolitude exist in relation to India. But, this ontological perspective, in its proper historical and social context, does not mean that the dream of those originating from India is to return there, despite carving out myths of their ancestral homeland . . . In fact, it would be more appropriate to say that coolitude may help the descendants of Indians abroad, to realise that they engage India, or the Indias, in the process of the creation of a mosaic self in Guadeloupe, Martinique, Guyana, Fiji, South Africa, Kenya, Zanzibar, Mauritius, or wherever they may be.

The craving for the 'mythical land of the ancestors' can create barriers in the elaboration of a wider identity, akin to the process of creolization, if it is not set against more exclusive definitions leading to a 'narrow identity'. Therefore, one has to be vigilant not to close on him/herself. However, the recourse to a lost origin is not in itself to be negated, provided this approach does not absolve an individual from the need to address the question of a present identity. A complex attitude can offer a balance to the interplay of relations in a number of social, human and cultural contexts.

Therefore, the India I would make reference to is one of Diversity, the Indies or Indias we spoke about, a reminder that even when searching for lost fragments of one's memory, to evolve a dialectics of identity, one should not forget that these origins cannot be exclusive of the differences of others, whether of language, creed or culture . . . The ontological approach must therefore be coupled with the approach of a complex identity, in which the source remains open to other sources.

MC: When Césaire read his famous verse 'l'Homme Hindou de Calcutta' did he express his fidelity to the concept of the original homeland to you? And since you say that the original homeland must also be subject to an open form of identity, or a complex identity, is this where you differ with his interpretation of the origins?

KT: Indeed, this is a major difference. The poetics of coolitude, engaged in complexity of societies and human situations, as you know, is itself not simple in its definition. It is a complex and dynamic one, in which, depending on the social, historical, and cultural context, a single aspect may at any time be highlighted, but which should not, in any circumstances, lead to an exclusive vision of identity. To go further, the original homeland should also be the country where one lives, even if this must be built everyday.

MC: Does this mean that coolitude proposes to build a bridge between *négritude, indianité* and creolization, as a necessary step towards the creation of a composite identity?

KT: This dynamic is already at work where 'the Indian element' is present and engaged in 'postmodern' creations, like music, literature or films, for example in the UK and Canada . . . But to come back to your question, coolitude posits an encounter, an exchange of histories, of poetics or visions of the world, between those of African and of Indian descent, without excluding other sources. In the broadest sense the coolie was a labour migrant without the word of his Voyage, and as I said earlier, there were 'coolies' from Britanny, as well as from Africa, China and India. The coolie is not an ethnic definition *stricto sensu*; it is also a juridical one, as worded in the contract which placed the wage labourer, whether European, Asian or African, in a relationship of salaried servitude defined by penal clauses. Viewed from this angle, coolitude does redefine the concept of *indianité* when it is a fixist set of 'Indian' values, leading to the acceptance of the presence of other cultural facets. Coolitude also seeks to emphasize the community of visions between the slave and the indentured labourer, shared by their descendants, despite the fact that these two groups, were placed in a situation of competition and conflict. As such coolitude may be seen as an attempt to bring the past and present of these groups into contact and to go beyond past conflicts and misrepresentations. The necessity of a reconciliation, from the outset, was fully understood by Césaire when we met. Allow me to tell you an anecdote to illustrate this. When Césaire accompanied me to the entrance of the Fort-de-France town hall where he is the Mayor, he drew the attention of his colleagues to my presence, holding my hand, and joking. 'Ladies and gentlemen, what do you see? A coolie and a negro? Isn't that great? It is coolitude (*N'est-ce pas beau? C'est la coolitude*)'. This reconciliation of the descendants of African and Indian migrants is important from the social perspective, from the point of view of living together, and of sharing a past, present and future.

MC: Was this encounter the trigger of your last book, *Chair Corail, Fragments Coolies,* as the West Indian History, together with Guadeloupean and Martinican landscapes, texts and words pervade this text?

KT: After this meeting, I remember re-reading *Le Cahier d'un Retour au Pays Natal* with the feeling that a powerful energy was at work in me. Two elements inspired this book. First, I was appalled to see that the people of Guadeloupe whom I met and some Martinicans of Indian origin, while participating in the *créolité* movement, felt that there was a lack, that something of their own presence in Caribbean History and culture, as expressed by arts and literature, was missing. This '*sens de la perte*' (sense of loss) is a locus of this society, and of many human communities torn by cultural violence. For the Indian descendants, there was no real founding text for their indentureship, and their presence on the islands – this was something I bore witness to, with different intensities in Guadeloupe and Martinique – was vitiated by a cultural uneasiness bordering on frustration. Expressing their presence in the Caribbean society remains an intense desire for them, in view of participating fully in it.

Secondly, there was something in the book of Césaire that thrilled me: essentially its rhythm, as part and parcel of its poetic force, even if the poet, like Senghor later, was to be criticized for restricting African culture only to emotions and rhythms. I worked on this element in the first part of *Chair corail*, as a bridge between négritude and coolitude, as an encounter of two *imaginaires*, two poetics. And also, while referring to Césaire's poetic music, I wrote of our thematic proximities and differences. Césaire says '*Ma négritude est une pierre* (my *négritude* is a rock)' and I defined coolitude starting from this metaphor, and blending it with the rhizome metaphor of creolization:

> '*Ma coolitude n'est pas une pierre non plus,*
> *elle est corail*
> *partage d'une terre de giboyeuse parole . . .*

(My coolitude is not a rock either
It is coral,
Fruit of an earth laden with speeches of birds and beasts)'[2]

In choosing the metaphor of the coral to define coolitude, I wanted to underscore the symbolic importance of the 'rock' for Césaire, in the context of the struggle for the decolonization of minds. It had to be forceful. The coral can be both soft, and hard, it can be found in two states, and it is traversed by currents, continuously open to new thoughts and systems. It is a living body with elements which are both vulnerable and solid, it is a symbol of the fluidity of relationships and influences. Moreover, it brings to mind another metaphor, that of the rhizome, as used by Edouard Glissant, the foremost West Indian theorist of creolization, who borrowed and acclimatized this image from Félix Guattari and Gilles Deleuze as first delineated in *Mille Plateaux*.[3]

The composite identity is assumed there to be a root conjoined with another root (the root of the other), without a predatory or central root, thus leaving identity open to *la relation* or the fact of bringing into the relation another component. By likening coolitude to a coral, I, in turn, blend the image of the stone of *négritude* and the rhizome of creolization. From this poetic marine metaphor, which again brings to the core of the meaning the seavoyage, emerge the following meanings: the coral is visited by many external cultural stimuli, it is a marine 'root' or rhizome, growing with no predatory centre in the process.

MC: If coolitude is not the 'Indian alter ego' of *négritude*, could it perhaps be described as the Indian version of creoleness or *créolité*?

KT: I wrote that 'Creoleness is to *négritude* what coolitude is to *indianité* (indianness)'.[4] In that formula I equated indianness to *négritude* (even though Césaire says that '*ce n'est pas par haine des autres races que je me réclame unique bêcheur de cette race*) [it is not because of a hatred for other races that I proclaim myself the sole tiller for this race]'), as defined by its essential relation to race and geographical origin and because of its geographical origin. I pointed to the danger of all exclusive celebrations of the origins, specifically the narrow definitions of *indianité*, forgetting the 'Indias': i.e. India as a cultural crossroads. In many countries to which indentured labourers migrated, whole sections of the diaspora celebrate a faithfulness to Mother India. In itself, there is nothing wrong with this first step in the process of cultural reappropriation. But this is often at the expense of their own emerging national identities in the host countries, which depend upon the meeting with, and convergence of, other cultures, coolitude posits a complex attitude. I likened, at this stage, coolitude to creoleness, because compared to restrictive definitions of *indianité, créolité* seems to be a more open concept, as it tries to go beyond the essentialism of *négritude* and the geographical limitations attached to a subsequent concept, that of 'Caribbeanness' or *antillanité*. In *Eloge de la Créolité*, Confiant, Chamoiseau and Bernabé define creoleness as the 'annihilation of fake universality, of monolinguism and of purity'.[5]

MC: But the concept of creoleness is not itself without some residue of confusion . . .

KT: I think this has been seen as such by many critiques. For Edouard Glissant, for instance, creoleness is an ethno-cultural space extending from the West Indies to the Indian Ocean, but instead of building its identity upon the process of relationships, creoleness seems to choose the 'unique root' at the expense of the rhizome, which Glissant defined as a demultiplied root with no centre, from which identity can be considered as also a construction deriving from a relationship to 'Otherness'.

In *Introduction à une Poétique du Divers*, Glissant is very clear:

> *'Pour moi la créolité est <u>une autre interprétation</u> (my own emphasis) de la créolization. La créolization est un mouvement perpétuel d'interpénétrabilité culturelle et linguistique qui fait qu'on ne débouche pas sur une définition de l'être. Ce que je reproche à la négritude, c'était de définir l'être: l'être nègre . . . il faut abandonner le prétention à la définition de l'être. Or, c'est ce que fait la créolité: définir un être créole. C'est une manière de régression, du point de vue de ce processus, mais qui est peut-être nécessaire pour défendre le présent créole. Tout comme la négritude a été d'une importance vitale pour la défense des valeurs africaines et de la diaspora noire. (For me, créolité is another interpretation of créolization. Créolization is a perpetual movement of cultural and linguistic interpenetration,*

which means that one does not necessarily end up with a
definition of being. That is what makes *créolité*: to define a creole
being. It's a type of regression, from the point of view of process,
but it is essential in order to defend the creole present. Just as
négritude was of vital importance for the defence of African values
and of the black diaspora)'.[6]

Glissant, by denouncing '*l'être*', 'the Being', as an invention of the West,
leading to conflicts and sectarian views, even in the hold of *créolité*, lays
stress on a <u>process</u>, on an infinite web of relationships. In any case, what
he underlines is the necessary predictable forms the relationships assume
at a particular moment of history. This also means that coolitude and
créolité must also take into account expressions and desires which form
part of the whole process of creolization. This explains why in particular circumstances the retrieval of India is an inevitable recourse, to
compensate for the 'sense of loss', but in the process, coolitude points to
the indispensable fact that this construction must be linked to a wider
process of identity.

**MC: Coolitude is a process very similar to creolization, in the sense that
it also springs from a complex situation in which cultural signposts,
interplay with other cultures, and *imaginaires* are mingled?**

KT: Coolitude is close to the spirit of creolization, even though, as I said
before, in order to enable creolization to be furthered, one must not visualize, in some contexts, the relation to past culture purely as a land of
desolation; one must endeavour to till this land again, in order to discover
the riches it can bring, and in the process one must be open to other
influences. Basically, the poetry of *métissage* (even if Glissant sees it as a
remnant of a colonialist discourse with a predictable basis) has been
taken to new heights by the author of *Introduction à une Poétique du
Divers*. When I developed the concept of coolitude in 1992 the idea of a
process, of a '*mise en relation*' or cultural interweaving, was very much in
my mind. I was not aware of the concept of *créolité* at that time. I became
interested in the creole writers after my meeting with Chamoiseau in
Lyon, just before he was awarded the Goncourt Prize.

The theoretical foundations of creolization were, *a posteriori*, to echo
intuitions and thoughts of paramount importance to me. The first

proximity is that our poetics are based on a continuous process of relationships. It is in this complex exchange that a mosaic identity is framed, of which we cannot predict the results. This represents, for any artist or poet, the unpredictability of creativity, and this may be more potent in a society where contacts are multiplied between cultures and where a transcultural movement is generated.

MC: Therefore, creolization offers a system of references through which identity can be reconsidered . . .

KT: For me, creolization is more a 'structure' than a system, similar to the semiological structure as defined by Umberto Eco in *L'Oeuvre Ouverte*[7], the 'structure' being open by nature, and able to enter into contact with other structures, whereas a system is quite closed by nature, being a construction with the idea of a totality, a centre. Therefore coolitude is for me a more formal relationship than a fixed content and as such very close to creolization.

MC: What is the consequence of this theoretical framework for identity?

KT: Coolitude is a process of identity construction which takes into account the impossibility of putting a full stop to this task, and not essentially a philosophy where the meaning is predetermined. It implies an approach in which the notion of a guiding culture, of a centre, of a *Logos*, becomes defunct. The questioning of univocity, of transparency, the decentralization of a *Sens Unique* (Univocal Sense) gives scope to the construction of a plural society. So often, people have been dismayed by the fact that creolization seems to be synonymous with chaos, as there is no peace or tranquillity in imagining a proteiform process. However, this 'chaos' allows us to determine a mental structure in which we can think, live, create and initiate a new definition for our own existence and identity.

Allow me to quote Glissant:

*'La créolization, c'est l'imprédictible. On peut prédire ou déterminer
le métissage, on ne peut pas prédire ou déterminer la créolization . . .
On peut résumer tout cela en posant l'opposition entre une pensée
archipélique et une pensée continentale, la pensée continentale étant*

pensée de système et la pensée archipélique étant la pensée de l'ambigu (Creolization is unpredictable. One can predict or determine métissage, but one cannot predict or determine creolization. This can be summarized by positing the opposition between an archipelagic thought and a continental thought, the continental thought being a systematic thought and the archipelagic thought being an ambiguous thought).'[8]

The important element here, is that my identity is not closed on others, it is not the ultimate centre, it is one identity among others and the awareness that one's identity is also framed by meeting that of others.

MC: Did you write *Cale d'Étoiles-Coolitude* in 1992, with this mosaic paradigm in mind?

KT: When I wrote *Cale d'Étoiles*, at the forefront of my thinking was my understanding of the history of Mauritius and the type of human relationships it engendered. When I brought to mind the odyssey of the coolie, I had the feeling that *Cale d'Étoiles* would perform a twofold task. It would recreate a voyage unknown or censored, to recover the 'loss' engendered by the sea voyage, and at the same time, concretize the recognition that India was left behind and that the descendants of the Indians had arrived in a new country, and were committed to founding a new vision of identity along with the other components of Mauritian society. I wanted to build on this notion of the sea voyage as a traumatic and regenerating experience.[9]

MC: How did this create an impact upon your writing style?

KT: *Cale d'Étoiles*, in its very structure and formal choices, aimed to highlight a modified vision of the world, a plural world born of 'chaos', and which is a renovated reservoir of forms and signs. What the word 'plural' here implies is not the mundane recognition that the island comprises many races and creeds as defined by Burton Benedict, but a more 'chaotic', tangible plurality which has a strong transcultural dynamic, an interplay between its diverse components.[10] The poetry of the book is modulated by this vision and this relation.

MC: Do you mean that in its very structure this founding text of coolitude reflected this poetic choice?

KT: *Cale d'Étoiles* is not linear or predictable in the sense that as well as being read from the beginning to the end, it can be read in two or more ways. It is divided into 'the Book of *Métissage*', 'the Book of the Voyage', and 'the Book of Departure'; 'the Book of the Voyage' being the pivot of this poetic experience, whether you read it from the beginning to the end or the other way round. Its cyclical aspect echoes the cyclical vision Oriental peoples have of time and history. The form of the book itself encompasses a vision of the world, the structure being part of the meaning, which is itself inseparable from the relation with diverse visions of culture and creation. This relationship with 'Otherness' is expressed in the use of words with Creole, Indian, old French, English and neologisms. Indianness here is redefined as part and parcel of a larger awareness resulting from a relationship between the *imaginaire* of a 'plural' society.

MC: So that in essence, the text allowed many *imaginaires* to converge?

KT: While writing a founding text of the coolie experience, my aim was to make it a mosaic piece of writing in which other social components would be able to find an echo of their own presence. This is also reflected in the form of the poetry, which by definition is open, and describes the process through which any and every person of coolie descent has been able to store memory by confronting the 'otherness' of the society to which he/she paradoxically belongs, and allowing these differences to merge into a new creation, a new language. Therefore, another implication of this book was the desire to take French language to my meanings, doing away with a certain *francotropisme* or excessive French linguistic or literary formalism. And, also, with the reticence of the Indian descendant towards the French language, which was in the 80s often perceived as the tongue of 'the Other'. This explains why I introduced so many words from Hindi, Bhojpuri, Creole and even a 'strange French lexicon' in *Cale d'Étoiles*, so that the spirit of coolitude could fully express itself, in a complex relation to words and identities.

MC: The fact that this book has a marine spirit, and emphasizes the voyage, is in itself one of the major premises of coolitude . . .

KT: Indeed, this point is very important, essential in the understanding of coolitude. The sea voyage bears very strange, troublesome, muffled and censored echoes among the Indian descendants. This is because it was a traumatic experience, which was 'censored' consciously or unconsciously by those whose reached the shores of the host countries. Bringing to the fore this problematic relation to the 'Voyage' was therefore not an innocent act of writing. By giving this marine essence to the text, what was sought was not only a poetic universe or atmosphere, but primarily a space where this trauma could be revisited, and once this has been done, the sea voyage was chosen as the space of the metaphorical construction of a new identity. An atavistic vision of the world had evaporated, a new, complex one was to emerge in this slow dissolution. Even though the indentured labourer made this voyage with the idea that going back to India was possible, at least, as was stated in his contract, many were to remain in the colonies. This thought of going back to Africa was impossible for the slave, chained as he was, with no legal paper to protect him as a human being. But the voyage remains central in both cases. I remember that when *Cale d'Étoiles* was presented in Mauritius, and in Guadeloupe, I could witness how those Indian descendants were stirred by the evocation of the ship bringing coolies to distant countries. Once, an old man even wept, as if something essential had been muffled in him for too long a time . . . It is also as if the coolie had been impressed by the goal of the voyage (I called this the 'Signified' of the voyage) rather than by its spirit (which I called the 'Signifier' of the voyage) . . . Very often, the passage from India to the island or elsewhere, this slow change of visions, of perceptions on board a ship, had been discarded, as what was important was reaching the land of 'gold and honey'. But for me, this transition also bore richness to the indentured, as this is the heart of this change of *imaginaire*, because on the ship different languages are heard, new techniques are displayed, and the ship is the first potent space of his hybridity outside India. The fact of getting hold of the sea voyage, of plying the coolie's *imaginaire* there, was therefore the acceptance of this severance from his atavistic land and culture, which, if fully mediated, can induce a complex attitude to identity and culture.

MC: What would account, therefore, for the lack of literary works visu-alizing the sea as a space for the liberation of the *imaginaire*, and as the prelude to new identities?

KT: The Indian, originally, is someone attached to the *Maati*, the Mother-Earth, and his *imaginaire* is rarely conversant with that seaspace, often perceived, specially for long voyages, as the place of foul spirits, as the immensity where the purity of one's life is lost. Furthermore, the sea as a source of inspiration of the celebration of courage and richness, seems, especially after the period of 'Great Discoveries', to be in the cultural and political wake of peoples of the West. So, putting one's words on this marine space was also an attempt to let one's *imaginaire* explore the space of the other, and putting oneself, metaphorically, in relation with 'Otherness', and let one's language engage itself in new webs of relation-ships. As you know, still nowadays, many of the Indian descendants seem to be oblivious of this voyage, as if their ancestors had come to many coun-tries by magic . . . And many tend to overlook the importance of this *coupure fondamentale* (fundamental act of severing ties), when they don't negate it. For example, in the secret, consensual speech of the Indian dias-pora, there is no 'distance' between the original homeland and the country of immigration. The Centre is paramount in the conception of a diaspora, which considers itself always in relation to the original homeland. By accepting the impact of the sea voyage, the *coupure*, the diaspora neces-sarily repositions itself, and is led to consider the lost homeland no longer as the only centre. The attitude to culture, identity, *imaginaire*, is thus a new one, a modern one in essence, as there is another relation to the host country, perceived as one of the centres of identity. And by positioning the sea voyage as a central process of one's relation to identity, one's attitude to identity can but be enlarged and complex. That is why in the diaspora this space of the 'Voyage', which reminds one that the centre, the land of 'Origins', is not the ultimate referent, is very often overlooked or negated.

2. Elements of the Coolie's 'Memory'

MC: As you said earlier, one of the principles of coolitude is to bring back part of a memory slashed by the violence of History, by conscious or unconscious censorship. Can you define the major constituents of the 'coolie's memory'?

KT: A very good way to answer this is to refer to Laurent Farrugia's book, *Les Indiens de Guadeloupe et de la Martinique* [11], which reveals, in many aspects, the tragic situation of the 'Indian' in the French Indies, and beyond. The author quotes Victor Schoelcher, the famous nineteenth century anti-slavery activist, who wrote that the indentured labourer was a '*serf de la glèbe vendu avec tête de bétail et outils aratoires* (a serf sold by the medieval land owner, with the cattle and the agricultural tools)'. The 'Indian coolie' oscillated between the slave and the wage worker – although he had a legal contract, his treatment approximated to that of a slave. The conditions of the indentured labourer differed from country to country, so that there were many situations and aspects of the first stages of coolitude, but, fundamentally, there is no serene voyage in coolitude. Therefore, though he/she was the bearer of an ancient, literate civilization, so much valued in the Western world, the coolie himself was treated as an 'object'. And even though he had his name on a contract, he had to fight to make his humanity respected. But the very fact of having this name on the contract is a highly significant aspect of coolitude, bequeathing on him a human status, at least from the legal point of view, thus, guaranteeing the coolie his/her *habeas corpus*. This scriptural mark, however, will also lead to the distortion of Indian patronyms as a sign of the 'scriptural wound' of identity. This original situation, as one can easily imagine, framed the later stages of the migrant's identity abroad. These early phases must be rediscovered. It is necessary to mediate this cultural and social trauma, through a new approach of identity, literature, culture . . . Therefore, a better knowledge of this period must not lead to a closed vision of identity, celebrating the past indefinitely, refusing the complexity of present societies, as the first stages implied contacts with languages, cultures and *imaginaires*.

MC: We know that many stratagems were devised by the coolie, from tragic scenarios to more indirect means of survival . . .

KT: One of the most tragic escape routes of the coolie was suicide. Farrugia has noted the prevalence of a particular way of killing oneself, – letting oneself pass away or as he calls it, 'suicide by nostalgia', for the 'expiation of a fault one did not commit'. This sense of guilt at having left the original homeland with its cosmogony, its sacred rules, the attachment to purity, the loss of one's place in the cycle of reincarnation, besides other traumatic forms of abandonment and renunciation, are pertinent paradigms of these (and later) stages.

Another common stratagem was a particular form of '*marronnage*', that is, *vagabondage*, or vagrancy. Thousands of Indians condemned as vagrants for deserting their work, or through inability to labour through sickness, were confined in specially constructed colonial vagrant *dépôts*. In 'Coolitude'[12], attention was brought to the fact that vagrancy was the most common form of revolt, an alter ego of the '*marronnage*' of the slaves, with its own specificities. Basically, the slave was a maroon, the coolie a vagrant. This difference of perceptions and resistances must also be explored in relation to the construction of 'mixed societies', and literary and artistic productions cannot ignore them.

MC: In these early stages, the way the coolie was seen by the other is inseparable from his/her own elaboration of a set of references born in exile . . .

KT: Contradictions were abundant in colonial societies – for instance, the perceptions of the coolie, this newcomer whose image oscillated between the docile agricultural labourer and the vicious, dirty, rebellious, immature, subhuman malingerer. This is also part of the coolie's memory. In this respect, the indentured labourer was not fully recognised as a citizen of the countries where he/she had settled, sometimes for several generations. In Guadeloupe for instance, it was only in the first quarter of the twentieth century that the coolie descendant was granted his citizenship rights, following the legal struggle of an eminent lawyer of Indian origin, Henri Sidambarom. Sidambarom desired to be '*un fils du sol à part entière*', that is, a fully recognized citizen, with cultural, moral and political recognition, to achieve the historical legitimacy of his presence, as an integral part of the host country. This marginalization of the indentured in the host country's social fabric is an important space of tension, frustration, and even, nowadays, in some countries, condones a sense of 'loss' and social trauma.

MC: Is it right to say, for eample, that when the coolie achieved his/her economic and social settlement objectives overseas, he/she in fact transfered or 'spoiled', in some cases, the potential creativity of exile?

KT: The adaptation process was long. First, one pragmatic reaction of the indentured labourer was to aspire to possess the land, and this was in keeping with rural Indian culture, even if, in exile, there was greater social and economic mobility in the process. This ownership was seen by the indentured as the means of procuring affective, political and cultural security. This was to condition much of the coolie's social mobility strategy. On a basic social level, the coolie was largely successful in retaining the family unit intact, through the migration process, with increasing recourse to chain migrations of spouse and family members; an option which was scarcely available to the slave. Families who migrated into indenture could also be subsequently bought out of the system; so that the indentured labourer always had the goal of earning his/her liberation. However, we cannot overlook the degree of creativity necessary in those pragmatic strategies. Often more subtle and long term stratagems, usually involving a degree of cultural subjugation were also evolved. Those reactions show that the 'plural societies', Mauritius, for example, were often framed by antagonizing forces, and endless tensions . . .

MC: The 'plural society', even in its embryonic form, showed that exclusion was at work at an early stage . . .

KT: Indeed. Many writers and historians have pointed to this 'exclusive' foundation. This was apparent even in the 'mixed racial' stratum. Creole society gave rise of a class of mixed ancestry, the *sang mêlé*, who came to occupy an intermediate political and cultural position in the binary social structure of the plantocracy. The Indians, often, were to come between the emancipated slave and the European planter, and in some way, competed with the *métis*, in that intermediary social margin. But, in many of the countries to which Indians migrated, in the immediate post-emancipation period, the fact of being the mainstay of the plantation system, after the abolition of slavery, earned him the reputation of salvaging the economy of the master, of being an 'ally' of the planter. This remains one of the principal causes of ostracism, and unspoken 'rivalry' between African and Indian descendants in many former colonies. This element of memory is still to be expressed, as it bears painful scars nowadays. This is why *Cale d'Étoiles* brings those two suffering memories face to face, more, it blends them in a common creation.

MC: According to you, a cultural and human *non-dit* (unspoken speech) needs to be expressed at the heart of coolitude.

KT: Yes, there is a sense of loss and silence . . . For instance, in the French West Indies, due to distance between the original country and the colony, and to the size of the indentured population as compared to other components of the plantocratic society, and also to the separation of coolie settlements and their geographical locations, the coolie experienced acutely the sense of the loss of his/her self. In Guadeloupe and Martinique, the written text of the original culture was lost, and this was accompanied by the subsequent loss of the mothertongue and languages. This led in turn to what can be described as the '*culture de la trace*', (vestige culture) and to the task of 'rememoration' of the lost meanings of the original culture. Those Indians who migrated in small numbers, as in the French Caribbean, experienced a complete revolution of their social fabric. Castes, creeds, entire ways of life which had been kept separate, become entangled, and ultimately, the 'purification of the paria' was one result of the abolition of caste distinctions.

This social revolution brought by the indentured and exile created a more homogeneous Indian group, and at the same time, imbued its participants with a lasting sense of guilt linked to the loss of one's creed and also, the suppression of a taboo (crossing the *Kala Pani*, mixing castes and creeds, for instance). Moreover, the silence or strategy of withdrawal often developed, as a natural attitude to preserve onseself, to try to come out of an inhuman system is framed against this background of exclusion and adjustments, and we can understand that reflexive attitudes and subsequently, resistance strategies, mainly on the economic and political planes, alongside with the preservation of Indian values, did not leave much time and energy to the indentured to explore his/her tormented identity on an aesthetic level, and to develop a creative *imaginaire* of exile. We have some examples of this desire to keep the signs of an original culture, and preserve them from the loss of the crossing. In the Coolie Museum of Mauritius, we have a copy of the Quran, entirely recopied by hand, in an attempt by an indentured to keep from loss his sacred text. Oral traditions, in Madrassas (Quranic schools) and Baitkas (Hindu sociocultural organizations) preserved what they could. This was the case in Mauritius, but not really in the French Indies. However, it is often reported that, there, the Indian story-tellers were really admired, but eventually, they also dwindled away . . .

MC: So the concept of a major guilt is important in coolitude . . . From this loss, and subsequent efforts to recapture, recreate and reinvigorate a new approach to identity, does coolitude call attention to those moments of trauma, both in literary and analytical terms?

KT: The 'primitive', symbolical trauma can be summed up in the emotive terms '*Kala Pani*', the Dark Seas . . . Indeed. This sense of guilt is significant with the prohibition of the crossing of the *Kala Pani*, a major taboo in Hinduism. The soul of the Hindu who left the Ganges was doomed to err perpetually, as it was cut from the cycle of reincarnation. So going on the high seas was a poignant existential decision, a major symbolical act, as the *Kala Pani* was peopled by *houglis*, foul spirits and monsters. Undertaking the 'Voyage' meant many deaths, a betrayal of one's beliefs, social tenets and culture. I have pointed to this guilt or fear in coolitude to explain why the trauma and the liberation of the voyage occupies an important position, so often neglected in collective consciousness. The crossing of, and the relation to the sea is an important unacknowledged aspect of the coolie's descendant's identity . . . In countries like Guadeloupe and Martinique, due to greater distance, the migration of souls cut off from the waters of the Ganges, produced a series of psychological disasters, as one can imagine. For example, there, the Hindu indentured labourers were forced to bury their dead, instead of burning the corpses as in their homeland. Many such factors or circumstances led, in varied degrees, to the dilution or loss of the Indian identity in many plantocratic societies. Needless to say that this sense of emptiness, of exclusion, of dereliction, needs to be transferred in a creative approach to exile and identity. People have often expressed their desire to be part of the countries where they were born, and this means moving out of the negating strategies of the past . . . Therefore, a more constructive, creative approach to this period is needed. I think that a new definition must be achieved when thinking of Indian, European, African or other cultures, in this context.

3. Aesthetics and Literature

MC: In your desire to extend your vision to other languages or 'reservoirs of signs', how far would you accept the well known definition of creoleness based on a 'triple negation' as propounded by its principal ideologues Confiant, Chamoiseau and Bernabé?

KT: When Chamoiseau, Confiant and Bernabé, in *Eloge de la Creolité*, said that Cesaire's *négritude* led the way to a possible *Antillanité* (Caribbeanness), they defined this concept by reminding us that the Caribbean identity was founded on a triple negation: 'We are neither Europeans, nor Africans, nor Asians, we proclaim that we are creoles'. However the limiting factors of this definition of *Antillanité* or 'West Indianness' are clearly race or territory or nationality, as many writers and critics later stressed. Thus, creoleness was to be the next concept on which Chamoiseau, Confiant and Bernabé worked. Soon, they were defining creoleness as 'an open specificity', an oxymoron in itself, and this has to be linked to what Glissant said about creoleness as being an 'interpretation' of creolization, the latter being defined by him as a more open process generating a new attitude to identities.

MC: Does this stance underlining the 'specificity' of creoleness, as stated by Confiant and his colleagues, account for a special attitude to the Indo-Caribbean in literary works from the West Indies?

KT: A survey of most of the novels of many West Indian writers will show that very often, characters of Indian origin seem to be relegated to a status bordering on absence and silence, as if they reflected the position imposed on the indentured by the violence of History. Whilst being aware of the specificity of the coolie experience, many of these authors, especially in their earlier works, have often reflected the status of object (out of speech) assigned to the coolies. The coolies were viewed almost as 'outsiders', not really forming part of the country, and this marginalization is in line with historical and social interpretations which have prevailed until recently. That is, the coolie saved the sugar master from bankruptcy, the coolie was an ally of the plantocracy, or he/she came too late after slavery to be fully considered a real Caribbean. *Sucre Amer*, for instance, a feature film directed by Christian Lara, from Guadeloupe, in 1997, echoes this ambiguous status of the Indian descendant in Caribbean societies, seen almost as an outsider in the Guadeloupean-identity construction.

Thus, aesthetic constructions, with some notable exceptions (I think of Glissant or Condé, for example, and some later writings of Confiant) have often failed to integrate the presence of the coolie in the West Indian novel leaving him/her on a marginal or borderline axis. The coolie remains an obscure presence in many constructions of Caribbean literature, in which, given the social issues of those societies torn by violent rejection of races and cultures, the social function and sense of historicity is strong. This also entails that the writer's attitude to culture is extremely important to all components of Caribbean society. Of course, we can understand that when evolving their aesthetic, social strategies and visions, the writers of *créolité* were already too preoccupied with the plight of their own *manque à dire* (speech deficiency or lack of expression), with the problems of their own society, mainly people of African origin, to enlarge their perceptions fully to the 'other'. From this 'particular/open' construction, however, they showed potentialities of a possible vision of complexity, and owing to the awareness of the poetics of coolitude (I am referring here to the foreword of Raphaël Confiant in my book, *Chair Corail, Fragments Coolies*), will lead to a more complex attitude at the core of creoleness..

MC: Would you say, that with the passage of time, literature has a role to play in integrating the problematics of coolitude?

KT: Indeed. The function of literature should reach other horizons and go beyond the limitations of the past. It is particularly important for literature to work in a political, social and cultural framework in which all the components of Caribbean and other societies could feel part of a wider community. People need identifications, representations to mediate their relation to the past and the present. Arts, culture and literature are highly significant spaces of expressing one's relationship to society, to history and new perceptions. Literature has a very significant role to play in societies where components of diverse origins and *imaginaires* come into contact. There have been, however, interesting changes in this attitude recently, and an awareness has been growing constantly in the French Caribbean and elsewhere as to this part of the mosaic.

MC: Do writers outside *Créolité* have a different view?

KT: Maryse Condé, while not forming part of the movement of *créolité*, has, through the construction and diversity of the themes and settings of her novels, shed an interesting light on what may be defined as the 'Complex Self/Identity'. For instance, in *Traversée de la Mangrove*,[13] Condé uses several voices in her narrative and brings her readers into contact with the kaleidoscopic identity of Guadeloupe. The coolie presence here is expressed through the Ramsarans and through the complex character of Francis Sancher, who is of mixed origin. Condé's novel is one of the rare works of literature which gives a full voice to persons of Indian ancestry in the French Caribbean, and echoes profoundly one aspect of the poetics of coolitude, i.e. the relationship of identities of different origins without a '*racine prédatrice*' (predatory root). Here the mangrove seems already to be the metaphor of a 'creole identity', a swamp where multiple roots become entangled, live, fight and die in the same virtual space. In the book, Sancher, the central enigmatic character, attempts to write about his 'roots': a task which is represented to be difficult, if not impossible, leaving the poetics of cultural diversity open to the possibility of failure. However Sancher, in allowing the different narrative identities to converge, to telescope with each other, offers a possibility of combining the mosaic presences of Guadeloupe into an articulation of diverse visions, despite the clash of its composite parts. Through this interplay of characters and psychologies, we reach the heart of a vision of the world which is dynamic. Condé sheds light on the *imaginaire* of a 'community' which does not stifle the voice of any of its components, though the entire discursive strategy rests on the enigmatic figure of Sancher, whose presence triggers an exchange of words and attitudes between the different components such as Vilma, Dinah, Dodose, Rosa and Mira. This recalls Glissant's theory of 'chaos and incompleteness' inherent to creolization and coolitude, as Condé's novel demonstrates the impossibility of creating a collective consciousness of the Guadeloupean community. This 'failure' is a metaphor of the process of creolization; a reminder that the totality of vision of this kaleidoscopic community is but a process with various possible combinations. It also underlines that there is no need of a predating identity capable of subsuming the others, or of achieving a synthesis in which otherness is reduced to sameness. Memories and histories are intertwined here like the roots of the mangrove, indicating that the various identities are engaged in an active interplay where new forms, and new *imaginaires*, are possible. The part which is unsaid, the silence, or the '*cri en cale*', (the cry from the hold) is transposed here as a possible material of complex attitudes in post-modern or creole identities. From this point of view, Condé's work is of fundamental importance to the understanding of *créolité*, creolization and coolitude.

MC: You mentioned earlier, that the presence of the 'coolie' has often not been fully taken into account in many texts of French Caribbean literature. In that context, would you say that coolitude is a corrective echo of creoleness, in the sense that it brings to the picture the fuller potentialities of creolization?

KT: Coolitude is an aesthetic blend, a kind of mix of a complex culture, bringing to the *imaginaire* a part of the other. It calls to attention 'Indianness' in relation with 'Otherness' as a premise which leads to a transcultural awareness. This is in keeping with the fundamental attitude of creolization. We must understand that in those texts of creoleness which often do not integrate coolies as fully fledged literary creations – a fact that does not live fully to the promises of creolization – a mirror is held to History, a moment of History, when the struggle between the descendants of slaves and the descendants of coolies was real, each fighting to carve out a place in the plantocracies.

   The literature of the Indies or of the Indian Ocean, as I said earlier, often reflects, in its borderline attitude towards the coolies/indiens/malabras, those conflicts, the suspicion and *non dits* (unsaid conflicts) between the children of slavery and indenturedship. *A l'Autre Bout de Moi*, for instance, by Marie-Thérèse Humbert explored this impossible encounter between an Indian descendant and a Mauritian creole[14]. This theme of friction is also encountered in literary works of writers originating from Indian immigration. This is the case of *Lal Pasina*[15] by

Abhimanyu Unnuth, a novel written in 1975 in Bhojpuri, in Mauritius. In this historical novel, Unnuth brings out the diverse, 'rival' components of Mauritian society in his plot, and shows their struggles and aspirations. Similarly, in Confiant's *Le Nègre et l'Amiral*, we come across flashes of this rivalry, even if, in this novel, Confiant confines the coolies to a marginal social role. His creole hero, very often from an urban area, with imperious sexual gusto has, almost all the time, the upper hand on the stereotyped, weaker coolie character coming from rural areas or from peripheral and ill-famed urban quarters. This reflects, consciously or unconsciously, the marginalization of the descendants of coolies in Caribbean literature and society. Literature here, even in this strategy of the *détour* used in relation to the coolie, reflects a type of social relation beset by the vagaries of colonization, slavery and indenturedship. The *non-dit* (unsaid) seems to be transmuted into *l'incommunicabilité* (non-communication) between the characters who belong to two worlds. This struggle for territory and identity is vividly portrayed in the novel of David Dabydeen *The Counting House*,[16] which describes a competition between Miriam the ex-slave, and Rohini, the coolie's wife, to win the favours of Gladstone, the master of the sugar cane plantation. In this novel, what seems to be contained as a virtuality in the novels of *créolité* is brought to aesthetic and social realization by Dabydeen, who, to quote him, 'uses the continuum of coolitude' to bring into contact the ex-slave and the coolie on a Guyanese plantation, in a confrontation between the *imaginaires* of those two actors of History, coupled with a Freudian exploration of the symbolical importance of sexuality in that violent encounter.

MC: You make frequent reference to History as a background, which is also part of your reservoir of signs. Don't you think that this can affect the aesthetic aspect of coolitude?

KT: As you know, there is no contradiction for any aesthetic proposal or vision to integrate a social and historical process, even if it also tries to transcend it. What would be Zola's *Germinal*, for instance, without the social background of his time, or Steinbeck's *Grapes of Wrath* without the American crisis? There are so many other examples . . . It is not incompatible for poetry itself to have a concrete relationship with History or the archives in *Vétiver* (Triptyque, Montreal, 1999), which may be transubstantiated, as many writings have proved, among which are those by Byron, Derek Walcott, Federico Garcia Lorca, Aimé Césaire, Edouard Glissant, V.S. Naipaul . . . I would also give an example of the poetic rewriting of the archives by Joël des Rosiers, a Haitian poet living in Montreal, who blends Indian, Haitian, creole and indigenous cultures, archives and history in a magnificent poetic composition.

MC: Is this transmutation of History, which is also a way of giving shape to the 'cry from the hold', a way of exploring new potentialities and convergences?

KT: In the case of coolitude, even if there is a very close similarity with the symbolism of the 'cry from the hold', this traumatic moment of a stifled utterance when the ship was leaving native Africa for the slave, I would refer to a 'murmur from the hold', given the ability of the indentured to see, sometimes move, and even speak when the ship was leaving native India. But, basically, something was repressed in the words of exile in both cases. It may be useful at this juncture to recall a central tenet of creolization as evolved by Edouard Glissant. Creolization is accompanied by a dynamics, a movement, that brings with it the possibility of entering into types of relationship, which, to simplify, may be seen as 'chaotic encounters' with unforeseen results. Glissant points to this fundamental aspect of creolization: '*Elle met en Relation sur un mode égalitaire et pour des premières fois . . . des histoires . . . convergentes* (It creates a relationship on an egalitarian footing and, for the first time, between convergent histories)'.[17]

This egalitarian perception, as well as this convergence, is central to coolitude and to its relation with *créolité* and postmodern identity in which each part should be, potentially, in an 'equal' position to enrich complex identities. This stems from the fact that, when considering this 'egalitarian mode' one should be reminded of its relation to complex identities, and the relations between those identities themselves. If not, ultimately, each group or community of individuals can view the world from the perspective of a unique set of values. The latter vision could also be the result of a strategic choice a writer has made, in which he/she expresses his/her philosophy of diversity, which may not comprehend all the facets of the mosaics. In this vision of diversity, one may come across a kind of arbitrary synthesis, which may be a reductive one, if it is dictated by his/her position of prevalence in Hhistory or a type of society, or if the writer doesn't take care to let the potentialities of the relationship open. This attitude is at work in some interpretations of *métissage*, in eurocentrism, sinocentrism, sometimes, in a vision of creolocentrism, where the '*racine prédatrice*' will hinder the development of a rhizome identity and may ultimately lead to the continuation of the *non-dit* and a predating vision, a centre.

This literary treatment of the '*non-dit*', for instance in the name of a complex vision of society, may sometimes just boil down to the construction or interpretation of one component's vision of how the rhizome-identity should be, and even this mosaic vision may be felt to be partial by the component(s) with the greater speech and cultural deficit. That is, there is one vision which tends to be *the* vision of the rhizome. This, paradoxically, just brings to mind another form of the '*confiscation de la parole*' (the confiscation of speech), and can just strengthen feelings of rejection or dereliction. We can see, for example, how recent action against globalization reflects the desire of nations and persons not to accept a 'synthetic vision' of the world imposed on them. They want to stress their own participation in fully enriching the concept of a 'global' planet, and express their own specificities and desires in giving a content to globalization. In doing so they inject into the concept, which has often been a mercantile one, their attachment to their own presence and diversity. People have been defending their regional/national products, cuisines and cultures in front of economic or cultural giants associated with standardization. I think the same logic applies to the poetics of complexity in which the egalitarian mode must be respected, as it leaves the process open to its potentialities, and does not make it a rigid interpretation of 'complexity'.[18] The concept of coolitude is in itself a mirror of many aspects of this problem, hovering between a past confined in silence or censorship, and creolization, without a subsuming identity as sometimes expressed in creoleness. It points to multiple identities in a dynamic interaction, in a 'dialectic of mutations'.[19]

MC: Your vision of identity, of present attitudes to supranational constructions makes room for plurality. It is, if I am not mistaken, baroque in spirit. Is the aesthetics of baroquism, defined primarily as a *mise en relation* of diverse perceptions important in coolitude? Your poetry often brings to light a complex architectonics.

KT: As you know, the baroque element has very often been the antonym of classicism in the sense that baroquism expresses 'surprising or extravagant' expressions or thoughts, extended to literature, music or architecture. The baroque element is also, and this is the point I would like to stress, the consequence of a type of historical relation which has brought into contact diverse mental structures, modes of life, languages and visions of the world. That is, through its asperities, its impurities, baroquism embodies an 'excess' of civilizations and, in a paradoxical movement, liberation in language and aesthetics, by the very fact of letting diversity express itself in works of art or literature . . . For the descendants of the oppressed, it would have been a greater crime to adopt a univocal system of references for the construction of identity, akin to, for instance, what Roland Barthes called 'classico-centrism', not far from the concept of 'purity'.

MC: The baroque poetics sustains, in your approach, a particular type of expression fraught with the refusal of a dominant cultural or colonial attitude . . .

KT: Indeed, this attitude derides an oppressive system resulting from this 'transparent' matrix of plantocratic systems, excluding the 'impurities' that were attached with the presence and culture of the other. I am referring to 'transparence' as founding the pragmatic 'culture' of the colonial society where efficiency was increased by using, for instance, basic words for several tasks, sometimes reducing creole language to a mere ghost of syntax and grammar. Often, the relation to productivity with its simplified, 'transparent' language, was the only type of relationship between the master and the oppressed. In that society, complexity was often a sphere left to the dominant planter and his collaborators. Language therefore, in the servant–master relationship, was divested of its poetic elements, of its creativity, I would say, of its baroque subversive capacities.

Subsequently, therefore, literature resulting from this universe, almost instinctively recuperated this creative characteristic, by having recourse to carnavalization of characters and of situations, as defined by Bakhtin. In the literature of *créolité*, the *ludique* (playful) creations and improvisations of the creole language reveal a mental structure, which, in the very act of creation, of inventing new words and images, points to a particular strategy of survival and resistance of the slave descendants in language and literature. By creating, the slave (or later the indentured), denied the objectal status deferred on him by the plantocracy. This is why I feel literature, artistic creations and culture at large constitutes the onus of a necessary construction of *imaginaires* and identities. Language, tradition, memory, viewed as 'a réservoir' of signs and as a potent source of relations to the world, to a new universe, of reconnecting with one's humanity in fact, is among the most important spheres of resistance to plantocratic or colonial societies, specially from people who 'left' their aesthetic universe, their symbolical status in language, as they were treated as objects or subhuman entities. This space still keeps its vivid symbolical dimension with the possibility of reconstructing what is thought as necessary for a fuller presence and participation in the society.

MC: Therefore, by using baroque elements, a density of language and identity is made more evident . . .

KT: It is significant that Edouard Glissant says in *Poétique de la Relation* that one has to resist reduction to transparency: '*Non pas seulement consentir au droit à la différence mais, plus avant, au droit à l'opacité . . . la subsistance dans une singularité non réductible* (Not simply to consent to the right to be different but, more importantly, to the right to opacity . . . subsistence in a non-reducible singularity)'.[20] The temptation of reducing otherness to sameness is a constant problem in human relations. Baroquism correlates to this opacity of language and, by being open to many *imaginaires*, to the irreducibility of identity to a monosemic construction.

MC: Baroquism therefore reflects a resistance to sameness, in fact, a type of reduction of the subject to a transparent vision which equates with a construction of the centre, the estate owner's truth in the planto-cratic context. Is it to be understood as a 'deviant' form of resistance?

KT: Opacity may be viewed as a symptom of identities crushed in the maelstrom of plantocratic societies. The coexistence of opacities, accord-ing to Glissant, avoids the 'prison of an impenetrable autarchy' or the reduction of the truth of the subject to the values and norms of the person with the domineering position in the 'exchange' (whose un-conscious desire is the reduction of the subject's otherness). Baroquism, by its 'impure', multiple, mosaic consistence, enables this coexistence of opacities. In fact, this poetics allows to use 'deviant forms and expres-sions' to break the order of a system whose language, for efficiency and domination, did not tolerate a spontaneous, dynamic or chaotic approach to language, and therefore favoured communication and social coercion. In fact, a baroque attitude which is a complex one, brings to the very heart of communication a kind of subversion, where the *imaginaire* becomes capable of exploding the 'productive language strategy' of the Centre. Cuban writer Alejo Carpentier clearly described baroquism as a 'creative impulse'. There is no better way of breaking a compelling strand of communication than by multiplying the levels of possible interpreta-tions, by turning language itself into a contaminated medium where the precedence of transparency is caught in the web of contradictory mean-ings, in what Eco has called a semiotic game, *'jeu de la sémiosis'* when referring to Joyce's *Finnegan's Wake*, for instance.

MC: So, as a poet, baroque language is often seen and employed by you as a major locus of the expression of the Diverse . . .

KT: Basically, yes . . . Robert E Burton has called this type of communi-cation *'un marronnage dans la langue'* (marooning with language). Baroquism and *marronnage* for me, are major figures in the creations of many writers of *créolité* and coolitude. Carpentier rightly said that *créolité* and baroquism are linked. The poetics of coolitude, therefore, often gives rise to a strangeness of language, *'l'étrangeté de la langue'*, and this aspect is in itself an intrinsic characteristic of poetry and literature.

MC: Does coolitude establish a firm correlation between the opacity of language and a complex attitude to identity?

KT: Language itself is unpredictable in the various relationships inherent to a creative process. It can also elude the meanings we wish to add to the texts and discourses. Frued was right to say that besides speaking, Man is also spoken. However, coolitude does not seek to champion either opacity or transparency, even if a form of literary baroquism reflects a complex approach to identity. It is a false debate to separate opacity and transparency on an arbitrary plane. Literary creation does not imprison a writer in one vision or the other. I would like to give an example here. If one reads *Bénarès*[21], a very surprising novel written by the Mauritian Barlen Pyamootoo, which some critics have qualified as a 'post-Durassian' work, one would not really go through a 'complex' use of language, with formal signs akin to the baroque or postmodern aesthetics. However, *Bénarès* represents a very strong current of coolitude in the sense that its 'transparent' language reveals a high degree of poetic concision and, above all, an interaction between language and a sharp literary vision. The *imaginaire* at work here, which gives this type of story and style, is one of a complex vision resulting from the coolitude poetics at work in the writer's approach to reality and its subsequent capture by literature.

On reading Sewtohul's *L'Histoire d'Ashok et d'Autres Personnages de Moindre Importance*[22] for instance, one comes across a 'chaotic', complex reality of characters with an ironic tinge, mixing fantasy and the dire reality of their island torn between divergent communities and visions. The novel has a strong baroque superstructure. Compared with Unnuth's work in a Bhojpuri mixed sometimes with Creole lexicon and expressions, the coolitude expressed by Sewtohul is in keeping with a postmodern attitude, twisting French language to fit the objective of a 'plural' approach of the *imaginaire*. Whereas Unnuth, in *Lal Pasina*, for instance, closely based his plot on historical and social realities, with coolie descendants still continuing the suffering linked to the betrayal of the contract and exclusion, Sewtohul construes another reality which multiplies social, cultural and literary landmarks, and irreality, to create a composite universe, where comic situations, delirium, the Sacred, desires, frustrations and love are conjoined with reflections on the hyperpolitization of the island, its surrealistic situations, and the quest for a Mauritian identity breaking away from communal models. The form encompasses this complex vision. Sewtohul's narrative is extremely creative in that respect. Languages mix in the text, we even have a parallel plot (the inner quest of the artist) in the Creole language, as a reflection of his complex attitude to identity, open to otherness of language. This plot sheds light on the main plot, the story of Ashok and Priya, in a *mise en abyme* of his characters and narrative. Having said that, everybody knows that opacity itself is a feature of poetry, of literature and of art. It is now admitted that we cannot understand everything totally, and that the opacity of something, of someone, their very otherness is in fact, part of their truth and mystery. This vision has been extended to human encounters, as a source of beauty and mystery. For instance, there is an interesting baroque definition of the creole self in *Le Nègre et l'Amiral* by Confiant:

> '*Etre créole . . . c'est manière de compromis entre le Blanc et le Noir, entre le Noir et l'indien, entre l'Indien et le bâtard-chinois ou le Syrien; au fond, que sommes-nous d'autres que des bâtards? Eh bien, revendiquons notre bâtardise comme un honneur et ne recherchons par, à l'instar des békés, des ancêtres héroïques dans une Guinée à chimère ou dans l'Inde éternelle. Voyez-vous, mon cher Amédée, tout ce mélange a produit une race nouvelle,une langue neuve, souple, serpentine, tout en étant conviviale et charnelle.* (To be Creole . . . is a type of compromise between the white and the black, between the black and the Indian, between the Indian and the half-Chinese or the Syrian; at bottom, what are we all if not bastards and half-castes? Well, let us proclaim our bastardy as an honour, and stop looking, like the white Creoles have done, for heroic ancestors, in a chimerical Guinea or an eternal India. You see, my dear Amédée, all this mixing has produced a new race, and a new language, which is supple and serpentine as well as being convivial and tangible)'.[23]

MC: How have you enlarged upon this concept of the creation of a 'new race' in your work?

KT: I would like to say that the notion of 'race' here must be understood as a concept beyond the strict sectarian definitions of race. The concept of self must also be thought of cautiously. One of the most interesting elements of *Le Nègre et l'Amiral* is the comparison made between the imaginary attempts to rediscover the 'purity' of the race through the ontological quest of 'heroic ancestors' from a chimeric Guinea or eternal India. This mental attitude to exile, coolitude or slavery, echoes the *béké*'s (white Creole's) own quest to glorify his ancestors. As a necessary reappraisal of the past, nowadays the white Creole acknowledges those of his/her ancestors, who, like the coolie, originated mostly from the lower, marginalized classes of society. The positive contribution of *Le Nègre et l'Amiral* is in the articulation of the desire to visualize and create a 'new race', let's say, a new identity, out of the 'victims' of History, whether they have passed through the furnace as colonizer or the colonized. In his definition, Confiant, on an ideological plane, states that a 'compromise' in the field of identity would put in contact the 'Indian' element, and the Chinese and Syrian components with the Black and the White.

MC: The literary world has recently begun to evoke themes which you describe as being central to coolitude. For example, you mentioned David Dabydeen, earlier . . .

KT: In *The Counting House*, David Dabydeen brings a new dimension to the fiction of the Indian 'diaspora', by the fact that he engages in the poetics of coolitude, through the paradigms of History, sexuality and gender. Vidia, the coolie male is once again in a secondary role: in relation to the omnipotent master and to his wife Rohini's attempts at seducing the master in order to attain respectability and power, in short to be like the 'superior white'. The coolie's role is determined by the place granted to him in the rigid plantocratic society. He saves every penny, thinking of the future of his children, and 'accepts' that his wife becomes little more than another form of 'currency' (*monnaie d'échange*) in a sexual game leading to the bed of the master. The tragedy here is that the 'male of reference' is the master (the position of 'normal' male being held by the '*békés*' or local whites in the West Indian novels) and this particular sexual dominance is but the expression of an economic system which moulds the presence, the desires, the dreams of the coolies on the alienating values on which the plantation system rests.

This situation is strengthened in the novel by the fact that a marooned coolie (with a textual spill over of the master/slave dialectics) becomes the lover of the African mistress who has been abandoned by the planter in favour of the younger coolie woman. This coolie is a symbol of a syncretic new culture in Guyana, since he possesses within him, both the outlook of a 'maroon' or run-away, and the will for a freedom which goes beyond his own creed and 'race'. He is ultimately vanquished by the dogs of the master, symbolizing the failure to carry through the egalitarian project of a 'plural' society.

MC: Dabydeen's writing, therefore, approximates to the 'contagion of *imaginaires*' which you underline as a major axis of coolitude writings . . .

KT: There is a narrative project in *The Counting House* in which the slave's and the coolie's *imaginaires* are brought into contact, even to the point of exchange, if not, of communion. But often, elsewhere, the plantation effectively 'castrates' the coolie male, which may explain the perception of him as a silent being, a mere shadow in the system. This has been delineated in Danielle Dambreville's novel, *L'Echo du Silence* (L'Harmattan, Paris, 1995), in Reunion, where the coolie character is named '*le muet*' (the mute). The 'Indian' character with wounded speech reflecting an absence in/from language and society, is recurrent in Ananda Devi's novels where women, mostly of Indian extraction, live in a claustrophobic atmosphere, confined in a traumatic universe of silence. Women like Aeena, nicknamed Gungi (the mute)[24], symbolizing exclusion from speech, is boldly delineated. She closes upon herself, in silence, 'so as not to hear the noise in her memory', and her coming to humanity, her overcoming of suffering, comes through an act of revolt against the husband's or the father's authority, who not only reproduce a traditional system where speech is the reserved space of male domination, but also induce the same type of censored relationship to language, speech and identity, a fact imposed on them by the plantocratic society. The same applies to another heroin of Devi, Mouna, with a '*bec de lièvre*', bearing a symbolical wound on her lips. This character is also a victim of exclusion from speech as 'her mouth is not a mouth'.[25]

MC: You wrote: '*Le bon indien est un indien muet*' (The good Indian is a mute Indian), playing on the words 'muet' and 'mort' (dead) . . . What else does this 'evanescent' status in fiction represent?

KT: This muteness, this 'frailty' of speech, is another form of the symbolic castration of the coolie as a result of his/her situation in History, in the plantocratic society, and as reflected in many writings, including those of *créolité* writers. This fictional treatment in fact emphasizes what has been repressed and what has to emerge, in a kind of therapy. I am here referring to the 'murmur from the hold' where memory has been repressed, speech inhibited and the relation to a complex identity forced into an attitude of recoil. That is why literary expression is so vital to carve out one's full presence in those societies. The encounter of *imaginaires*, leading to a type of convergence, brings those muffled expressions to a social, aesthetic space where a more profound type of work can be accomplished. This type of creation also allows one to conjoin one's imagination to others. For instance, in *The Counting House*, the marooned coolie carries within him the revolt of the blacks alongside his desire to change the world, and this is the result of a psychic cross-breeding between two imaginative approaches. Sexuality here is central to the literary representation of underrated males in an oppressive system and illuminates the core of the problem between coolies and blacks (and the whites). But sexuality must also be understood as a competition for the mastery of language, a major tool of power, also a sign of cultural resistance . . . By trying to be the mistress of the planter, Rohini, the coolie's wife, eventually dreams of possessing the culture of the master . . .

MC: The texts you refer to show characters in situations where identities are dissolving, and new ones emerging . . .

KT: Françoise Lionnet rightly holds that '*métissage*' and 'indetermination' are indeed synonymous realities for our postmodern condition.[26] I quoted another woman writer, Ananda Devi, who often explores female characters in crisis, people silenced, cut off from others, or showing the symptoms of a non-relationship with 'Otherness'. Two worlds coexist, often juxtaposing that of the plantation owner, the 'White' in general, to the world of the small planter. This universe is linked to the muffled universe of women, exploited and often brutalized by those men who are themselves frequently at odds with their own caste or community groups. This impossible relation with the other is at the heart of the narrative tragedy. A dialectics of History, linked to the fabric of a society based on the plantocracy, drives the plots of Devi's novels. Her characters cannot master their own fate, which is inextricably linked to the dominance of sugar cane production or to the pursuit of economic wealth among rural communities. The characters live in a 'no-history zone/no-discourse zone', and are the victims of a slow decay, which is the source of their neurotic behaviour (for example Mouna in *Moi l'Interdite*, is denied her very humanity, hardly uttering a word, lapsing into animality, with the curse of *'enfant l'orage'* [child of the storm] on her lips).

The characters explore the emptiness of the meaning of their own existence . . . The sufferings of Devi's characters find their cause in the traumatic past, censored, buried in those women, which weighs so much on their current existence, because it has not been fully expressed and debated. As pointed out in *Cale d'Étoiles*, the space of this original trauma, on a collective plane, is the hold of the ship in which coolies were transported to the sugarcane fields. In *L'Arbre-Fouet*, Devi echoes this necessity of returning to this 'hold of stars', symbol of an existential, linguistic and cultural uprooting. This is why in Dabydeen's novel, or in Naipaul's writings, with his own specificities the Voyage remains a central metaphor.

MC: These texts already show an array of attitudes in the field of coolitude . . .

KT: Indeed. But it is also important to underline that in this process and those literary strategies, discourse and speech acquire a specific substance and status. For instance, in Nando Bodha's novel, *Beaux Songes*[27], words of Bhojpuri coexist with standard French. Language itself becomes the space where the past is recalled, and where the present is reconsidered, remodelled, and in his/her quest to preserve the past, the writer often brings to the forefront elements of the archives. Bodha's text is quite revealing in the sense that it hovers between the archives and literature, and this has a specific impact on the writer's overall style. Bodha mirrors a painstaking effort of recapturing a profound Indo-Mauritian memory in the field of literature, and brings out vibrant 'traces' of a vanishing rural community. The same can be said of Idriss Issop Banian's

Indianités (éditions Pages Libres, Reunion, 1990) which is a celebration of his Gujerati ancestors who came to Réunion in the nineteenth century. This poetry-book blends many words of Indian origin in its first part, with a very interesting feature: facing the French translation is the Gujerati text, written with Latin letters, to keep trace of a language many youngsters in Reunion may not read or recall otherwise . . . In its second part, 'Identité', the poet writes in French, without the need of translating in his ancestral language, and meets the *créolié* of his island by extolling his '*moi mosaïque*'. Jean-Claude Carpanin-Marimoutou, another poet, uses his Tamil and Reunionnais origins in his quest for a larger community in the Indian Ocean, and has engaged in an interesting blend of words at the apex of coolitude. The same vision is apparent in the very successful Ziskakan maloya and fusion music group from his island. Language as a distinctive element of this form of literature is also evident in Carl de Souza's *La Maison qui Marchait vers la Mer*, where creole merges with the French language and visions of two communities mix and clash. The same can be said of the novels of Marcel Cabon and Unnuth in the Indian Ocean. From the point of view of Caribbean literature, Dabydeen provides numerous examples of this linguistic *métissage*. With their own militant and feminist tinges, we may also call attention to the texts of Ramabhai Espinet and Mahadai Das.

MC: The same relation to language can be said to be conspicuous in the French Indies, for instance, among writers of *créolité* . . .

KT: Proponents of *créolité* like Chamoiseau and Confiant also give a great deal of importance to this, more even than most of their Indian Ocean counterparts. Among Caribbean novels, *Texaco* is a powerful testimony of this play and work on language and the *imaginaire*. Throughout the work of Raphaël Confiant, language also acquires a character of its own. There is a constant interplay between the oral language and the written text, leading to what is called '*oraliture*' (oral speech transposed in a written literary code). Speech inventiveness acts here as the mirror of creole vivacity and comic irony, from which '*le réalisme magique*' ou '*le réel merveilleux*' (magic realism) can spring. Reader and writer share a pact or a '*code de reconnaissance*' (code of understanding) as they accept the twists and turns of the languages used, because they share with the authors the *imaginaires* of

'Diversity', which has rejected the essentialist notion of purity of race or of language. Here, in a singular reappropriation of words, their histories meet, are exchanged, and are recomposed. The art of speech is central to creole societies, and functions as a point of intersection where problematic memories, and experiments with identities are expressed. Literary speech reflects this dual status: it constitutes a space of resistance and of residence.

MC: In spite of this linguistic *métissage*, you still spot absences and silences in the existing Caribbean literature of *créolité*, as regards the Indo-Caribbean dimension. Can you expand further on this, specially on the attitude of this literature as to the choice of language?

KT: We spoke of this aspect earlier. Indeed, we have very few examples of this language resulting from an imaginary contagion between the African and the Asian in *créolité* novels, and this may be because the original language of the coolies was lost. This was also complicated by the fact that whereas the African descendants, in the French Antilles eventually 'lost' their language, even in their relation to the 'Sacred', the 'Indians' kept remnants of Tamil, the tongue of the majority of the coolie descendants there, or Tamil as the mysterious language of the spirits and and the lost land, even if, in the course of time, many could not speak or understand it, a fact, which, *a contrario*, may have increased this 'impossible conversation' of the African with the Indian's *imaginaire* . . . The vestige of an original language, among other factors of opposition, may have meant incommunicability between two imaginations of exile. But we believe that what has been lost or has remained opaque in the words, a language can be revisited in the spirit associated with those who spoke/speak it, and who have their own perceptions of reality expressed by the words of any language. This is apparent in the attitude to language, for instance, in Raphaël Confiant's novels. The writer evolves two structural discourses, which may have been considered antagonistic in Martinique. He refers to oral traditions and the French tradition of '*papa de Gaulle*' in *Le Nègre et l'Amiral*. He constantly brings these two into contact, with inventive tones and twists, giving rise to a powerful language with baroque overtones. However, a third dimension seems to be left in the margins . . . It is that of the citizens of a second zone, the coolies, who seem here to be outside the discourse, as shown in *Le Nègre et l'Amiral*, out of the territory, in limbo. When Confiant's characters engage in a flight of oratory, whether light-heartedly or in a serious vein, the coolie seems to be only a passing shadow, voiceless, almost invisible and here, inaudible. The master, or white colonist, and his coloured representative have 'a speech of their own' in the novel, but the coolie's words seem relegated to a third, muffled and therefore unwanted, disturbing part.

Thus the coolie, at this stage of Confiant's writing, was not an autonomous character as he was, for instance, in Condé's novel. He was frequently a non-identity, a non-being in the West Indian mosaic. This particular status of the coolie may be said to reflect a deeper attitude at work in those societies shaken by plantocratic violence: the relation between the Master and the Slave excludes the third party, who is an undesired presence between the 'Father' and the 'Son'. He/she thus becomes *l'être sans parole* (wordless being).

In what is a disruption of this code of the '*Divers*', the coolie is out of the discourse because he is between the Master and the Slave, out of the binary Manichean model or seen as an 'unmediated' presence. Indeed the title of the novel is very clear: it is an 'opposition' between the 'negro and the admiral' and a third chaotic presence, the coolie, is clearly not included in Confiant's narrative project. At this point, however, we reckon that it takes time to come to this unsettling term of the relation, to its chaotic heart. The fact that the coolie is only seen on the periphery of the plantation in *Le Nègre* points to a particular vision of the Indian descendant, who is not yet comprehended as an integral part of Caribbean discourse. He is represented as having come to the West Indies only to crouch with his hoe in the sugarcane fields, with nothing to say in the elaboration of a mosaic identity. This is where coolitude brings a humane dimension to light. It reminds one of the necessity of the principle of equality of social, cultural and historical components at the theoretical core of creolization. No projection or presence of the other should be censored or ignored in its wake.

MC: The identity delineated in coolitude is thus a reapraisal of the components, of all the components of creole societies . . .

KT: In throwing light on this egalitarian dimension, coolitude recalls that the building of an *imaginaire* from a traumatic past and memory, with a sense of alienation in language, needs a composite approach. That's why in *Le Nègre et l'Amiral*, as in some other créole novels, the coolie who is left out because of his own 'opacity', (or the créole narrator's 'conjunctural' inability to integrate his presence, not to speak of his/her discourse/speech), doesn't live to the full potentialities of a richer literary, social and cultural construction. Of course this non-presence in the narrative is often an unconscious act. The coolie, as compared to the ex-slave, was weaker in his discourse when he/she entered the process of the interaction between the Black and the White. Therefore, this 'deriding' attitude, interpreted by the coolie descendant as a non presence, a *non-parole*, and by extension, a non-Caribbean or a non-being, ultimately leads to a sense of exclusion. This is mainly because, paradoxically, the coolie did not use words and culture as the slave descendant did to overcome plantocratic violence. This was also complicated by the fact that whereas the African descendants, in the French Antilles 'lost' their language, even in their relation to the 'Sacred', the Indian descents kept remnants of Tamil, which may have increased this 'impossible conversation' of the African with the Indian's *imaginaire* . . . The vestige of an original language, among other factors of opposition, may have meant incommunicability between two imaginations of exile.

MC: Has Mauritius, in your view, offered more than the West Indies, as regards this exchange of imagination and fantasies (*imaginaires*)?

KT: A writer who was a pioneer in this field originated from Mauritius. I am referring to Marcel Cabon, a creole writer, specially in his later period. Sometimes critics have called his novels *'romans pastoraux'* (pastoral novels). This statement stems from an overly traditional view of literature, close to the taxonomy of French literature. For me, the pastoral setting of the novel is dictated by the very nature of the people Cabon was writing about, that is, the Mauritians of Indian origins, the descendants of the coolies. The pastoral setting pervades his style and acts profoundly on the human nature of his characters, and this is because the village is a highly symbolical place for coolitude, just as the *mornes*/mounts are for the people of creoleness. The village and the slave/coolie camp are a central location in the novels of Unnuth, Devi, Dabydeen and Naipaul . . . The geographical space imposes a treatment of form and plot, a choice of words, language, of the psychology of characters, and cannot be bypassed in the poetics of a writer. In Cabon's novel, the village, is thus, in itself a character of the novel.

MC: Don't you think that Cabon was too idealistic in his treatment of those coolie descendants in that 'traditional' setting?

KT: In his later novels, the communal life, the recreation of something 'Indian', the preservation of pastoral traditions and culture, was encapsulated and prolonged. We might call this a traditional approach, with an idealistic flourish, which sometimes causes Cabon to extoll the virtues of this 'innocent' rural life untouched by the vices of urban civilization. This rural factor is itself a prolongation of one basic aspect of Indian civilization in which the rural setting is predominant. However, the important aspect of Cabon's work is that he moved from ethnic narrowmindedness, and his work must be assessed in the context of cultural exclusions which prevailed in the Mauritius he wrote of, and seen from this angle, Cabon was a courageous pionneer. Even if there was suspicion between the creoles and the 'Indians', Cabon, through humane and political convictions, believed that the oppressed, creoles or coolies, were to unite against exploitation. As a militant creole, his political analysis explains greatly why he went to explore the profound humanity and misery of the village people.

He observed the villagers minutely, and learned much about their culture, at a time when the 'Indians' were thought of as negligible culturally. He even made a voyage to India, and not to Africa, the land of his ancestors, to learn more about the people he wrote about. A process of exchange of *imaginaires* is clearly at work in Cabon's novels, a rather new configuration at the heart of complex perceptions. Cabon describes perfectly the daily details of village life, mixing Creole and Bhojpuri, and this inclusion of an authentic lexicon in classical French was an audacious act of affirming a non mainstream cultural identity. In Cabon, we can say the literature of coolitude finds out one of its noblest novelists, who was realistic enough to understand the social and political issues at stake.

MC: Can you give a precise example of this 'literary struggle'?

KT: In *Namasté*[28], Cabon goes back to the village and portrays Ram, who thinks when seeing on the river the *bateaux-langoutis* (languti ships), of the *thowlias* which carried the coolies to the island. He remembers his grandparents who suffered so much, who died without quenching their thirst for land. His descriptions also bring new tones and tastes to French language as used in Mauritian literature. Besides, Cabon portrays Ram with two mental attitudes to space. He is a transitory migrant, having in mind both the village where he lived, a burning desire for his past and a concrete aim, to be part of the island where his parents migrated: 'He didn't know why, the fire rekindled in him times and people he had not known: his father who died in the very month following his wedding; his grandfather, coming from India, in a "languti-ship" with other coolies . . .' But Ram is already aware that Maurtitius and not India is his motherland, and there is much to do here. But there is a great paradox: Ram becomes mad, living solely on time past or an idealized present when Oumaouti, his wife, dies. Cabon portrays here the ideal Indian labourer, hardworking, loving the land, but unable to find peace and happiness in Mauritius. Cabon himself said that in Ram he described the suffering of the Indian immigrant in Mauritius. But what is interesting in the personality and moral stature of Ram the villager is that, to enable his child to come to existence, he would like to teach that 'the souls can love beyond races, beyond castes and nothing is better for the burns of offenses than forgiveness'. The madness of Ram is at the heart of this paradox: he is the coolie descendant torn between a past made of exile of his coolie ancestors, the bad treatment of the '*grand missié*' (the sugar master), and a problematic present. This delicate position in the host country, made of the nostalgia of the land of his ancestors and the hardships of daily life, coupled with a sense of dereliction in view of the negative consensus at the basis of Mauritian society, annihilating his projection in the future, symbolizes the quandary of the first generations of coolie descendants born in Mauritius. This paradoxical situation, framed very acutely on cultural and economic negationism plays havoc on the 'Indian' or Indo-Mauritian.

With this novel, Cabon, as a social chronicler coupled with a talented creative novelist, allows us to understand the paradox at the heart of the coolie descendant's relation to past and present, to India and the host country. One of the extreme forms of this 'chaotic' position in identity, besides madness, is the 'denial' of the host and/or the original country. This is the case of Sir V S Naipaul, who decided to discard his native Trinidad, seen as a land where the reconciliation with memory and History is impossible. The sense of loss here, symbolized by the death of Ram's, and his wife's Ouamati's, baby, exemplifies what exile requires from one, that is the loss of a part of one's memory and history, to be able to put together, as in a puzzle, fragments of the past, the present, the future, with diverse references, in order to carve out a new identity. These are symptomatic signs of the relation to 'Otherness', with different forms of hardships. One of the worst results cultural alienation causes, as we know besides severe disruptions of the personality, is death. Therefore, what is striking in Cabon's later writing is that in spite of some sweeping generalizations, he goes to the heart of the 'Indian' a bit like Loys Masson in his realistic approach, leaving behind exoticism, or fake empathy. But what is really new is that his characters try to build a new nation, a plural one, echoing his own desire to be a plural Mauritian. He shows a real poetics of relation, a rare, genuine insight in the *imaginaire* of people outside his community, and this is an honest construction in itself, beyond its intrinsic literary qualities.

MC: But beyond Cabon's open, complex attitude, other Mauritian writers have mixed attitudes towards the descendants of the Indians . . .

KT: In fact there are, basically, three types of attitudes, as stated earlier in the first part of this book. First, the 'Indian' mirrors oriental mystery, as in *Ameenah*. Secondly, the 'Indian' is the barbarian, as in *Polyte* by Savinien Mérédac, where the creole hero sees the 'Indian' as an invader: '*La terre, oui ils la connaissent, ils nous la volent assez, morceau par morceau*' and '*Sale nation va! C'est dans leurs mains que reste le profit . . .* (As for the land, they know it so well, they have been grabbing it away from us, bit by bit . . . Damned nation! It is in their hands that the profits are to be found . . .)'.[29] In *L'Etoile et la Clef* by Loys Masson, Zinovief states: '*Entre les blancs et nous il y a tout de même des points communs. Nous avons la même nature, plus ou moins les mêmes goûts. L'indien est un barbare* (Between the Whites and ourselves, there are common points.

We have the same nature, more or less the same tastes. The Indian is a barbarian)'[30]. Thirdly, the 'Indian' is an ambassador of exoticism and sensuality. This is apparent in Arthur Martial's *Poupée de Chair*. Here, the woman has captivating looks, she charms with her body shaped fantasmatically by the Greek canons of Beauty. In the Indies, the 'straight' hair of the 'coolie' is a somatic element, which often comes in the description of coolies, whereas, in Mauritian writings, it is the eyes which have this function, as they carry suggestive messages and reflect the magic world of another culture. Furthermore, in *L'Etoile et la Clef*, the body of the woman is beautiful and celebrated as an object of perfection. In West Indian novels, to make a quick comparison, the male coolie's body is an object of mockery, compared to the powerful negro. In *Ameenah* by Clément Charoux the heroine is 'a frail bibelot', and as such, triggers a paternalist, protective attitude. Whatever their foils, these writings at these early stages, abring many elements of the Otherness of the 'Indian' to 'contact' with language and literature.

MC: What is the importance, at that stage, of incorporating a human or social component in literature?

KT: This linguistic/literary function is the backbone of a social construction, of a complex identity. The presence of the coolie in 'mosaic' novels makes of him/her a partner of a complex identity. Many writers and readers would agree with Eco when he says that 'Literature, by contributing to "create" a language, contributes to the formation of an identity and a community'. When the coolie is out of literature, he/she is clearly left out of the *imaginaire* of complex identity and of society itself, out of its authentic spirit and frame. An 'evanescent' coolie character in a mosaic novel brings out an element of exclusion, as he/she is considered as an outcast in the ferment of the identity of the country or region. I mean, the coolie is out of the society if he/she is out of its creations. This has been understood, though not always brought to full expression, by novelists of *créolité*. They have recourse to '*figures de l'autre*' (representations of otherness) in their carnivalization of Caribbean society, by convoking the Syrian, the Lebanese, the Chinese and the Coolie (the major marginal figure), in view of showing the 'Diversity' of their *imaginaire*. They may be genuine in making this formal choice. But very often, those 'figures' aimed at bringing the complex vision of identity are only passing, evanescent or secondary ones, as if the stylistic expression of variety was more important than a real grasp on the plurality of perceptions and creations founding the mosaic society at the basis of the novelists' quest . . . There is a notable exception, however, in *La Vierge du Grand Retour*[31]. In this novel of Confiant, all oppressed people, coolies, mulattoes, blacks . . . seem to converge towards a comprehensive, consensual creole society, with a more balanced narrative technique, giving more importance to many human components of the Caribbean in the process. Here, even if the portrayal of the coolie is still marginal, as compared to Condé's, Confiant goes further than most of the *créolité* writers when he explores the coolie's inner visions, his dreams, his poeticity, in short, and all that this entails. This novel clearly marks a sharp aesthetic twist in Confiant's mental and narrative universe.

It indicates that one of the results of the conscious or unconscious censorship, or marginalization of the coolie is the denial of a richer Creole discourse (*discours créole*). Having said that, *créolité* can also be expressed in other ways than through simple literary tools. Confiant wrote a preface to a historical book, *Mémoire d'Au-Béro* (Jean-Pierre Arsaye, Ibis Rouge Editions, Guadeloupe, 1998) where he stresses the plight of the coolies, the ostracism they have suffered, and underlines their contributions to the creole society, in terms of cuisine and religion. I think the recent reactions of Confiant show that the coolie component is now being reconsidered . . . However, this 'lack of speech' has led some new writers to express their history in the Caribbean. I would refer to L Moutoussamy and C Minatchy, who explored the coolie's memory and plight in two books, in 2000. This also indicates that it is interesting to see that writings from Indian descendants are cropping up, with a view to revisiting their past, of reassessing elements of memory and History, keeping in mind, however, that they must engage in this perspective without losing sight of complex attitudes to identity.

4. Tradition, Society and Indianness

MC: Where would you situate coolitude in literary and intellectual history? Can it be said that coolitude comes just after creoleness, in a kind of chronology, as the coolie came after the European and the African in the process of cultural interactions?

KT: Coolitude projects itself from a continuum, from a colonial and postcolonial memory. Having said that, any new literary vision is the result of unconscious and conscious investments, and the text resulting from a new aesthetics, as JM Rey puts it, 'is never to be read in the field of the logic of identity . . . it is never simply inscribed in the space of a linear historicity'. From this angle, every work has its socio-cultural and historical context, which in turn it tries to transcend. This dialectic of tradition and creation is broadened by the outlook and approach of the individual's own take on language and literary history. I think his/her grasp on identity/ies is also a factor governing his/her attitude to novelty. An appropriate metaphor of such poetics would be the palimpsest, on which earlier inscriptions have faded, but whose content is the result of subsequent reappropriations of linguistic signs and meanings. Chronologically, what can be said is that coolitude reflects on the recent stages of creoleness and brings more aspects of the mosaic to mind, integrating more perceptions and experiments, to which 'Indias' in exile, India in the poetics of the relation, are conjoined. It therefore brings another root to the rhizome, conjoining former visions, interpreting them, and proposing an enriched scope, while leaving open new attitudes to identities.

MC: What is the main desire behind this approach of reformulating, reassessing history, culture and societies . . .?

KT: For the coolie (here I am referring to the coolie's strategy of '*repli*'), it was 'convenient' (this was also a reaction to exclusion) to be invisible and indecipherable, but this meant also that he was, as a consequence, absent from cultural interactions through literary creation. In the West Indies, as in the Mascarene islands, the space of language, the cultural sphere in short, were fields where social ostracism was expressed and fought, and as such, this field had (and still has) a crucial symbolical and political importance. For instance, the '*mulâtre*' (mulatto/half-caste) placed particular emphasis on culture for his social recognition. This also was the case in Mauritius, except that this libertarian attempt was affected by the tendency of the coloured men of letters to use language to aspire to participate in the world of the dominant class. He, in the end, made his intrusion in literature an exclusive field in which he voiced his own aspirations, and those of his ethnic group.

Literature remains a space in which contradictory impulses resulting from a 'negative consensus' continues to be an important factor in societies such as Mauritius or the Indies. We can understand that the pragmatic strategy of social and economic ascension, the ability to recreate the Indian village in some countries, and the fact that language was acquired much after the 'créole' component, diverted the coolie from an aesthetic projection of his self in the plantocratic society. He was in the claimant's position (letters, complaints, petitions, accountancy) in the use of linguistic signs, and less in the aesthetic projection of his self in a literary and thus, transubstantiated social dimension, that is, he was not in a creative position. Nowadays, more than ever, I believe the Indian descendants desire to participate in the elaboration of meanings, of reinterpretations of the world around them, through aesthetics, artistic projects and productions . . . They cannot ignore the major social and cultural issues, or turn a blind eye on composite aesthetics as societies are more than ever engaged in a process where atavistic certainties are questioned by modernity. It is so important for a person to restore an *imaginaire* born from trauma and which is still in a dilemma, in fact, make of this 'uncertainty' a proposal for complex reactions to identities.

MC: Let's go back to this construction at the beginning. How did the coolie – or his/her descendants – begin to reconstruct or reappraise his/her identity in the colonial situation?

KT: First, the coolie, as I said before, reconstructed 'India', to negate, in his turn, the '*regard réifiant*' (deifying look) of the other. Of course, the nostalgic reverence for and reference to a form of mythical, original India born out of the trauma of exile has held him/her together. But, ultimately, the coolie became involved in the building of a new identity in the land where he/she had settled. In this *mise en relation*, new patterns were evolved, though the process was difficult, as you know. This was due to the fact that the arrival of the coolie complexified a creolization process already under way, upsetting the social strategies of the former slaves, bringing new demographic realities. In Mauritius, the Indian element was to outnumber the former plantocratic components. This also meant for the newcomer to come to grips with a creolization phase he/she couldn't easily integrate as he/she was the 'odd person out'. Today anthropologists and historians agree on one fact in Mauritius: that the coolie, though adopting the values of the coloured classes – '*valeurs des métis*' – were quite rapidly disqualified by the latter. This in turn resulted in an inward-looking identity '*repli identitaire*', leading to the movement or concept of Indianity or Indianness, which has been often a reaction of '*repli*' or looking back to India, warding off the crossing of the *Kala Pani*, the latter being for me the most important 'act' of withdrawal from identity, literature and history . . . In short, it constitutes an act of symptomatic denial of the 'cut' the Voyage brought, and this 'distance' with atavistic India was a possible means of getting engaged in a relationship with a mosaic perception and identity. The fact of withdrawing to the original land certainly meant that the challenge of modernity was delayed.

In the West Indies, due to the smaller number of the coolies in those societies, a similar sociocultural exclusion took place, based however, on other specificities. But new attitudes also cropped up. The coolie himself began, beyond the system of castes, to adopt the social strategy of the creoles of Mauritius and the other societies which he joined, by climbing the social ladder through schooling and occupation of posts in the Civil Service . . . In the Mauritian case, this social progress was strengthened by Gandhi's visit in the early twentieth century, who advised the descendants of Indian labourers in Mauritius to invest massively on education as a way of preparing the coolie descendants to new political and social challenges.

MC: This adoption of a new code of social conduct, alongside traditional structures preserved in the coolie villages or camps, show that, even in that stage of tension, the stricter proponent of Indianness no longer lived in a monosemic universe, even if the relation to the other was often perceived as a source of alienation or acculturation . . .

KT: Chronologically among the the late-comers to these 'plural' colonial societies (Chinese in Mauritius or Lebano-Syrians in the

Caribbean), after the settlement of the European and the African communities, the coolie came into contact with pre-existing 'pluralistic' communities, with all their contradictory characteristics of exclusions and exchanges . . . In Mauritius, the mainstream cultural space was the exclusive domain or '*chasse-gardée*' of the dominant class and of its allies, the *métis* or coloured class. The coolie thus oriented himself towards the land, working on it, saving money from the sale of its produce and acquiring the title to this land. With the processs of collective purchase and parcelling out of lands in small plots, groups of Indians succeeded in recreating a semblance of the Indian village settlement in Mauritius, replicating its basic social organization, sacred topography and so on, even though this recreation entailed that something was lost in the essence and had to be recaptured. I also want to bring out here that there was the continuation of an ancestral relation to the land, in keeping with Hindu mythology, for which the land is the *maati*, the 'mother-land'. Even in 'isolation', the coolie was already engaged in 'pluralism'. He spoke Creole earlier than we think, learned French and English when he was more at ease economically . . . The fact of speaking a different language, living in a different political system, of being away from the homeland, must not be underrated, as the coolie and his descendants were engaged, in so doing, in a poetics of relations. Indianness, even if it brought back the undying values of India, was already taking into account, consciously or unconsciously, that there was the barrier of the sea between the coolie and his original country, even if, as a form of defence, it also fostered an attitude of 'recoil'.

MC: Could you explain how coolitude relates to this process of Indianity, how it redefined the values of eternal India, India as seen as a plurality, the relation, in short, to the 'Original Land' when one has to settle in a new country?

KT: Coolitude, in its first definition, set against this background of 'mutual exclusions' between Blacks, Whites, Mulattoes, Coolies . . . aims at recapturing or recreating a problematic memory caught in the reaction of '*repli*', which I partially defined earlier, as the strategy of recoil – the reconstruction of an identity in the new land, using a mythical India as the 'Signifier' or 'Ultimate Referent', and Indianity, as a means of keeping the values of the 'Original Land' beyong the 'Voyage'. This led to the construction of an 'Indian' identity abroad, unconsciously taking into account that the coolie is now in another land, in exile, though trying to 'negate' the Voyage, which is a response to the unknown, an attitude so apparent in migrations. With time, the original Indianity has had some changes in its appreciation, with shifts in its definitions. For instance, in the last ten years, in Réunion, poet Issop Banian wrote *Indianités*, with a more open definition of Indianity, as irrigating and being irrigated by *créolite*. The same attitude, though more in keeping with a rehabilitation of the coolie's memory by historical research, has cropped up in the concept of *'malabarité'* as put forward by Sully Santa Govindin. Coolitude, set against this context, broadens the concept of the 'Indian abroad' or the indian diaspora into the consciousness of a mosaic, complex vision, acknowledging the traumatic and constructive potential of the Voyage/exile. It entails the inclusion of Indianity into a mosaic poetics, which involves an interweaving with 'Otherness' (*altérité*).

MC: Can you, at this stage, remind us of some basic constructions of coolitude?

KT: The chief characteristics of coolitude are, to sum up, the redefining of 'India', of the relation to India, to other cultures, in the setting of their adoptive homelands. A crosscultural *vagabondage* (cultural vagrancy) is at its heart. This is particularly important, in view of the significance of suspision and exclusion which accompanied the first stages of coolitude in social, historical and political fields in many countries. Coolitude clearly states that the *'désir de repli'* (the desire of recoil) is a reaction to exclusion, but also the expression of a fear of becoming engaged in the process of 'Otherness' (*altérité*). This attitude reflects a rejection of modernity and the present state of the world seen a complex one. Therefore, coolitude as a living process shows that, while adhering to Indianity as a major set of references, one should also put this in contact with other visions of the world, a process, which is in any case, already at hand in many societies. This implies that the attitude to identity can no longer be thought of alongside the narrow visions of atavistic desires.

5. Some Literary Characteristics of Coolitude

MC: What are, at this point, to expand on the poetics you have just defined, the principal literary characteristics of coolitude?

KT: It is difficult to be exhaustive, as we continue to participate in a process which is relatively new, in its analytical, even in its literary and aesthetic aspects, compared to, for example, the creations of a plantocratic culture, movements of *négritude, antillanité, créolité* and creolization.

First, of course, we can say that the content reveals one of the chief characteristics of coolitude. A text about a coolie, a descendant of an indentured labourer, or related to this labour migration, can be considered part of this poetics. But this definition needs to be broadened because what is important is the approach of complexity, in which the Indias are in relation with exile, the Voyage and other conceptions of the world.

Secondly, naturally, its form: whether the text is about the indentured period, or about the descendants of coolies or not, is essential, as it reflects the attitude of the person to history, society, cultural situations . . . We spoke of baroquism earlier and its philosophical premises. Therefore, this would include writers ranging from Naipaul to Dabydeen.

MC: Don't you think that Naipaul really harmed the coolies' image by pointing to their inability to see the world differently, and by showing that they were trapped in their narrow ambitions and desires?

KT: Even if Naipaul has been very critical of the coolie's descendants, he is one of the very first writers of coolitude . . . *Miguel Street, The Mystique Masseur, A House for Mr Biswas*, have been among the first books to show a coolie, an immigrant character and perspective in literature . . . In some ways, his texts have the same sociological and literary value as Cabon's, as this part of the reality of Indian migrants was nearly out of focus at that time. While Naipaul expresses more than reticence about his Trinidadian origins, the very fact of writing across borders motivates his desire of being a witness of the hybridity of the world, of his time. He explores the plurality of visions, and even if he seems to condemn 'chaos', his approach to reality is basically framed on a plurivocal basis.

Exile and indenturedship, whether he rejected the latter, have left a major impact on his poetics, and this cannot be ignored when assessing Naipaul's work. Furthermore, Naipaul himself acknowledges that the Voyage is at the heart of his writings. In a recent interview, Naipaul stated that his books 'represent a part of (his) attempts to fill the emptiness he felt when (he) started to travel'[32]. In this respect, his works show relevance to our paradigms. Coolitude is a poetics taking into account Movement as a factor giving rise to a particular poetics, and this is, broadly-speaking, to the foundation of Naipaul's relation to the world and literature.

MC: You wrote an article about 'Naipaul, a writer of coolitude' in *La Quinzaine Littéraire*[33], stating, briefly, that this writer can be understood more thoroughly if approached through coolitude. How can this concept shed a new light on his literary vision?

KT: Naipaul's vision is inseparable from his birthplace, the immigration of his ancestors to Trinidad, who came as coolies. His grandfather was a cane cutter, even, if originally his ancestors were 'high caste'. We cannot fully understand his style and attitude to identity, with its paradox and contradictions, if we do not bring to mind his personal experience, closely linked to those coolies trapped in their Caribbean exile, and the fact of finding antagonistic views of Naipaul when relating to that phase of his history will not discard the correctness of our reading. In fact, these very contradictions are relevant to coolitude. One remembers his father, Seeparsad Naipaul, who hid himself in the toilets of the docks of Port of Spain when his parents were waiting for the ship which was to take them back to the 'India of the Origins'. This 'primitive scene' of the 'end' of exile, will reveal the reality of an impossible return to India. This awareness is at the heart of coolitude: the tie with India was severed by the *Kala Pani*. Needless to say that this new, consented exile, left an indelebile impact on young Naipaul. Subsequently, Naipaul's relation to identity was to be modelled by travelling, as he dreamt of leaving his native Trinidad very soon, considering that the coolies there were torn between a problematic integration and an impossible return to their atavistic homeland. This 'return voyage', virtually possible in coolitude – one remembers the contract stipulating a possible return to India – admitted as undesirable by Naipaul's father, and prolonged by Naipaul's desire to leave Trinidad, has been transferred into writing and travelling as a therapy of the *coupure* (cut) resulting from severing ties both with the mythical homeland and the native island. We must also remember that Naipaul's father refused to go back to India because he wanted to write, and for him, the only place he could do that was in 'exile'. Naipaul wrote also as a means of coming to terms with this chaotic relation to memory, History and territory. By rejecting India as the 'Centre', the 'Ultimate Reference', thus redefining the notion of the diaspora (we know that the diaspora always considers itself as a periphery as set against a centre, the original land), Naipaul's work is, in fact a poignant testimony of coolitude, of the relation to the Voyage, the importance of which we dealt about earlier.

MC: Naipaul has been very critical of the coolie descendants in Trinidad. Doesn't that mean that he has to be understood as a writer outside coolitude?

KT: The predicament of the coolies in Trinidad influenced Naipaul's first thoughts about identity, exile and the Voyage, which he later continued to explore through incessant travelling. The fact that he rejected their 'lack of ambition' or vision doesn't mean that he is a writer to be interpreted *ex nihilo*, outside this human, sociological or cultural frame. In fact, may be, his revolt against the Trinidadian coolies meant that their relation to history, to identity was not in keeping with something he desired, and this attitude in itself reveals an awareness to identity stemming from the coolie's inadequate relationship to history. Very soon, the writer concluded to the impossbility of a serene identity, and as such, showing that he did not adhere to the 'phantasm of purity' sometimes alive in the exiled's relation to an 'original' identity. Thus travelling and writing about societies, seen to be shaken by nationalism, extremism and chaotic relations to modernity gave rise to writings which give a major insight into the transubstantiated attitude of Naipaul to memory, the past, or identity. I believe that the Swedish Academy, by awarding the Nobel Literary Prize to Naipaul, a non-consensual writer if any, has rewarded the first writer of a 'paradoxical' coolitude, even if he is often refered to as a modern Dickens, in the best British literary tradition.

MC: Can you expatiate on this foremost event, or 'primitive scene', which expresses the relation to the original land, to Voyage, and the founding act of Naipaul's writing? In fact, it seems that the relation to geography, real or imaginary, is essential in your approach . . .

KT: This is in fact, one of the basic expressions of coolitude. The founding act of Naipaul's father's relation to writing was the awareness that there was no going back to India, to settle there for good. This would have meant, for him, the end of his desire to write. Seeparsad's son continued this act of refusal of the 'Original Land', in order to adopt a new territory, a new *imaginaire*, in fact, through language and literature. The fact of displacing the quest for identity, social mobility and recognition, in the field of literature is highly telling of the symptomatic condition of the coolie descendants, of their situation related to the expression of an aesthetic self, of their sense of suffering related to a deficit in language and literature, a sense of dereliction still pervading many coolie descendants in the Indies, in the Indian Ocean, in Fiji . . . nowadays. Here, we have a rare example of the projection of a 'torn' identity into words, as a way of expressing it beyond traditional limits of land and culture. This is a major step in the coolie descendant's attitude to a very difficult situation: how to express the contradictions, even the challenges, of two worlds. This means that Naipaul, at this stage, had decided to quit the 'recoil' strategy of his forbears, even, if many contradictions later cropped up, as in the case of Ram, the character of Cabon, who was led to an *impasse*, as some challenges were not met with, given the conditions of the times, or due to regrettable personal choices . . .

MC: When speaking of the parallel between Naipaul and his father, I have the feeling that we are in presence of an Oedipal relation to writing . . .

KT: There is much to say in that parallel. Indeed, when young Naipaul continued his father's desire to stay on the island of exile, he in fact prolonged his scriptural act, a form of revolt against the ancestral land. Naipaul in turn left his father's native island and went to England, then to societies which seemed to have come to terms with their identities. One of his father's reasons of staying in Trinidad, allow me to stress this point again, was that he wanted to write. He wrote short stories and became the reporter of *The Guardian* there. So, in the heart of exile of the Indian coolie descendants, there is a founding act: the pro-jection of a stranded self in an aesthetic space, that is, in literature. This goes beyond the political or economic dimensions, or 'traditional' means of social mobility of the coolie descendants. Writing itself is viewed as a means of getting across the obstacles inherent to the coolie's quandary. The coolie descendant chose no longer to be invisi-ble or silent . . . By refusing the return to India, because he wanted to write, which is in itself the founding act of Naipaul's relation to what could be termed a postmodern attitude to identity (with limitations in his case), Naipaul's history yields a symbolical scene of the poetics of coolitude: he gives a language, an aesthetic project to the descendants of the coolies.

MC: But, ultimately, didn't Naipaul return to the land of his ancestors, that is, didn't he show revolt towards his father by going there and writing three books, as a means of recapturing India and atavistic identity?

KT: In fact, by going abroad, Naipaul delayed his encounter with India. He severed ties with Trinidad, his native island, preferring to go to England for his studies, and from there, he wandered through the world, as we know, to observe societies, but also, to reflect on the state of soci-eties, the fate of empires and their/his relation to identity. He, in the end, accomplished the 'return' voyage to India, which his father had refused, but only to say that there is no reconciliation with memory or atavistic identity, even if there have been contradictory attitudes in his itinerary. I believe that the writer lived with an 'incomplete identity', hovering between the English gentleman's, the English Brahmin's, the apatrid's or the reconquered high caste Indian's . . . This construction shows that this 'uprooted Indian' conceives his relation to identity in a complex manner, doing away with all forms of certainties of an old atavistic culture, even if some disquietening aspects later contradicted with his 'complex' attitude. In fact, what is to be brought in the lime-light is that Naipaul wrote that he saw no solace in restoring memory, as it can be a formidable prison. The past, if not reconsidered, can be the end of history. In fact, travelling, in his perspective, reveals identity as a perpetual relation to movement. Identity is thought in a dynamic rela-tion, in the poetics of otherness. This tension means that Naipaul's exile would never end, and this allows us to say that a vigilant, alert attitude to identity construction is inherent to our poetics. We see, in fact, that Naipaul often imagined identity through this paradoxical, complex relationship. He seems to be eternally in *l'entre-deux* (in-between two worlds and perceptions) . . .

MC: Why is this tension important in the creation of standpoint and style?

KT: This problematic relation to his past and identity is important in the creation of Naipaul's style, termed classical, in his use of English. But I would stress the fact that Naipaul has a baroque point of view, and this is apparent in his obsession with details. In his third book[34], Naipaul weaves a 'spontaneous vision of culture and civilization', to quote him, through 'small personal mutinies'. This baroque attitude cannot be withered from his relation to the exile of the indentured and the culture resulting from it, even if there is a paradox . . .

MC: Indeed, he adopted the English nationality and expressed sympathies to Indian ultranationalistic views. Can you be more explicit when you speak of Naipaul's 'paradoxical coolitude'?

KT: Naipaul's coolitude is paradoxical because he seems to be oblivious of Trinidad, the very island which gave him this terrible and powerful awareness of being an 'other Indian or indo-Trinidadian'. This does not mean that Naipaul is ignorant of indenturedship or of its main debates. In 1989, *A Turn in the South* brings back three questions which are essential in the work of Naipaul: Trinidad's discovery by Colombus, slavery and the coming of Indian coolies . . . I am quoting his own assessment. In those three events, we have the *mise en relation* of the Europeans, the Africans and the Indians, and the matrix of the plantocratic society . . . We have the the basic geographical ingredients of a new *imaginaire*.

MC: But Naipaul seemed to be ill at ease with this baroque geography . . .

KT: Recently, he seemed oblivious of Trinidad. This refusal, or unconscious censorship of the *lieu* (place) of indenturedship emerged when I heard the writer speaking on the French radio, following his Nobel Prize.

I will quote him: 'This Nobel Prize is a hommage to England and the land of my ancestors, India . . .'. He never mentioned Trinidad, a fact which led to confusions in French media. Journalists reported that the prestigious prize was awarded to a 'Hindu British', 'An Indian of British nationality', or to 'a British of Indian origins' . . . I have met persons who have been upset and confused with this rejection of the native island.

MC: This rejection of the island is not an innocent act. Don't you think that the paradox of Naipaul here expresses a refusal of the 'purification of the paria', which is important in coolitude? I would also quote journalists stating that Naipaul was awarded the Nobel as a result of the attacks of September 11, as he is a staunch opponent of Islam . . .

KT: I think this prize has triggered mixed, if not many hostile, responses in the literary world. Recently, in the last issue of *Le Monde Diplomatique*[35], the literary critic Pascale Casanova has been virulently against Naipaul whom she accuses of favouring 'the shock of civilizations' so widely publicized recently, in view of the international situation of war in Afghanistan. For her, Naipaul just shows a very narrow vision of identity, specially in view of Islam, which in some of his texts, Naipaul accuses of all the evils that have befallen on the colonized countries. He even said that it was Islam and not colonization which precipitated the fall of India and which killed all intellectual life in all Muslim countries. Islam represents for him a cruel form of barbarism. I feel we have to be more objective by not mixing interpretations and religion itself. In any case, this attitude would mean that either Naipaul is biased against this religion and its civilization, which leads him to overlook its contributions to science and culture, and its role as a catalyst of European Renaissance, or that he is simply ignorant about it, which would be very surprising as he has widely travelled in Muslim countries . . . He cannot ignore what Moghul civilization has brought to architecture, music and arts in India. Pascale Casanova shows an even more disquieting aspect of Naipaul's relation to identity. Naipaul is sympathetic to the caste system, the social injustice it generates and supports the extremist views of the ultranationalist parties in India . . .

MC: How would you account for this contradictory position?

KT: This contradictory attitude may be linked, unconsciously, to Naipaul's refusal 'the purification of the paria', of the *harijan*, the lowest in the caste system, for whom Gandhi had a special affection. The Voyage, as you know full well, meant putting in contact different castes, either in the dépôt where the indentured waited for a ship to carry them to the colonies, or on board of the ship, where the pangs of exile and the dangers of the Voyage, brought the coolies together. They even developed the expression, *macchan*, 'brothers of the ship' to express the new bonds woven between the Indians in face of adversity, irrespective of caste or social positions.

This levelling possibility of the Voyage and exile thus 'purified' the paria, and this has been more prevalent in societies where the coolies were in small numbers. This relation between visions of the world among Indians is at the heart of coolitude, even if, in Mauritius, for instance, elements of this system were weakened, and another form of the caste system was to emerge. In fact, Naipaul's itinerary is highly interesting, in line with that paradoxical coolitude we developed earlier. We know that his ancestors were brahmans, of the high caste, and that his ancestors went to Trinidad in hope of securing material prosperity. His grandfather became a canecutter, a coolie. This 'fall' may have been badly resented by the family, and the island, paradoxically, was probably perceived as the place of the deterioration of the family's condition. So the 'purification of the paria' here operated at his expense, if I may say. This purification is accompanied by a *'souillure du brahmane'* (the fouling of the brahman). We can see how this 'fantasm of purity' is at work on both sides of the social system of the indentured: both the high and low castes feared to cross the foul seas, in fact, the ocean was seen as a source of contaminating one's spirituality, of ruining one's identity. The traditional social substructure cannot be separated from the relation to the Sacred in India. This may account for the pulsion of restoring one's purity lost in the Voyage, as a response to the exclusions the coolie met with in 'plural societies'. In this process, the sacred and social definitions of purity coincided with each other. Indianness, as a social and intellectual construction, as a form of cultural resistance, therefore tried to 'suppress' the loss of a part of the Indian self on his/her way to the colonies.

MC: We cannot ignore, however, that the quest for a better social position is inherent in all migrations . . . When Naipaul left Trinidad, he in fact did what many coolie descendants did when they left their native lands for studies abroad . . .

KT: Naipaul's decision to go to England for studies follows a quest for ascension. Of course, this has been a normal process for many coolies. But in Naipaul's case, he became, in the end, an 'English Lord', when he was made a knight by the Queen. He restored his lost 'high caste' status, and became a kind of 'English brahman'. With this position, symbolically, the 'fall or fouling' of the Brahman was warded off. He reconquered the social position lost by his ancestors, and this may have accounted for his denial of the 'parentheses of Trinidad'. The island is marked with the seal of the 'fall of the brahman', that is, a land to be obliterated. The purification of the paria is reversed here because the nobility of the origins was restored in the system of references to the master, and Trinidad, was left behind, as a stigma of the fall. Trinidad, as the censored birthplace, highlights this paradox.

MC: Do you think, that even if Naipaul is often perceived as a subversive writer, he in fact didn't go through an essential act of revolt, which, ultimately, made him reject the land of his exile?

KT: In fact, to make a quick reference to Freudian and Lacanian theories, we may consider that Naipaul did not 'kill his father' symbolically, as he continued the process of writing initiated by him. Naipaul knew full well his father, though, could not live fully to his aspirations as a writer. His relation to his father is quite organic in any case . . . Later, when Naipaul visited India where his father had refused to return. This 'opposition' to the father is to be understood within the family's dramatic experience of exile, in which literature became a therapy. Shiva, Naipaul's brother also wrote as a means of perpetuating the founding act of the father, as a means of proving his social and cultural identity. Both travelled in Africa, Europe, Asia to write. So, we must stress this fact: in a kind of symmetical act of denial, we may say that Naipaul's father refused India, and Naipaul rejected Trinidad. This 'censorship of the *lieu*' shows a great contradiction with Naipaul's theories concerning memory and past, and indeed a postmodern relation to identity.

MC: Why is it important not to amputate one part of this 'lieu' (space)?

KT: When you reject part of your history, you reflect you have not come to terms with it, and this is the source of many tensions, complexes and, even, of self-denial. The egalitarian approach of a complex identity is floundered here, as the place also contributes to frame your attitude to identity, because it has its own culture, memory, identity, even if they have still to be reinterpreted or furthered into new configurations. This contradiction is even more apparent, to come back to Pascale Casanova's article opposing Naipaul as a recipiendary of the Nobel, when the writer supports the Indian far-right political parties, because, paradoxically, Naipaul says, 'this movement comes from the base', mainly from the *harijans* (parias). This 'movement' favours a rigid social system and has an exclusivist attitude which is in full contradiction with the attitude of complexity at the core of Naipaul's poetics. Did Naipaul try to recapture Original India by censoring Trinidad?

I think here we are given to fully understand the paradox of Naipaul: the Voyage has been instrumental in giving a modern relation to memory and identity, and at the same time, the Voyage has never been able to close a social, symbolical wound as his family 'lost its brahmanic caste' due to its exile on the island. This has led to censorship of the *'lieu'* as it crystallizes the symptom of the fall. This latter attitude may account for the deep reticences of Indian descendants towards the acceptance of the Voyage as a space of dissolution and creation of identities, and a suspicion towards the social mobility triggered in the social fabric of the host country. Losing one's place in the social fabric entailed losing one's relation to Transcendence. The contradiction is indeed sharp when we consider that Naipaul was very cautious when weighing the past and memory, regarded as prisons capable of leading to the petrification of historical consciousness or identities. The fact of not 'accepting' the island as a place of convergences may have led, in the end, Naipaul to engage in a contradictory movement of return to India, but not in keeping with his analysis of complexity, because the geography of the loss, of exile, I mean Trinidad, was refused in the Voyage . . . I think that the fact of not mediating the passage to Trinidad fully is important in this contradictory vision of Naipaul's modernity. As you know, accepting the land of exile, which in turn became a new homeland for many coolies, as the place of one's new identity is central in coolitude, and this phase seems to have been overlooked by Naipaul. I think that instead of connecting again with Trinidad, which would have been a logical conclusion of Naipaul's intellectual construction, he made an ontological connection with India, unconsciously warding off the 'cut' (*coupure*) of the *Kala Pani*, and the result is that Naipaul restores a social fabric, the caste system, which the Voyage brought to new definitions, and sometimes, to dissolution.

MC: Would this acceptance of the space of exile, I mean the symbolical acceptance of Trinidad, have conditioned Naipaul's literary style and vision differently?

KT: I believe that probably Naipaul may have been more creative in his use of language . . . His 'transparent style' and fidelity to nineteenth century writers like Dickens and Balzac, have led to remarks from Casanova, stating that Naipaul was only content at reproducing narrative models of the nineteenth century. Casanova rightly points to the fact that, basically, Naipaul remains a conformist, having written more journalistic books than real literary creations, even though I would be more reserved in my remarks because Naipaul, in his descriptions and obsession with details, couples this language with a baroque attitude, as I said earlier. However, when Naipaul holds that, for him, Joyce, a master of experimentations of style, remains 'incomprehensible', this casts a light on his own attitude to innovations in literature.

MC: Was this classical style in conformity with Naipaul's defence and illustration of the grandeur of British civilization, as stated by Pascale Casanova?

KT: Naipaul's sharp vision of his contemporaries, specially through his acid portrayal of the poor peoples of the Third World and the South, have often been perceived, understandably, as contemptuous. His vision is in fact different from Dickens's empathic treatment of the poor Londoners in *Oliver Twist*, for instance. Naipaul is 'cold, disdainful' towards the poor of the Third World, probably as a continuation of the '*effacement*' (denial) of his origins. Pascale Casanova even speaks of Naipaul's betrayal of the have-nots of the South, an ambiguous position he derives from his 'origins' stemming both from the West and the Third World. This ambiguity, sadly, often mars the attitude of Naipaul to

identity, specially in his later books. To point again to Naipaul's attitude
to space and identity, and to the importance of space in identity-construction, we will bring to attention that Naipaul decided, as a second
birth, to live in the English countryside, learning the names of the flora,
the history of the land, voluntarily cutting himself from the Indian and
Pakistani immigrants' problems and aspirations. This choice of space
induces a relation to the world and to Naipaul's literary and social perceptions and style, and this is not a neutral attitude . . . Pascale Casanova
rightly quotes Salman Rushdie's remarks on 'Naipaul's Olympian contempt' and Derek Walcott's statement that 'Naipaul doesn't like
negroes'. She holds that Naipaul is a propagator of the hate of Islam, as
if he favoured a war of religions. Coupled with his essentialist views of
the caste system as propounded by the Far Right Shiv Shena Party in
India, this troublesome part of Naipaul's vision goes against Coolitude as
a complex process . . . We are of course dealing here with the contradictory elements which undoubtedly weigh heavily on Naipaul's work.

**MC: But one could object that by becoming a Wiltshire English gentle-
man, Naipaul showed that he lived his *métissage* . . .**

KT: I think that the writer is free to make choices and he has to feel at
ease with them. He can choose the society he wants to integrate.
Basically, Naipaul seems to be content with this choice, even though he
also criticized British society, as a reminder that he is a non-conformist.
But I would recall here the necessity of an egalitarian mode in the relation to otherness, and that the coexistence of differences is at the heart
of coolitude. In Naipaul's case, we seem to have a reduction of differences and opacities, to sameness, to the 'transparence' of a chosen
identity (the Wiltshire gentleman, far from the immigrants' preoccupations in UK, cut from Rushdie's tropicalized London, for instance), at the
expense of the other (Indo-Trinidadian, the exiled Indian . . .). Nothing
would have prevented Naipaul to have been, in a complex attitude to
identity, an English gentleman, a Trinidadian coolie orginating from India
of a brahmanic family, and much more, or none of this. Here, we would
have had a mosaic coexistence, in keeping with the more interesting
polysemic observations of the writer. I believe that Naipaul must be
regarded as a transitional phase in the history of coolitude, caught
between colonial representations and the necessities of modernity, point-

ing to possibilities of facing the complexity of the situation, and under-lining the attitudes which prevent the emergence of a liberating attitude to the mosaic *imaginaire* of cultures and civilizations.

MC: Let's come back again to the 'denial' of Trinidad which is a central point of this issue. Wasn't Naipaul, when he left the island, rejecting the exclusivist views about identity, about exile considered as a prison, even if, at the end, this contradiction got on the writer himself?

KT: There is much scope to think so in his obliteration of his passage to Trinidad, even if later positions of Naipaul weakened this stance. I think chronology is important to assess Naipaul's work. By leaving the island, he developed his polysemic intuitions about identity. Maybe, Trinidad for him represented the space of an impossible identity, and we know that in those times, the coolies were a minority, the political situation was diffi-cult there, with a potential situation of civil war. In fact, this refusal, paradoxically brings to light three factors which reflect important para-digms of coolitude: India as the land of an impossible return (even if references are kept in the relation with other cultures), the acceptance of the Voyage as the premice of a relation to complex identity and the *imaginaire* and memory as a space of the possible decay of history and modernity. These tenets interact with each other to give rise to a per-ception of an 'open' relation to the world. In fact, this is in keeping, schematically, with the modernity of coolitude. Therefore, Naipaul's 'desertion' of his native island, the non acceptance of his passage to Trinidad, which initiated an interesting process as I said in view of cooli-tude, led Naipaul's poetics to a major paradox: his intellectual recognition that there is no serene, simple, approach to identity, to memory, the past and history, and, in a contradictory impulse, his rejec-tion of the poetics of space, the denial of the wound of exile (the fall of the family, the fouling of the brahman . . .) by espousing the dominant values of British civilization, coupled with his acceptance of essentialist visions of Indian society. This non resolution of contraries led, utlimately to Naipaul's quandary in face of complexity. An enigma seems to be the result of this paradox.

MC: Why is coolitude operational in this paradox?

KT: Coolitude is present in Naipaul's 'complex' attitude, which, whatever its twists and bends, questions atavistic identity. This is a *sine qua non* condition towards a new consciousness, a complex vision of societies and identities. Naipaul admitted recently that travelling (the Voyage) was inseparable from his academic quest. The metaphor of the Voyage, through a dynamic observation, distance, new relations initiated by movement, is central in coolitude. To come to another standpoint, which is a negation of the potentialities of this polysemic vision of societies, Naipaul refuses that complexity when he adheres to essentialist views. This choice, even in its limited aspect, is also operational in coolitude, *a contrario*, as it brings out a regressive attitude which is still alive in many countries, and which sometimes might take the shape of a modern form of 'recoil', leading to communalism or ethnicity. Regarding this choice, we stress that vigilance must be deployed to prevent this type of regression which spoils the potentiality of the relation.

Naipaul, at the heart of this paradox, is therefore exemplary of some of the contradictions, fears and prejudice Indian descendants have not been able to overcome and which have induced exclusivist attitudes . . . I think that Naipaul's paradox also points to the fact that the relation to *la poétique du lieu* (poetics of geographical space) is an important factor in the construction of a complex attitude to memory, history and culture.

MC: In coolitude, the *lieu* (geographical space), therefore, is not seen as a prison, but rather, is conceived as a creative axis . . .

KT: Naipaul's refusal of Trinidad brings out the fact that that while working at expressing the potentialities of space, as in any creative process, the relation to it must be transfigured or transcended, a fact which seems to have been left out by him. What is important is not the geography, but one's attitude to it; the same can be said about one's relation to identity. Naipaul, however, developed an interesting, paradoxical, scripturary relation to travelling, as a meeting and a clash of worlds, and these works have to be approached with this idea of complexity in mind. In those writings, coolitude is fully significant.

I think the flaw of the Nobel Prize winner is that he did not leave the island for the world but he *discarded* it for the world. The island could have continued to be one of the foundations of the world. This is where his poetics shows its major limits. I believe that the family trauma may have prevented the closing of the wound of exile. For instance, Naipaul holds *The Enigma of Arrival*[36] as an essential book in his production. He talked about this intertextual reference to Chiricco's painting, which shows two migrants having just landed in an English port, with the ship still visible in the background. I believe this book could also have been entitled 'The Enigma of Identity', as this representation of the space of exile, in reference to this painting, is inseparable from Naipaul's migration to the Wiltshire. In any case, this relation to space, to Trinidad lost and Wiltshire adopted as the created homeland, thus, to a new identity, reveals an interesting, though troublesome, aspect of Naipaul's itinerary . . .

Becoming a writer in England, living far from immigrants, as an English gentleman, in some way reflects Naipaul's father's decision to write from a distance, an act which meant that his relation to the land of his origins, India, was a complex one. Naipaul says that his settlement in Wiltshire was 'a second birth', and this aspect makes the relation to complexity ambiguous as the first birth was left in/to the past . . . In my perspective, the 'relativization of India as the Centre' doesn't mean an elimination or a shameful censorship of one's relations to one's origins. It doesn't mean an obliteration of India, but rather a connection of its potentialities with other *imaginaires*, a confrontation of India with other geographies on an egalitarian basis . . .

There is another text of Naipaul which throws light on what I would call the 'erasing of one's origins'. It is *The Abyss of Conrad*, an essay Naipaul wrote about Joseph Conrad, another immigrant of English Literature. We know about Conrad's problematic relation to his orgins, which he suppressed, to become a perfect English writer. Conrad gave rise to a powerful work. Naipaul develops a close identification with Conrad's attitude, and we may seize this '*relation en miroir*' (close, speculative identification) as a revealing aspect of the rejection of his Indo-Trinidadian origins. This same act of rejection of the birthplace is also apparent in Naipaul's nephew's attitude, who is a writer living in Canada. Indeed, Neil Bissoondath says that he has nothing to do with Trinidad where he was born, that he has gone beyond the 'question of identity', and that he is a 'North Canadian writer', even though, paradoxically, the island seems to be unavoidable in his work. The same *retour du refoulé* (the recurrence of the repressed) seems to be constantly plying this paradoxical attitude, and must be read, again, as a symptom of a paradoxical coolitude.

MC: Can we then consider Naipaul's work as a *prefiguration* of major themes of coolitude?

KT: Naipaul's work may be regarded, in our paradigm, as a transitory phase of coolitude. It points to the contradictions of the trauma of the indentured's exile, explores some of its avenues of liberation, and in the process, brings a redefinition of one's identity enriched by the Voyage. This paradigm operates in many of Naipaul's books. However, Naipaul's writing also indicates an impossible relation to identities, as it finally closes on an implosion of those contradictions, on an *aporie* or an *impasse* (deadlock), with, in the end (and as the end) of this process, the emergence of an exclusivist relation to identity. I think we have to assess Naipaul's work through this paradoxical angle, as it allows us to sieve more meanings out of it, rather than through an approach stating that the writer, owing to his condemnable essentialist views, brings nothing to the construction of a complex identity. One has to be vigilant in approaching Naipaul's contradictory attitudes, which in themselves, can offer food for thought as to the potentialities of coolitude, and the consequences of their denial.

MC: Would you mean that Naipaul's contradictions offer readable material from the point of view of the history of the symptoms, and the expressions of a wider process?

KT: There is the paradox, and there are the contradictions. We have to differentiate between these two terms. I mean the paradox is meaningful, in keeping with a vision of complexity, and the contradictions reveal the part of coolitude which, when not fully mediated, may lead to a negation of the Voyage, with all its *coupure* (cut) initiated, as a creative space and standpoint in postmodern (some would say postcolonial or postindustrial) identity. Viewed from this angle, Naipaul's work must be read as a document of a paradoxical phase of coolitude, trapped in the contradictions of an epoch, of a personality. Coolitude allows to weigh those contradictions against a literary, historical, aesthetic and poetic background. It points to the pitfalls of a vision of identity which negates the 'discoveries' of the relation, basically because the island, as the *lieu de la blessure symbolique* (the space of the symbolical cut), has not been integrated as part of a modern attitude to identity, and this refusal leads to a regressive stance to cultural differences and a mosaic poetics.

MC: Is David Dabydeen's relation to space and identity, as seen through *The Counting House*, different from Naipaul's?

KT: Dabydeen, from another generation, reflects the attitude of the descendants of Indians in exile who have decided to compose their identity in the host country, British Guyana. For instance, he conjoins two cultural paradigms when at the beginning of *The Counting House*, the recruiter states that Guyana is the land of the Ramayana. Similarly Vidia, one of the revolted coolies of Dabydeen's novel, is conversant with the negro spirits sleeping in the hollow bark of trees, hearing their complaints of their inability to return to Africa. We have here an *imaginaire* at work across texts, borders and race, with a transcultural frame and a poetics of relations. This is also apparent in his lexical choice and use of language. This paradigm is important, because we can see an 'imaginary contagion' in it. This literary creation echoes *La Quarantaine* by J M G Le Clézio, who, while speaking about the coolie odyssey, uses words from *Cale d'Etoiles*, in an intertextual relation, 'authentifying' (anchoring to local realities) French language with the use of Hindi/Creole/Bhojpuri words; this relation to history through the narrative corroborates the spirit of coolitude, which is the meeting of *imaginaires* from India, Africa, Europe, China or other spaces, and where the perception of India, experienced by the coolie or not, is modified by the voyage.

MC: There are other writers who echo this vision of the world . . .

KT: Indeed. Novels by Rushdie, with their generalizing narrative techniques, and a baroque perception and use of language, participate in this complex definition of 'open Indianness'. In his work, the writer has 'displaced' Indianness from a closed definition, and has given full expression to the multiplicity of the *Indies*, embracing the otherness of language and the *imaginaire*. In this type of postmodern constructions, the signifying intention becomes more emphatic; the poetic function of language is primordial – a normal consequence of plurivocity. In this type of poetics, the writer is constantly redefining meanings, and a metalanguage, assessing and devising codes . . . Rushdie has displaced the relation to India in a poetics of space, as his London is a tropicalized one, characterized by the *'réalisme merveilleux'* we would meet in the universe of Garcia Marquez, for instance. He needs constantly to mix Persian, European, Indian myths, with, sometimes, the lyrics of Elvis Presley . . . He sustains that myths, in a baroque attitude, are reversible – and this is a very forceful aspect of the egalitarian mode in making histories converge. For instance, the myth of Orpheus, in an Indian context, would be operational if it is the woman who saves the man . . .

This complex attitude comprehends voices ranging from Arundathi Roy, Vikram Seth, or Michael Oondatje and other 'Indian' postcolonial or 'World fiction' writers, and in some way, echo Rushdie – who defines himself as a 'plural Indian', that is, a poetics which confronts Indians with otherness, an attitude which is at the heart of coolitude. One can say, in a nutshell, that the whole gamut of writing corresponds to coolitude, when it is essentially India considered from another geographical or aesthetic standpoint, from a mosaic stance, where the coolie, or his modern alter ego, the migrant or the traveller, is engaged in the poetics of Relation. This is distinguished by a particular vision, style, use of language, narrative, where post-modernism is often prevalent, in the sense that univocity is often put under strain.

MC: This complex vision, with the central aspect of the Voyage, as seen in many writers' works, in many spaces of literature, reveals the tensions, desires, in short, the expression of a trauma . . .

KT: I believe that this *'traversée de signes/d'imaginaires'* or crossing of signs and imaginations and fantasies, constitutes a preoccupation with form and language which is a symptom of the lack of speech, which is apparent in the field of literary discourse. By breaching the 'arbitrariness' of forms, and of language, by often opening them to a spiral of meanings (*'la signifiance'*), the poet of complex identities brings to mind that there is no serene vision of identity therefore, in language or culture, as seen in atavistic prisms. By redefining codes, words, techniques of the narrative, of poetry, he/she mocks at the order of the world, by enlarging it to the possibility of many centres of meaning, of a 'contagion' of *imaginaires*. One correlate, opacity in writing, gives this discourse a logic where worlds can meet and can converge from various standpoints. This is what I mean by 'scriptural equality' – *'une égalité scripturaire'* I quote from Glissant. In baroque aesthetics, as in postmodernism, many realities seem to coincide, to correlate with each other, questioning the predominance of one vision. I believe that this relation at the core of coolitude marks the end of a forced or self-imposed exile in language and other major issues of present societies.

This is pregnant in the fields of music with the bhangra and fusion music in London, or the Bhojpuri Boys and Kaya, in Mauritius; the same applies to arts, cinema, literature (C Marimootoo, M Das, R Espinet, Lindsey Collen, Shenaz Patel) . . . where coolitude is often in the forefront. And there are many heartening examples from artists and writers who resort to their mosaic identity, expressing openness, and this is where the definition of coolitude applies fully. Just to mention a few names: Khalid Nazroo, N Treebooben, G Teker, D Dausoa . . . in visual arts . . . Y Kadel, Dev Virahsawmy . . . in stage writing, J Moopen (dance) and many others . . . I think there are many interesting creations to arise. A new creative and analytical field is now being expressed and explored.

Conclusion:

Revoicing the Coolie

The forging of a new identity in exile took the migrant far from the confines of official platitudes and historical appraisals. The experiences of the coolie place him on a par with migrants of whatever hue, across a range of climes and times. And yet the coolie imbued his or her places of settlement with a defiant, distinctive Indianness. The specificities and parallels of the coolie experience are summed up in this concluding chapter. Coolitude confronts the experience of Indians beyond the seas, and traces the elaboration of the awareness of the Indian who has accepted his exile, and acquired new forms of expression, to become part of the history of the nations in which he has settled.

This volume has sought to rediscover the coolie, firstly through an exploration of the stereotypes which evolved about the Indian labour migrant in official documents and in the early literature, and secondly through an assessment of more recent writing which has explored Indian identities in diaspora. The purpose of this exploration has been to redefine and reappropriate the concept of the coolie. Through coolitude, an articulation and an evocation of the Indian labour diaspora, the coolie can effectively be revoiced.

Contemporary texts which described – and often distorted – our image of the coolie, whether travellers' observations or accounts of colonists and residents of the territories to which Indians migrated, have been characterized by exoticism. Succeeding generations of writers have attempted, with varying degrees of success, to capture the essence of the migrant experience and to define their place in the societies where they have settled. This has given rise to what Nelson has identified as 'customary grand narratives of displacement, nostalgia and loss'.[1]

Coolitude has emerged from the rich francophone tradition of writings about Creole societies. Creole poetry and prose has been characterised by twin preoccupations: the appropriation and subversion of the French language, and the quest for an identity.[2] Principally linked to French Caribbean writers, Raphael Confiant has nevertheless reserved his highest accolade for an Indian Ocean poet: *'de l'Ile Maurice, nous vient ... la première poésie de la Créolité* (from Mauritius comes, the premier poetry of Creolite).'

> *'La Négritude sut assumer le mot 'nègre', insulte jetée par l'Occident à la face des fils de mère-Afrique. La Coolitude cherche a son tour a assumer le mot 'coolie' ... la Coolitude vient, aux côtés de la Négritude ... apporter son indispensable pierre a l'édifice que nous sommes tous en train de construire depuis des siècles: la créolité.*
> (Negritude was able to take on the word 'negro', an insult thrown by the West in the faces of the sons of mother Africa. Coolitude searches in its turn to take on the word 'coolie' ... Coolitude comes, at the side of Negritude ... to bring its indispensable brick to the edifice which we have been in the process of constructing for centuries: créolité.)'

Thus, as Khal Torabully has explained, coolitude should be considered as a reflection of a twin process: firstly the rediscovery of the coolie memory where appropriate, such as in the Caribbean, and secondly, where the aesthetics of loss is less prevalent, the necessity of a complex attitude to culture. In the latter case, the construction of identity has much in common with creolization – traversing phases imposed by social, historical and political realities without losing sight of the philosophy of linking with otherness and rejecting a sectarian identity: *'La Coolitude n'a rien d'un cri ethnique. Elle prolonge la créolité en Inde insulaire. Elle est acclimation de la culture de l'Inde en terre plurielle.* (Coolitude has nothing of an ethnic cry. It takes *créolité* into insular India. It represents the acclimatization of Indian culture to a plural landscape).'[4]

Creolization texts have sought to reclaim the history of forced migrations and the *metissage* which resulted. Creolization has permitted the class of *'sous-hommes'* which resulted from the involuntary diasporas to: *'devenir des hommes, des hommes vrais – c'est-a-dire des Créoles – et c'est cette force secrete-la que chante si bellement la poesie de Khal Torabully* (to become men, real men – that is to say, Creoles – and it is of this secret strength that the poetry of Khal recites so beautifully)'.[5]

It may not be considered so surprising that it is Mauritius, rather than the Caribbean, which has provided the inspiration for this poetry of *créolité* and for the birth of coolitude. Francoise Lionnet sees Mauritius as a 'true site of *metissage* and creolization', while Turcotte and Brabant have argued that as a microcosm of world cultures, Mauritius is well placed to provide future human bridges: '*hommes-ponts*' who may become the real interpreters of the North-South dialogue and precursors of world understanding. [6] In the 'post-ethnic society' of Mauritius where the 'impact of modernity' has rubbed away at competing ancestral cultures, Khal Torabully has emerged to become a '*homme-pont*', or human bridge.[7]

Poetic and Critical
Texts of Coolitude

Poetic texts in prose

Coolitude: parce que mes pays foisonnent de nouvelles traces de mémoire. Et si des gestes nègres sont venus à nos mains en tranchant les cannes, il nous reste encore des craquements et des danses de doigts habitués au tabla que la ravanne a souvent harmonisés d'un grand cri des coeurs à la derive.

Coolitude: parce que je suis créole de mon cordage, je suis indien de mon mât, je suis européen de la vergue, je suis mauricien de ma quête et français de mon exil. Je ne serai toujours ailleurs qu'en moi-même parce que je ne peux qu'imaginer ma terre natale. Mes terres natales?

Dans nos langues, nous sommes à la frontiere féconde des codes, pour ouïr une parole entre nos vocables d'esclaves et de maître. Est-ce pour cela que ma vraie langue maternelle est la poésie? Que ma seule terre natale est la Terre?

Aussi, je suis prêt à faire taire toute querelle de frontière pour faire voir notre étoile, pour partager notre héritage commun: chair et sang.
   K Torabully, *Cale d'Étoiles, Coolitude*, p. 105.

Coolitude: because my country heaves with new traces of memory. And if negro gestures come to our hands as we cut the canes, there remains in us those movements of fingers used to the tabla and which the ravanne often harmonised in the great cry of hearts left to wander.

Coolitude: for I am a Creole by my rigging, an Indian by my mast, a European by my foreyard, a Mauritian by my quest and French by my exile. I will always be elsewhere than in my own self. I can but imagine my native land. My native lands?

In our tongues, we are at the fertile frontiers of codes, to hear speeches between our vocabularies of masters and slaves. Is this why my real mother tongue is poetry? That my only native country is the Earth?

For all this, I am ready to silence all border quarrels, to show our star and share our common heritage: flesh and blood.

Coolitude: parce que tout homme a droit a une mémoire, tout homme a droit de connaître le port de sa première errance. Non pas que ce port soit un havre; mais parce que dans ce lieu a jamais innommable il peut remonter des ancres qui parfois le raccrochent a sa vérité.

Oui, tout homme a droit de connaître les flammes qui embrasent ses rêves et ses silences. Jusqu'à être phalène de son histoire.

Par coolitude je veux dire cet étrange fracas de langues qui craquèle le for intérieur de millions d'hommes pour une histoire de cristaux et d'épices, de tissus, et de bouts de terre.

Musique insoupçonnée au seuil des mots d'horizons différents.

Et rencontre en moi-même de ceux qui prennent les bateaux à rebours.

En cale d'étoiles.

K Torabully, *Cale d'Étoiles Coolitude*, p. 29.

Coolitude: every man is entitled to a memory, each has the right to know the port from which he departed. Not because this port is a haven, but because in this eternally unnamed place, he can pull up those anchors which sometimes attach him to his truth.

Beyond doubt, every man has the right to know the flames that set his dreams and his silences ablaze. Even to be the nightfly of his history.

By coolitude I mean that strange mingling of tongues, which shatters the hearts of millions of men, for a history of crystal and spices, of cloths and clods.

At this new dawn, my hopes of an Encounter . . .

So that my Odyssey and my voyages as a coolie will not sink into vacuity, I launch my cargo of stars towards nascent horizons.

As I know my crew will firmly dissolve frontiers to widen the country of Man.

Coolitude pour poser la premiere pierre de ma mémoire de toute mémoire, ma langue de toutes les langues, ma part d'inconnu que de nombreux corps et de nombreuses histoires ont souvent déposée dans mes gênes et mes îles . . .

Voici mon chant d'amour à la mer et au voyage, l'odyssée que mes peuples marins n'ont pas encore écrite . . . mon équipage sera au nombre de ceux qui effacent les frontières pour agrandir le Pays de l'Homme.
K Torabully, Cale d'Étoiles Coolitude, p. 7.

Coolitude: to lay the first stone of my memory of all memories, my language of all tongues, that part unknown which numberless bodies and histories have often cast in my self, my genes and my islands . . .

Here is my love song to our travels and our sea, the odyssey
which my seafaring people have never written . . . As I know my
crew will firmly dissolve frontiers to widen the country of Man.

Coolitude non seulement pour la mémoire, pour le passé de notre
première traversée de la Terre. Mais aussi pour ces valeurs d'hommes
que l'île a échafaudées à la rencontre des fils d'Afrique de l'Inde de
Chine et de l'Occident.
                        K Torabully, *Cale d'Étoiles Coolitude*, p. 107.

Coolitude not only for the memory, for the history of our first
crossing of the Earth. But also for those values of Man that the
island carved at the encounter of the children of Africa, India,
China and Europe.

Coolie, parce que ma mémoire perdue choisit ses racines dans mes
vérités.

Mais je ne prends la langue que pour autant qu'elle m'adopte, pour
ne plus etre coupé à la parole.

Et, au seuil de la langue française, je frappe aux voyelles et aux
consonnes différemment. Car j'aime les mots d'abord, plus que mes
blessures.
                        K Torabully, *Cale d'Étoiles Coolitude*, p. 98.

Coolie because my lost memory chooses its roots in my veracity.

But *if* I seize this tongue, *it is* because it has adopted me, and no
longer cuts me from my word.

At the threshold of vowels and consonants I knock at meanings
differently. For I love words before all, even before my wounds.

Poetic texts

Le langage m'a coolie . . .
L'eau pure ignore les sangs
Coulé calé calqué:
Deviner mes prochains itinéraires
Est ma vraie moisson d'images de mer.

K Torabully, *Cale d'Étoiles Coolitude*, p. 19

For all time
Language has coolied me.
Pure water
Pappadumbed, curried away, coiled.
Guessing at my forthcoming routes
Is my real harvest of dreams.

Définissez moi je vous prie:
qu'est-ce qu'un coolie?
Celui qu'on lie au cou
pour écouler sa longue vie?
Je suis lascar, malabar
madras tamarin de bazar
Télégou, si tel est mon goût.
Marâtre marathi ou tiamar.
Qu'importe, je suis nègre d'inde,
cobaye, de Port-Louis à Port-d'Espagne
pour remplacer mes grands esclaves de Zanzibar.
Pour mémoire, ma seule langouti, un pagne,
ma langue engloutie.
Si vous me reconnaissez, je vous prie,
appelez-moi esclave prête-nom,
homme de paille ou bouche-trou
kapok des champs ou vertèbres d'océan.
Mais sachez que mon sabre de sang
m'a déraciné jusqu'à la moelle.

K Torabully, *Cale d'Étoiles Coolitude*, p. 25.

Define me pray:
What is a coolie?
One caught by his neck
And thrown over deck?
I am Lascar, Malabar,
Madras tamarind from the bazaar
Telegu to tell all to you.
Cruel mother Marathi or Chamar
Whatever, I am Indian negro,
Guinea pig, from Port Louis to Port of Spain,
To replace mighty slaves of Zanzibar.
For memory, my only langouti.
My tongue swallowed by the sea.
Please if you recognise me
Slave or figure head call me
Straw me or man to fill all that's empty,
Field kapok or ocean vertebrae.
But please know my blood sabre
Has uprooted me to the marrow.

Je suis
Seul nègre marron
N'ayant pas fui à l'écrasement du volcan
A la fureur du corail
A l'éboulement du ciel
Seul nègre marron
Qui ne marronna pas.

I am
the only marooned nigger
who did not wriggle out
of the crumbling crater.
To the fury of coral
and the tumbling sky
the only nigger *marron*
who never marooned.

Coolitude: à se soumettre à la parole -
sans oublier la mémoire
qui ne se souvient encore de rien . . .
         K Torabully, *Chair Corail Fragments Coolies*, p. 26.

Coolitude: to submit to the Word
Without losing the memory
Who yet remembers nothing . . .

Car voici l'histoire du péril sans nom
captifs silencieux mutilés de confessions –
         K Torabully, *Chair Corail Fragments Coolies*, p. 80.

For here is the perilous, nameless history
Silenced captives with mutilated confessions.

Dans ma mémoire sont des langues aussi
Ma coolitude n'est pas une pierre non plus,
elle est corail
         K Torabully, *Chair Corail Fragments Coolies*, p. 82.

In my memory are languages too
My coolitude is not a rock either,
It is coral.

non plus l'homme hindou de Calcutta
mais chair corail des Antilles
         K Torabully, *Chair Corail Fragments Coolies* p. 108.

No longer the Hindu man from Calcutta
But coral flesh from the Indies

Malabar, moi la barre,
moi motte de terre
moi de sel moi de chair:
mon âme lascar lasse
quart malais tiers malaise
sera fragments
poutres de ciel rompues
corps rompu
à larguer les amarres.

K Torabully, *Cale d'Étoiles Coolitude*, p. 37.

Malabar, male at the helm
me at the clods of earth
me at salt me at flesh,
my alms lascar last and least,
quarter malay third malady,
me to be fragments
pillars of broken skies
me body in tatters
in pulling up the anchors.

Coolitude: m'enraciner. Je plie ma résistance en refus
de me faire offrande

K Torabully, *Cale d'Étoiles Coolitude*, p. 25.

Coolitude: to lay down my roots. I show my resistance in
    refusing
To make an offering of myself.

Mon pays n'aura pas de statue
de l'homme d'orage aux pieds nus

K Torabully, *Cale d'Étoiles Coolitude*, p. 16.

My country will have no statue
Of the barefoot man of storm

Je ne suis pas cristal
de la Compagnie des Indes
Je suis pollen d'humain
. . . accroché au gouvernail des mers.

Et mon éternité commença
Aux amarres du tout premier marin
A son superbe voyage d'azur
K Torabully, Cale d'Étoiles Coolitude, p. 23.

I am no crystal
From your India Company . . .
I am human pollen
Hooked on the helm of waves.

And my eternity began
At the moorings of the first sailor
On his first azure voyage:

Mon chant est donc coolie; ma coolitude est mon
seul partage d'une mémoire balayée par les vagues.
K Torabully, Cale d'Étoiles Coolitude, p. 102.

My song is therefore coolie; my coolitude is my
Only share of a memory tossed by waves.

Vous de Goa, de Pondicheri, de Chandernagor, de
Cocane, de Delhi, de Surat, de Londres, de Shangai,
de Lorient, de Saint-Malo, peuples de tous les bateaux
qui m'emmenèrent vers un autre moi, ma cale d'étoiles
est mon plan de voyage, mon aire, ma vision de
l'océan que nous traversions tous, bien que nous ne
vissions pas les étoiles du même angle.

En disant coolie, je dis aussi tout navigateur sans
registre de bord; je dis tout homme parti vers l'horizon

de son rêve, quel que soit le bateau qu'il accosta ou
dût accoster. Car quand on franchit l'océan pour naître
ailleurs, le marin d'un voyage sans retour aime replonger
dans ses histoires, ses légendes, et ses rêves. Le
temps d'une absence de mémoire.

> K Torabully, *Cale d'Étoiles Coolitude*, p. 89.

You from Goa, Pondicherry, Chandernagore
Cocan, Delhi, Surat, London, Shanghai
Lorient, Saint-Malo, people of all the ships
Who took me towards another me, my ship-hold of stars
Is my travel plan, my space and vision of an ocean which
we all had to cross, even if we do not
See the stars from the same angle.

In saying coolie, I am also speaking of every navigator without
A ship's register, every man who has gone towards the horizons
Of his dreams, whatever the ship he had to board.
For when one crosses the ocean to be born
Elsewhere, the sailor of the one-way voyage likes to plunge
    back
Into his history, his legends, and his dreams.
Even during his absence of memory.

Motifiez-moi
âmez-moi
humainez-moi
hommez-moi.

> K Torabully, *Cale d'Étoiles Coolitude*, p. 35.

Word me
Soul me
Humanise me
Man me.

Notes

Introduction

1. Senghor, L S, *Littérature Nègre*, Paris, 1990, p. 33.
2. Ashcroft, B et al., *Key Concepts in Post Colonial Studies*, London, 1998, pp. 12–16.
3. James, C L R, *The Black Jacobins*, London, 1980, appendix, p. 401.
4. Prosper, J G, *Histoire de la Littérature Mauricienne de Langue Française*, EOI, 1978. p. 236–40, p. 277–284.
5. Fanchin, G, 'La littérature francophone de 1945 à nos jours', in *Littérature Mauricienne*, Notre Librairie, no 114, 1993, p. 53.
6. Prosper, op. cit., p. 275.
7. Joubert, J-L et al., *Littératures francophones de l'Océan Indien*, EOI, 1993, p. 51
8. Leblond, Marius & Ary, *Après l'exotisme de Loti, le roman colonial*, Paris, Rasmussent, 1926, p. 8; 'La Marche sur le feu', Paris, 1937; Joubert, p. 54; J G Prosper, 'L'Apocalypse mauricienne', in *Chants Planétaires*, Proag Printing, Mauritius, 1990, p. 115.
9. de Rauville, C, *Indianocéanisme, humanisme et négritude*, 1970.
10. 'Raphael, creole is a patois spoken by savage negroes and dirty coolies'. From 'Ravines du devant-jour' by Confiant, cited in Bayle, T, 'Plaidoyer pour la Créolité', *Magazine littéraire*, no 320, Paris, April 1994.
11. Glissant, E, *Le Discours Antillais* Paris, 1981, translated by M Dash as *Caribbean Discourse*, Virginia, 1989; Bernabé et al, *Eloge de la Créolité*, Gallimard, 1989, p. 13
12. 'Créolité is the foundation and extension of an authentically humanist Négritude' quoted in Hookoomsingh, V, 'So near, yet so far: Bannzil's pan-Creole idealism', *International J. Soc. Lang.*, 102, 1993, p. 32–3.
13. Lionnet, F, *Autobiographical Voices: Race, Gender, Self-Portraiture*, New York, 1989, p. 4.

14. Hookoomsingh, V, 'So near, yet so far: Bannzil's pan-Creole idealism', *International J. Soc. Lang.*, 102, 1993, p. 33.

15. 'If the constellation of Creole islands were gathered in the same ocean, it would assert itself as a dynamic original culture and civilization. But divided between the Caribbean, the Americas, and the Indian Ocean, mixed in an ambiguous fashion through the intersections of different civilizations, subject to powerful centrifugal forces, it conjures up, above all, the remains of a shattered universe' Benoist, J (ed.), *L'archipel inachevé: culture et société aux Antilles françaises*, Montréal, 1972 p. 6.

16. Hall, S, 'Cultural Identity and Diaspora' in Williams, P & Chrisman, L (eds), *Colonial Discourse and Post-Colonial Theory*, UK, 1994, p. 396.

17 Parekh, B, 'Some reflections on the Hindu diaspora', *New Community* 20(4) p. 617.

18. Burton, R D, 'Penser l'indianité. La présence indienne dans la réflexion martiniquaise contemporaine' in Etan, G L (ed.), *Présences de l'Inde dans le monde*, Paris, 1994, p. 211.

19. Schnepel, E M, 'The Creole Movement and East Indians on the Island of Guadeloupe, FWI', in Motwani, J et al., *Global Indian Diaspora: Yesterday, Today and Tomorrow*, New Delhi, 1993, p. 233. Coolitude can be distinguished from a purely diasporic stance because it points to the necessity to shun a centre (for example the notion of 'mother India', India as an ultimate reference) and adopts instead the host country as another centre. In this respect coolitude can be likened to postmodern constructions of identity based on complexity rather than on monoculturalism.

20. Benoist, J, *Hindouismes Créoles. Mascareignes, Antilles*, Paris, 1998, p. 205.

21. Naipaul, V S, *The Mystic Masseur* (1957) quoted in Singh, M I, *V S Naipaul*, New Delhi 1998, p. 98.

22. Quotations are from N Bissoondath, *Digging up the Mountains*, Toronto, 1986, p. 97, and *A Casual Brutality*, New York, 1988, p. 123.

23. Baxi, S, 'The World of Neil Bissoondath: Ideology In/And Practice' in Jain, J, *Writers of the Indian Diaspora*, New Delhi, 1998, p. 136–7.

24. Rushdie, S, *Imaginary Homelands: Essays and Criticism*, London, 1991. Rushdie's observation is akin to coolitude, which characterises the descendant of the indentured or overseas Indian as one who has already accepted life in a new homeland, which interacts with the primary homeland (India), in the form of a creative attitude to the imaginary or constructed homeland.

25. Natarajan, N, 'Reading Diaspora' in E S Nelson (ed.), *Writers of the Indian Diaspora*, USA, 1993.

26. Jain, J, *Writers of the Indian Diaspora*, New Delhi, 1998, p. 17–18; Bakhtin, M M, *The Dialogic imagination: Four Essays*, USA, 1981.

27. Prosper, J G, op. cit., p. 218–19.

28. Bragard, Véronique, 'Gendered Voyages into Coolitude: the Shaping of the Indo-Caribbean Woman's Literary Consciousness' in *Kunapipi: Journal of Post-Colonial Writing* vol. 20:1,(1998), 99–111 and 'Coolitude or the Interw(e)aving of Plural Identities', XXIII Annual Conference of the Association for the Study of the New Literatures in English (ASNEL) (Liège and Aachen 2000).

1 The Coolie Odyssey: A Voyage in Time and Space

1.   Calcutta Commission of Enquiry Report, Appendices, in *Parliamentary Papers* 1840 (58).
2.   ibid.
3.   *Fiji Sun*, 19 March 1979, p. 9. Maharani's story is related in N Mahabir, *The Still Cry*, New York, 1985, pp. 77–88.
4.   Indian Immigrants Commission Report, Natal, 1887, evidence of Aboo Bakr.
5.   Quoted in S Bhana and Pachai, pp. 20–21.
6.   Gillion, K L, *Fiji's Indian Migrants*, London, 1962, p. 132.
7.   Vatuk, V P, 'Protest Songs of East Indians in British Guiana', *Journal of American Folklore*, 1964, p. 224.
8.   Quoted in Lal, B V, *Girmitiyas: The Origins of the Fiji Indians*, 1983, Canberra p.111.
9.   MA BIA Beyts Report, 1861, p. 44.
10. ibid., pp. 45–6.
11. MA RA 1844 Manley to Burton, 25 April 1866; RA 2075 Emigration Agent Madras to Colonial Secretary, Mauritius,10 June 1871.
12. MA PL 46 Protector to Manager, Sans Souci Flacq, 2, 10 and 13 Oct 1882.
13. Calcutta Commission of Enquiry Report, Appendices, in *Parliamentary Papers* 1840 (58).
14. MA RA 1176 Emigration Agent Madras to Colonial Secretary, 16 Jan 1852.
15. Jain, R K, *Indian Communities Abroad. Themes and Literature*, New Delhi, 1993, p. 1.
16. Kolff, D H A, *Naukar, Rajput and Sepoy*, Cambridge 1990, pp. 169–73; A A Yang, 'Peasants on the Move: A Study of Internal Migration in India', *Journal of Interdisciplinary History*, X, 1979, 43.
17. MA RA 1641 Emigration Calcutta to Colonial Secretary Mauritius, 3 October 1863; MA RA 1788 Emigration Agent Calcutta to Colonial Secretary Mauritius, 27 July 1865.
18. Yamin, G, 'The Character and Origins of Labour Migration from Ratnagiri District, 1840–1920', *South Asia Research*, vol. 9, no. 1, 1989, p. 51.
19. Pitoeff, P, 'Yanaon et les Engages de la Réunion: Trois Experiences d'Emigration au XIXe Siècle' Conference Proceedings, p. 230; MA RA 1314 Emigration Agent, Madras to Colonial Secretary, Mauritius, 21 December 1854.
20. MA RA 1788 Emigration Agent Madras to Colonial Secretary Mauritius, 26 August 1865.
21. Yamin, G, op. cit., pp. 44–6.
22. MA BIA Beyts Report, 1861.
23. MA RA 2075 Emigration Agent, Madras to Beyts, 8 February 1871.
24. Bhana and Pachai, p. 27.
25. Samaroo, B, 'The Indian Connection' in Dabydeen and Samaroo (eds), *India in the Caribbean*, Hansib, 1987, p. 44.
26. Uttar Pradesh Ke Lok Geet, quoted in Lal, B V, 'Approaches to the Study of Indian Indentured Emigration with Special Reference to Fiji', *Journal of Pacific History*, p. 67.

27. Quoted in Lal, B V, *Girmitiyas: The Origins of the Fiji Indians*, 1983, Canberra, p. 113.
28. ibid., p. 114.
29. 'They Came In Ships' by Mahadai Das in Dabydeen and Samaroo (eds), *India in the Caribbean*, 1987, p. 288.
30. Quoted in Lal, B V, 'Approaches to the Study of Indian Indentured Emigration with Special Reference to Fiji', *Journal of Pacific History*, p. 68.
31. Vinson, A, *De l'Immigration Indienne*, Réunion, 1860, p. 15.
32. MA RA 1129 Secretary of the Government of Bengal to Emigration Agent Calcutta, 17 April 1851.
33. Nandan, S, *Voices in the River*, Suva, 1985, p. 54.
34. *Fiji Sun*, 20 March 1979, p. 6.
35. 'Coolie Odyssey' by David Dabydeen in Dabydeen and Samaroo (eds), *India in the Caribbean*, 1987, p. 281.
36. Bhana and Pachai, pp. 22–3.
37. Quoted in Mahabir, N K (ed.), *The Still Cry*, New York, 1985, p. 85.

2 Thrice Victimized: Casting the Coolie

1. Earl Grey, *The Colonial Policy of Lord John Russell's Administration*, vol. 1, London, 1853, pp. 81–2.
2. PRO CO 167 Note of James Stephen, 8 December 1832.
3. IOLR Bengal Public Proceedings, Secretary to Indian Law Commission to H. Prinsep, Secretary to Government of India, 16 September 1836.
4. IOLR Indian Public Proceedings, Range 186 Vol 99 Colonial Secretary to Secretary to the Government of India, 9 August 1841.
5. Calcutta Commission of Enquiry Report, printed in Parliamentary Paper 1840 (58).
6. IOLR Bombay Public Proceedings Range 347 vol. 71 November–December 1838, Report of the Committee on Indian Labourers, Bombay, 20 September 1838.
7. PRO CO 167/235 Major Archer to Lord Stanley 28 September 1841.
8. *The Christian Advocate*, 24 April 1841; PRO CO 167/210 Minute of Russell, 14 October 1839.
9. Crooke, W, *The North Western Provinces of India: their History, Ethnology and Administration*, London, 1897, p. 326.
10. Quoted in Tinker, H, *A New System of Slavery*, London, 1974, p. 123.
11. IOLR Report on Colonial Emigration from the Bengal Presidency, 1883, p. 6.
12. Jenkins, E, *The Coolie, his Rights and Wrongs*, London, 1871, pp. 94–5; J Beaumont, *The New Slavery*, 1871, p. 84.
13. IOLR Bengal Emigration Proceedings Range 434/22 Protector of Emigrants at Madras, 1869.
14. Mouat, F J, *Rough Notes of a Trip to Reunion, Mauritius and Ceylon; with remarks on their eligibility as sanitaria for Indian invalids*, Calcutta, Thacker Spink & Co, 1852, p. 9.

15. PRO CO 167/210 Extract from Petition of Planters, 18 May 1839.

16. 'The Indians are remarkable for their gentleness and submissiveness', quoted in Singarevelou, *Les Indiens de la Guadeloupe*, p. 70.

17. *Le Cernéen*, 30 May 1851, Mauritius. The original French version read '*Des gens sans aveu, sans nom même pour la plupart (car souvent leurs tickets portent leurs nombre de bord, comme ils disent, c'est à dire les noms de ceux qui les ont envoyés à leur place) des gens d'aucune instruction, sans principes quelconques, . . . nomade et presque sauvage encore . . . une véritable invasion de barbares . . . des parias, le rebut de la société indienne.*'

18. Simonin, 'La Réunion' in *Revue des Deux Mondes*, 1861 p. 368.

19. Naz, Sir V, *Conférence sur l'Immigration Indienne*, 1891 p.91–20.

20. Beaumont, J, *The New Slavery*, op. cit., p. 65. For the 1910 quote see M Ramesar, 'Indentured Labour in Trinidad 1880–1917' in K Saunders (ed.), *Indentured Labour in the British Empire*, 1984, p. 67.

21. Merven, T, *L'Indien a Maurice*, 1896.

22. A Bengal Civilian, *Journal of Five Months' Residence in the Mauritius*, Calcutta, 1838, p. 91.

23. Mouat, op. cit., pp. 34–5, 104.

24. Maillard, *Notes sur l'Ile de la Réunion*, Paris, 1862, p. 187; Andrews, C F & Pearson, W W, *Indentured Labour in Fiji, an independent enquiry*, Madras, 1916.

25. Anderson, J, *Descriptive Account of Mauritius*, 1858, pp. 69–70.

26. Morris, James, *Monographie de l'Ile Maurice*, Bordeaux, 1862, p. 33.

27. Vinson, A, *De l'Immigration Indienne*, Réunion, 1860, p. 17.

28. Gordon, A H, *Mauritius – Records of Private and Public Life, 1871–4*, vol. 1, p. 125.

29. Bronkhurst, H V P, *The Colony of British Guiana and its Labouring Population*, London, 1883, p. 244.

30. Marimoutou, Michèle, 'Femmes Indiennes et Engagement au XIXe Siècle à la Réunion', Conference Proceedings, p. 290.

31. Quoted in Lal, B V, 'Veil of Dishonour. Sexual Jealousy and Suicide on Fiji Plantations', *Journal of Pacific History*, 1985, p. 139.

32. Andrews, C F, *Indian Review*, July 1922.

33. Andrews and Pearson, op. cit., p. 6.

34. '*Une solidarité profonde, une sorte de cousinage moral qui exclut tous les autres groupes ethniques*' (Alix d'Unienville, *Les Mascareignes*, quoted in Callikan-Proag, Callikan-Proag, A *Marcel Cabon: Rêve et Réalité*, 1982, Mauritius, p. 62).

35. '*Entre les blancs et nous il y a toute de meme des points communs. Nous avons la même nature, plus ou moins les memes goûts. L'indien est un barbare*', Masson, L, *L'Etoile et la Clef*, p. 220 ; Paus, V 'Des indianités dans la littérature coloniale de l'Océan Indien', DEA 1999.

36. Hookoomsing, V, 'Races et classes dans les romans mauriciens des années 30', Conference Paper, Martinique, 1991, p. 26.

37. '*Ces femmes-là ne peuvent pas monter, mon cher, c'est vous qui descendrez.*' *Ameenah*, p. 205.

38. Joubert, J L, 'La vieille dame dans l'ombre. Une littérature bi-séculaire: des origines à 1945', '*Littérature Mauricienne*', Notre Librairie, no. 114, Paris, 1983.

39. Hookoomsing, V, 'Races et classes dans les romans mauriciens des années 30', Conference Paper, Martinique, 1991, p. 10.

40. '*Ce qu'il aimait par-dessus tout, c'était le contact quotidien avec ces paysannes indiennes, belles ou laides, jeunes ou vieilles, mais toutes attrayantes par la volupté paisible de leur yeux de jais*'. Martial, *La Poupée de Chair*, p. 31.

41. '*Tellement opposée de moeurs, de coutumes, de traditions, et si parfumée de pittoresque, si curieuse, par ses dieux multiformes, ses voiles, ses danses, ses joyaux.*'

42. Prosper, J G, *Histoire de la Littérature Mauricienne de Langue Française*, EOI, Mauritius, 1978, p. 35.

43. '*Une petite indienne qui passe, porte dans ses yeux la profondeur de vingt civilisations révolues*' (Ameenah, p. 92).

44. '*Les lois et la poésie de l'ancienne race, les Védas et les Ramayanas, les fastes religieux ou guerriers des siècles primitives, et la poésie aussi des temps modernes, née des contrastes exhalée d'un sol où tout est couleur et magnificence, les fruits, les fleurs, les femmes, le ciel, le soleil, la pluie ou le haillon, la richesse et l'indigence.*'

45. *Guyana Daily Chronicle*, 25 June and 3, 7 and 10 December 1899; Mendes, A, 'Boodhoo', in *From Trinidad*, ed. R Sander, 1978; E Mittelholzer, *Corentyne Thunder*, London, 1941; V Ramraj, 'Still Arriving: The Assimilationist Indo-Caribbean Experience of Marginality', in E S Nelson (ed.), *Reworlding the Literature of the Indian Diaspora*, USA, 1992, p. 78; J Poynting, 'East Indian Women in the Caribbean: Experience, Image and Voice', *Journal of South Asian Literature*, 21, no. 1, 1986, p. 14.

46. '*Pas le temps de penser, pas le temps de voir passer la vie, rien que la pioche, la fosse qu'ils creusent.*' Quoted in Callikan-Proag, p. 67.

47. L'Essor, September 1934.

48. Quoted in Prosper, p. 170.

49. Callikan-Proag, A Marcel Cabon: Rêve et Réalité, 1982, Mauritius, p. 68. '*On constate, chez Cabon, que les qualités typiques de l'indo-mauricien comme le goût de l'épargne, une vie fruste, et le sens du travail, qui étaient généralement objets de derision de la part des autres ethnies, inspirent maintenant de l'admiration.*'

50. Fanchin, G, 'La littérature francophone de 1945 à nos jours', pp. 46–7.

51. 'In *Namasté* and *l'Enfant Bihari* I describe the labour which propels men and women from their homes at the first sound of the cockerel, which drives them to the woods and to the fields in all weathers, the disregard for obstacles, and the spirit of thrift.' The Triveni, Mauritius, June 1970.

52. '*Allant et venant, elle sentait le poids des regards sur son ventre, comme un défi.*'

53. '*Il touche à une des préoccupations les plus importantes des femmes et même des hommes de civilisation indienne: les femmes qui ne sont pas enceintes quelque temps après leur mariage, sont presque les parias de la société. Elles ont droit au mépris des hommes et des femmes: elles-mêmes ont un sens aigu de culpabilité qui rend leur vie intenable.*' Callikan-Proag, p. 11–12.

54. '*Si grand et si fort, – et ce maintien – que je me plais à l'imaginer sous l'uniforme de quelque général de Shah Jahan, dans les vêtements de quelque prince du Pendjab ou du Cachemire.*'

55. Chazal, in *Le Mauricien*, 29 April 1960.

56. For details of these early works see R Confiant and P Chamoiseau, *Lettres Créoles, tracées antillaises et continentales de la littérature*, Paris, 1991, pp. 45–6.

57. 'Day's End', in Dabydeen, D (ed.), *Coolie Odyssey*, Hansib, 1988, p. 34.

58. Sewtohul, *L'histoire d'Ashok et d'autres personnages de moindre importance*, Gallimard, Paris, 2001, p. 164.

59. Moore, B, 'Sex and Marriage among Indian immigrants in British Guiana during the Nineteenth Century', Conference Paper, Trinidad, 1984, p. 4.

60. Marimoutou, Michèle, 'Femmes Indiennes et Engagement au XIXe siècle à la Réunion, Proceedings, p. 290.

61. Parekh, B, 'Some reflections on the Hindu diaspora', *New Community* 20(4), p. 608.

62. Mishra, B, *Rama's Banishment*, London, 1979, p.7, in particular his deconstruction of Chandra Sharma's *Pravas Bhajamnamjali*, 1947 work.

63. Lal, B V, 'Fiji Girmitiyas: the background to Banishment' in R Mishra, *Rama's Banishment*, op. cit., p.28.

64. Brereton, B, *Race Relations in Colonial Trinidad, 1870–1900*, Cambridge, 1979, pp. 186–9.

65. Rodney, W, 'Guyana: the making of the labour force', *Race & Class*, xxii, 4, 1981, p. 351.

66. Parekh, B, op. cit., p. 613.

67. Northrup, D, *Indentured Labor in the Age of Imperialism, 1834–1922*, Cambridge, 1995, p. 154.

68. Kale, M, *Fragments of Empire: Capital, Slavery & Indentured Labor in the British Caribbean*, Philadelphia, 1998.

3 Surviving Indenture

1. Quoted in Lal, B V, and Shineberg, B, 'The Story of the Haunted Line', *Journal of Pacific History*, 1991, p. 111.

2. Statement of Indians returned to Madras on the *Red Riding Hood*, April 1871, Meer, op. cit., p. 157–60; Singavarelou, p. 73; *Natal Mercury*, 14 July 1866, quoted in Y S Meer, *Documents of Indentured Labour. Natal, 1851–1917*, pp. 111–12.

3. Quoted in the *Fiji Sun*, 22 March 1979, p. 10.

4. Quoted in Lal, B V, 'Approaches to the Study of Indian Indentured Emigration with Special Reference to Fiji', *Journal of Pacific History*, p. 70.

5. PL 20 Petition of Urjoon, Cote d'Or village, to J Trotter Esq, Protector of Immigrants, 29 June 1908.

6. Bhana & Pachai (eds), *A Documentary History of Indian South Africans*, p. 3.

7. MA PL 47 Rughoonuth and Coopen to O'Connor, 14 May 1883.

8. Royal Commission Report, British Guiana, 1871, p. 5.

9. Evidence given before West India Royal Commission of 1897, quoted in T Ramnarine, 'Over a Hundred Years of East Indian Disturbances on the Sugar Estates of Guyana, 1869–1978: An Historical Overview' in Dabydeen & Samaroo (eds), *India in the Caribbean*, 1987, p. 122.

10. Quoted in Beall, J, 'Women under Indenture in Natal', in S Bhana (ed.), *Essays on Indentured Indians in Natal*, UK, 1991, p. 106.
11. Her story is recounted in the Express newspaper, Trinidad, 30 May 1991.
12. IOLR Statement of Ramasawmy, Madras Police Office, 1842.
13. Statement of Indians returned to Madras on the *Red Riding Hood*, April 1871, Meer, op. cit., pp. 157–60.
14. Calcutta Commission of Enquiry Appendices, Statement of Boodhoo Khan, 1838.
15. Laval, J C, op. cit., p. 307. Mauritius Papers, Dalais murder enquiry, 1865.
16. MA PL 50 Protector to Emigration Agent Madras, 31 March 1896; MA PL 28 Departmental Minute Paper, 14 June 1908.
17. Quoted in Lal, B V, 'Veil of dishonour', op. cit., p. 142.
18. Quoted in Beall, 1991, op. cit., p. 109.
19. MA PL 3 Letter of Gopaul, 19 February 1895.
20. Quoted in Tinker, H, *A New System of Slavery*, 1974, p. 176.
21. MA PL 32 Protector to Juggoo, old immigrant no.1,068, 1848.
22. CO 167/565 letter of Beehary Sing, Mauritius to the Secretary, APS, London, 14 October 1875.
23. Bhana & Pachai, op. cit., p. 38.
24. MA PA 60 Inspector French to Protector, 11 March 1884.
25. F Lacpatia, 'Quelques Aspects de l'Insertion des Indiens à la Reunion au XIXe Siècle' in Colloque, p. 402.
26. MA PL 32 Protector's Report, 27 November 1848.
27. Tinker, op. cit., p. 234.
28. 'They Came In Ships' by Mahadai Das in Dabydeen & Samaroo, op. cit., p. 289.
29. Bhana & Pachai, op. cit., p. 4.
30. Calcutta Commission of Enquiry Report, Statement of Djooram, Ayah, 1838; Statement of Heemgun, Calcutta, 1841; an official in Surinam, quoted in Tinker, op. cit., p. 209.
31. MA PL 46, Declaration of Ismael, 1883.
32. Meer, Y S, *Documents of Indentured Labour. Natal, 1851–1917*, pp. 138–9. Evidence.
33. Cited in Marimoutou, M, 'Cabanons et Danse du Feu: La Vie Privée des Engagés Indiens dans les Camps Réunionnais du XIXème Siècle' in Wanquet, C (ed.), *Fragments Pour Une Histoire des Economies et Sociétés de Plantation à la Réunion*, St Denis, Réunion, 1989 p. 241–2.
34. Singaravelou, op cit., p. 78.
35. MA PA 22 Petition of Bahooram, 29 June 1874.
36. Bhana & Pachai, op. cit., p. 5–6.
37. Vatuk, V P, 'Protest Songs of East Indians in British Guiana', *Journal of American Folklore*, 1964, p. 224.
38. Quoted in Laval, J C, 'Les Problèmes Liés à la 'Criminalité Indienne' Pendant la Période de l'Engagisme à la Réunion', Colloque, p. 305.
39. 'We have Survived' by Arnold Itwaru in Dabydeen & Samaroo (eds), *India in the Caribbean*, 1987, p. 292.

40. Quoted in Rafiq, F, *Aurat Durbar, The Court of Women. Writings by Women of South Asian Origin*, Canada, 1995, p. 224.

41. Chandran Nair's poem 'Grandfather' in *Once the Horseman and Other Poems*, Singapore, 1972, p. 9.

42. Quoted in Poynting, J, 'East Indian Women in the Caribbean: Experience and Voice', in Dabydeen & Samaroo (eds), *India in the Caribbean*, 1987, p. 251.

43. 'Coolie Mother' by David Dabydeen, in Dabydeen & Samaroo (eds), op. cit, p. 284.

44. 'Slave Song', Dabydeen, D, UK, 1986, and see the discussion of the poem in D Dabydeen & N. Wilson-Tagore, *A Reader's Guide to West Indian and Black British Literature*, Hansib, 1988, p. 162.

45. 'Poems in Recession', 1972, quoted in 'Cyril Dabydeen: Remembrance of Things Indian' in A L McLeod (ed.), *The Literature of the Indian Diaspora. Essays in Criticism*, New Delhi, 2000, pp. 189–204.

46. Ahmed Ali, *Plantation to Politics: Studies on Fiji Indians*, 1980, p. 6.

47. 'Ritual Songs and Folksongs of the Hindus of Surinam', quoted in B V Lal, 'Approaches to the Study of Indian Indentured Emigration with Special Reference to Fiji', *Journal of Pacific History*, p. 68.

4 Reclaiming the 'Other':
Diaspora Indians and the Coolie Heritage

1. Bhana & Pachai, op. cit., pp. 33–4.

2. *Collected Works of Mahatma Gandhi*, vol. 1, pp. 147–57; vol. 3, pp. 86–90.

3. Ibid., vol. 5, pp. 144–52.

4. Tredgold, J H, *The Export of Coolies, and other Labourers to Mauritius*, London, 1842, p. 32, pp. 55–6.

5. Quoted in Adamson, A H, 'Immigration into British Guiana', in K Saunders (ed.), *Indentured Labour in the British Empire*, London, 1984, p. 49; MA PL 44 Petition of Kesaddat to the Chief Clerk of the Immigration Department, January 1881.

6. Quoted in Beall, J, 'Women under Indenture in Natal', in S Bhana, (ed.), *Essays on Indentured Indians in Natal*, UK, 1991, p. 97.

7. MA PA 40 Petition of Jubboo, 18 June 1879.

8. MA RA 675 Petition of Boyjoo; Finniss Report 29 March 1841.

9. Bhana & Pachai, op. cit., p. 15.

10. MA PL 3 Letter of Gopaul, 19 February 1895. This is reproduced in full in Chapter Four.

11. MA HA 113 Petition of Porunsing 31 May 1841; police report, 9 June 1841.

12. MA PL 47 Ganaputhy Pillay to Protector 4 October 1883; Immigration Office Minute of 22 October 1883.

13. MA PL 47 Petition of Peerally, and report of C. Hughes, Deputy Superintendent, 15 January 1883.

14. PP 1840 (58) Coolie Commission of Enquiry, Calcutta, Appendices.

15. MA PA 205 Petition of Laligadoo to Sir Charles Bruce, 2 August 1899.

16. MA PA 202 Protector to Stipendiary Magistrate of Moka, 13 and 14 April 1899 and enclosures.

17. Parekh, B, 'Some reflections on the Hindu diaspora', *New Community* 20(4) p. 613.

18. MA PA 201 V. Moonsamy Pillay to Protector, 30 January 1899; Owen L O'Connor to Protector 25 February 1899; Protector to V Moonsamy Pillay, 8 March 1899.

19. Dabydeen, D, *Coolie Odyssey*, Hansib, 1988, p. 10.

20. Bhana & Pachai, op. cit., pp. 16–17.

21. De Verteuil, A, *Eight East Indian Immigrants*, 1989, quoted in K. Mahabir, *East Indian Women of Trinidad & Tobago, An Annotated Bibliography*, Trinidad, 1992, pp. 19–20; MA PA 40, J Austen British Consul, Rio de Janeiro to Protector of Immigrants, Mauritius, January 1879.

22. MA PL 48 Protector, Mauritius to Protector, Natal, 17 February 1896.

23. 'Coolie Odyssey' by David Dabydeen in Dabydeen & Samaroo (eds), *India in the Caribbean*, 1987, p. 282.

24. Parekh, B, op. cit., p. 615

25. Dabydeen, D, *Coolie Odyssey*, op. cit., p. 12.

26. Quoted in Poynting, J, 'East Indian Women in the Caribbean: Experience and Voice', in Dabydeen & Samaroo (eds), *India in the Caribbean*, 1987, p. 256.

27. Dabydeen, D, *Coolie Odyssey*, Hansib, 1988, p. 9.

28. Virassamy, M, *Le Petit Coolie Noir*, Paris, 1972.

29. In Rafiq, F, *Aurat Durbar, The Court of Women. Writings by Women of South Asian Origin*, Canada, 1995, p. 224.

30. Quoted in Poynting, J, 'East Indian Women in the Caribbean: Experience and Voice', in Dabydeen & Samaroo (eds), *India in the Caribbean*, 1987, p. 248.

31. Cook, D & Rubadiri, D (eds), *Poems from East Africa*, London, 1971.

32. 'Atlantic Song' by Cyril Dabydeen in Dabydeen & Samaroo (eds), *India in the Caribbean*, 1987, p. 295.

33. Remtulla, A in Maira, S & Srikanth, R (eds), *Contours of the Heart – South Asians Map North America*, New York, 1996, p. 124.

34. Jamal, S, 'Making of a Cultural Schizophrenic' in Rafiq, F, Aurat Durbar, The Court of Women, *Writings by Women of South Asian Origin*, Canada, 1995, pp. 119–30.

35. Walcott, D, *The Star-Apple Kingdom*, 1979, pp. 33–5.

36. Nelson, E, *Reworlding. The Literature of the Indian Diaspora*, USA, 1992, p. xiii.

37. McLeod, A L (ed.), *The Literature of the Indian Diaspora. Essays in Criticism*, New Delhi, 2000, p.192.

38. McLeod, A L, 'Cyril Dabydeen: Remembrance of Things Indian', in McLeod (ed.) op. cit., 2000, pp. 189–204.

39. Walcott, D, *The Star-Apple Kingdom*, 1979, pp. 33–5.

40. Her short stories are published in Alexander, M and Mathew, R, *Time of the Peacock*, Sydney 1965. See also Sharrad, P, 'Mena Abdullah's Untranslatable Diasporic Identity', in McLeod (ed.), 2000.

5 Some Theoretical Premises of Coolitude

1. Senghor, L S, 'De la liberté de l'âme ou éloge du métissage', in *Liberté I. Négritude et Humanisme*, Seuil, Paris, 1964 (1950), pp. 98–103. (Our vocation as the colonised has been to overcome the contradictions inherent in the dichotomy artificially erected between Africa and Europe, our heritage and our education. It is from the grafting of the one onto the other that our freedom will be born).

2. 'My coolitude is not a rock either It is coral Fruit of an earth laden with speeches of birds and beasts'. Khal Torabully, *Chair corail, fragments coolies*, Ibis Rouge, Guadeloupe, 99, p 82.

3. Deleuze, G & Guattari, F, *Mille plateaux*, Paris 1980.

4. Khal, 'Coolitude', Notre Librairie, CLEF, Paris, October 1996.

5. Confiant, R et al., *Eloge de la Créolité*, Gallimard, Paris, 89, p. 28.

6. Glissant, E, *Discours Antillais*, Gallimard, Paris, p. 127. 'For me, créolité is another interpretation of créolisation. Créolisation is a perpetual movement of cultural and linguistic interpenetration, which means that one does not necessarily end up with a definition of being. That is what makes créolité -: to define a creole being. It's a type of regression, from the point of view of process, but it is essential in order to defend the creole present. Just as négritude was of vital importance for the defence of African values and of the black diaspora.'

7. Eco, Umberto, *L'Oeuvre ouverte*, Seuil, Paris.

8. Glissant, E, *Introduction: une poétique du Divers*, ibid, p. 89. 'Creolization is unpredictable. One can predict or determine métissage, but one cannot predict or determine creolization. This can be summarised by positing the opposition between an archipelagic thought and a continental thought, the continental thought being a systematic thought and the archipelagic thought being an ambiguous thought.'

9. Véronique Bragard's works are extremely relevant on this point. This researcher from Belgium is presently working on a PhD thesis on 'Gendered voyages into coolitude'. She has extensively written on feminine voices in coolitude. Glissant, E, *Introduction: une poétique du Divers*, ibid.

10. Benedict, B, *Politics in a Plural Society*, 1972.

11. *Les Indiens de Guadeloupe et de la Martinique*, (Paris, 1975), an article published in Notre Librairie.

12. Khal, 'Coolitude', Numéro 128,CLEF, Paris, October–December 96.

13. Maryse Conde, *Traversée de la mangrove*, Stock, Paris, 92.

14. Humbert, Marie-Therese, *A l'autre bout de moi*, Stock, Paris, 1992.

15. Unnuth, A, (Lal Pasina) *Sueurs de Sang*, Gallimard, Paris, 2001.

16. Dabydeen, D, *The Counting House*, translated in French, *Terres Maudites*, Dapper, Paris, 2000.

17. Glissant, E, *Le Discours antillais*, ibid, p. 462. (It creates a relationship on an egalitarian footing, and for the first time, between convergent histories).

18. See articles by various writers in *Dictionnaire critique de la mondialisation*, Le Pré aux Clercs, Paris, 2002.

19. Glissant, E, *Poétique de la Relation*, p. 1990, p. 27.
20. Glissant, E, ibid, p. 159. (Not simply to consent to the right to be different, but, more importantly, to the right to opacity . . . subsistence in a non-reducible singularity).
21. Pyamootoo, B, *Bénarès*, Editions de l'Olivier, Paris, 1999.
22. Sewtohul, A, *L'Histoire d'Ashok et d'autres personnages de moindre importance*, Gallimard, Paris, 2001.
23. Confiant, R, *Le Nègre et l'amiral*, p. 128. (To be Creole . . . is a type of compromise between the white and the black, between the black and the Indian, between the Indian and the half-Chinese or the Syrian; at bottom, what are we all if not bastards and half-castes? Well, let us proclaim our bastardy as an honour, and stop looking, like the white Creoles have done, for heroic ancestors, in a chimerical Guinea or an eternal India. You see, my dear Amédée, all this mixing has produced a new race, and a new language, which is supple and serpentine as well as being convivial and tangible).
24. Devi, A, *L'Arbre fouet*, L'Harmattan, Paris, 1997.
25. Devi, A, *Moi, l'interdite*, Dapper, Paris, 2001, p. 30.
26. Lionnet, F, *Autobiographical Voices: Race, Gender, Self Portraiture, Reading Women Writing*, Ithaca, Cornell University Press, NY and London.
27. Bodha, N, *Beaux Songes*, Bénarès, Mauritius, 1999.
28. Cabon, M, *Namasté*, Royal Printing, Mauritius, 1965.
29. 'As for the land, they know it so well: they have been grabbing it away from us, bit by bit . . .' and 'Damned nation! It is in their hands that the profits are to be found . . .'.
30. 'Between the Whites and ourselves, there are common points. We have the same nature, more or less the same tastes. The Indian is a barbarian . . .'
31. Confiant, R, *La Vierge du grand retour*, Grasset, Paris, 1996.
32. 'V S Naipaul revisite une quête littéraire entre fiction et non-fiction', by Jean-François Fogel and Laurent Greilsamer, in *Le Monde*, Paris, 7/12/01.
33. Torabully, K, 'V S Naipaul, un écrivain de la coolitude', in *La Quinzaine Littéraire*, Paris, Octobre 2001.
34. Naipaul, V S, *L'Inde, un million des révoltes*, PLON, Paris, 1990.
35. Casanova, P, 'Le Nobel à V.S. Naipaul, le prix du reniement', Le Monde Diplomatique, No 573, December 2001, Paris).
36. Naipaul, V S, *The Enigma of Arrival*, Penguin, London, 1987.

Conclusion

1. Nelson, E S, *Writers of the Indian Diaspora*, USA, 1993, p. xvii. An example of this is the novel by Beeharry, D, *That Others Might Live*, which sought to recreate indenture conditions.
2. Fanchin, G, 'La littérature francophone de 1945 a nos jours', in Littérature Mauricienne, *Notre Librairie*, no. 114, 1993, p. 52.
3. Confiant, R, Preface to *Chair Corail Fragments Coolies*, Guadeloupe, 1999, pp. 7–9.

4. Torabully, K, 'Coolitude', *Notre Librairie*, April 1997, p. 71.
5. Confiant, R, op. cit., p. 9.
6. Lionnet, F, *Autobiographical Voices: Race, Gender, Self-Portraiture*, p. 6; Turcotte, P, & Brabant, C, 'Ile Maurice: Nuvo Sime', *Peuples Noirs/Peuples Africains*, 31, 1983, p. 106.
7. For a further discussion of these issues in the Mauritian context see Eriksen, T H, *Us and Them in Modern Societies*, Oslo, 1993, p. 91, and Hookoomsing, V, 'Preserving pluralism in the context of development and modernization: the case of Mauritius with particular reference to the Indo-Mauritians', Conference Paper, 1994, pp. 12–16.

Bibliography

A Bengal Civilian, *Journal of Five Months' Residence in the Mauritius*, Calcutta, 1838.

Ahmed, A, *Plantation to Politics: Studies on Fiji Indians*, 1980.

Alexander, M, and Mathew, R, *Time of the Peacock*, Sydney, 1965.

Anderson, J, *Descriptive Account of Mauritius*, 1858.

Andrews, C F, & Pearson, W W, Indentured Labour in Fiji, an independent enquiry, *Madras, 1916*.

Andrews, C F, Indian Review, *July 1922*.

Ashcroft, B, et al, *Key Concepts in Post Colonial Studies*, London, 1998.

Bakhtin, M M, *The Dialogic imagination: Four Essays*, USA, 1981.

Baxi, S, 'The World of Neil Bissoondath: Ideology In/And Practice' in Jain, J, *Writers of the Indian Diaspora*, New Delhi, 1998.

Bayle, T, 'Plaidoyer pour la Créolité', *Magazine littéraire*, no 320, Paris, April 1994.

Benedict, B, *Politics in a Plural Society*, 1972.

Benoist, J, (ed.), *L'archipel inachevé: culture et société aux Antilles françaises*, Montreal, 1972.

Benoist, J, *Hindouismes Créoles. Mascareignes, Antilles*, Paris, 1998.

Bernabé et al, *Eloge de la Créolité*, Gallimard, Paris, 1989.

Beaumont, J, *The New Slavery*, 1871.

Bhana, S, & Pachai, B, (eds), *A Documentary History of Indian South Africans*.

Bhana, S, (ed.), *Essays on Indentured Indians in Natal*, UK, 1991.

Bissoondath, N, *Digging up the Mountains*, Toronto, 1986.

Bissoondath, N, *A Casual Brutality*, New York, 1988.

Bragard, V, 'Coolitude or the interweaving of plural identities', XXIII Annual Conference of the Association for the Study of the New Literatures in English (ASNEL), Liége and Aachen, 2000.

Bragard, V, 'Gendered voyages into Coolitude : the shaping of the Indo-Caribbean woman's literary consciousness', Kunapipi: Journal of Post-Colonial Writing, vol. 20:1, 1998, p.99–111.

Brereton, B, *Race Relations in Colonial Trinidad, 1870–1900*, Cambridge, 1979.

Bronkhurst, H V P, *The Colony of British Guiana and its Labouring Population*, London, 1883.

Burton, R D, 'Penser l'indianité. La présence indienne dans la réflexion martiniquaise contemporaine' in G L'Etang (ed.) *Présences de l'Inde dans le monde*, Paris, 1994.

Callikan-Proag, A, *Marcel Cabon: Rêve et Réalité*, Mauritius, 1982.

Charoux, C, *Ameenah, Roman Mauricien*, Port-Louis, Mauritius, 1935.

Confiant, R, et al, *Eloge de la Créolité*, Gallimard, Paris, 1989.

Confiant, R, and Chamoiseau, P, *Lettres Créoles, tracées antillaises et continentales de la littérature*, Paris, 1991.

Cook, D, & Rubadiri D, (eds), *Poems from East Africa*, London, 1971.

Crooke, W, *The North Western Provinces of India: their History, Ethnology and Administration*, London, 1897.

Dabydeen, D, and Samaroo, B, (eds), *India in the Caribbean*, 1987.

Dabydeen, D, & Wilson-Tagore, N, *A Reader's Guide to West Indian and Black British Literature*, Hansib, 1988.

Dabydeen, D, (ed.), *Coolie Odyssey*, Hansib, 1988.

Deleuze, G, & Guattari, F, *Mille plateaux*, Paris 1980.

Eriksen, T H, *Us and them in modern societies*, Oslo, 1993.

Fanchin, G, 'La littérature francophone de 1945 à nos jours', in *Littérature Mauricienne*, Notre Librairie, no 114, 1993.

Gillion, K L, *Fiji's Indian Migrants*, London, 1962, p. 132.

Glissant, E, *Le Discours Antillais* Paris, 1981, translated by M Dash as *Caribbean Discourse*, Virginia, 1989.

Glissant, E, *Poétique de la Relation*, p 1990.

Gordon, A H, *Mauritius – Records of Private and Public Life*, 1871–4, vol. 1.

Grey, Earl, *The Colonial Policy of Lord John Russell's Administration*, vol. 1,London, 1853.

Hall, S, 'Cultural Identity and Diaspora' in Williams, P, & Chrisman, L, (eds) *Colonial Discourse and Post-Colonial Theory*, UK, 1994.

Hookoomsingh, V, 'Races et classes', paper presented at the *Colloque international 'Canne à sucre et littérature'*, Martinique, March 1991.

Hookoomsingh, V, 'So near, yet so far: Bannzil's pan-Creole idealism', *International J. Soc. Lang.*, 102, 1993.

Hookoomsingh, V, 'Preserving pluralism', paper presented at the *International Conference on* The Maintenance of Indian Languages and Culture Abroad, January 1994, Central Institute of Indian Languages, Mysore.

Jain, J, *Writers of the Indian Diaspora*, New Delhi, 1998.

Jain, R K, *Indian Communities Abroad. Themes and Literature*, New Delhi, 1993.

James, C L R, *The Black Jacobins*, London, 1980.

Jenkins, E, *The Coolie, his Rights and Wrongs*, London, 1871.

Joubert, J, 'La vieille dame dans l'ombre. Une littérature bi-séculaire: des origines à 1945', 'Littérature Mauricienne', Notre Librairie, no. 114, Paris, 1983.

Joubert, J, et al, Littératures francophones de l'Océan Indien, EOI, 1993.

Kale, M, *Fragments of Empire: Capital, Slavery & Indentured Labor in the British*

Caribbean, Philadelphia, 1998.

Kolff, D H A, *Naukar, Rajput and Sepoy*, Cambridge, 1990.

Lacpatia, F, 'Quelques Aspects de l'Insertion des Indiens a la Reunion au xixe Siecle' in Conference Proceedings, Reunion, 1984.

Lal, B V, *Girmitiyas: The Origins of the Fiji Indians*, 1983, Canberra.

Lal, B V, 'Veil of Dishonour. Sexual Jealousy and Suicide on Fiji Plantations', *Journal of Pacific History*, 1985.

Lal, B V, and Shineberg, B, 'The Story of the Haunted Line', *Journal of Pacific History*, 1991.

Lal, B V, 'Approaches to the Study of Indian Indentured Emigration with Special Reference to Fiji', *Journal of Pacific History*.

Laval, J C, 'Les Problèmes Liés à la 'Criminalité Indienne' Pendant la Période de l'Engagisme à la Réunion', Conference Proceedings, 1984.

Leblond, M & A, *Après l'exotisme de Loti, le roman colonial*, Paris, Rasmussent, 1926.

Leblond, M-A, 'Moutousami', in *Les Sortilèges*, Fasquelle, Paris, 1905.

Leblond, M-A, 'La Croix du Sud', in *Etoiles*, J, Ferenczi et fils (éd.), Paris, 1928.

Lionnet, F, *Autobiographical Voices: Race, Gender, Self-Portraiture*, New York, 1989.

Mahabir, K, *East Indian Women of Trinidad & Tobago, An Annotated Bibliography*, Trinidad, 1992.

Mahabir, N K, (ed.), *The Still Cry*, New York, 1985.

Maillard, Notes sur l'Ile de la Réunion, *Paris, 1862*.

Maira, S, & Srikanth, R, (eds), Contours of the Heart – South Asians Map North America, *New York, 1996*.

Marimoutou, M, 'Femmes Indiennes et Engagement au XIXe Siecle à la Réunion, Conference Proceedings, Reunion, 1984.

McLeod, A L, (ed.), The Literature of the Indian Diaspora. Essays in Criticism, *New Delhi, 2000*.

Meer, Y S, Documents of Indentured Labour. Natal, 1851–1917.

Merven, T, *L'Indien a Maurice*, Mauritius, 1896.

Mishra, R, *Rama's Banishment*, London, 1979.

Moore, B, 'Sex and Marriage among Indian immigrants in British Guiana during the Nineteenth Century', Conference Paper, Trinidad, 1984.

Morris, J, *Monographie de l'Ile Maurice*, Bordeaux, 1862.

Mouat, F J, Rough Notes of a Trip to Reunion, Mauritius and Ceylon; with remarks on their eligibility as sanitaria for Indian invalids, *Calcutta, Thacker Spink & Co, 1852*.

Nandan, S, *Voices in the River*, Suva, 1985.

Natarajan, N, 'Reading Diaspora' in Nelson, S, (ed.), *Writers of the Indian Diaspora*, USA, 1993.

Naz, V, *Conférence sur l'Immigration Indienne*, 1891.

Nelson, E S, (ed.), *Reworlding the Literature of the Indian Diaspora*, USA, 1992.

Nelson, E S, *Writers of the Indian Diaspora*, USA, 1993.

Northrup, D, *Indentured Labor in the Age of Imperialism, 1834–1922*, Cambridge, 1995.

Parekh, B, 'Some reflections on the Hindu diaspora', *New Community* 20(4).

Paus, V, 'Des indianités dans la littérature coloniale de l'Océan Indien', DEA 1999.

Pitoeff, P, 'Yanaon et les Engages de la Réunion: Trois Experiences d'Emigration au XIXe Siècle' Conference Proceedings, Reunion, 1984.

Poynting, J, 'East Indian Women in the Caribbean: Experience, Image and Voice', *Journal of South Asian Literature*, 21, no. 1, 1986.

Prosper, J G, *Histoire de la Littérature Mauricienne de langue française*, EOI, 1978.

Prosper, J G, 'L'Apocalypse mauricienne', in *Chants Planétaires,* Proag Printing, Mauritius, 1990.

Rafiq, F, *Aurat Durbar, The Court of Women. Writings by Women of South Asian Origin*, Canada, 1995.

Ramesar, M, 'Indentured Labour in Trinidad 1880–1917' in Saunders, K (ed.), *Indentured Labour in the British Empire*, 1984.

de Rauville, C, *Indianocéanisme, humanisme et négritude*, 1970.

Rodney, W, 'Guyana: the making of the labour force', *Race & Class*, xxii, 4, 1981.

Rushdie, S, *Imaginary Homelands: Essays and Criticism*, London, 1991.

Schnepel, E M, 'The Creole Movement and East Indians on the Island of Guadeloupe, FWI', in Motwani, J, et al, *Global Indian Diaspora: Yesterday, Today and Tomorrow*, New Delhi, 1993.

Senghor, S L, 'De la liberté de l'âme ou éloge du métissage', in *Liberté, Négritude et Humanisme*, Paris, Seuil, 1964.

Senghor, L S, *Littérature Nègre*, Paris, 1990.

Sewtohul, *L'histoire d'Ashok et d'autres personnages de moindre importance*, Gallimard, Paris, 2001.

Simonin, 'La Réunion' in *Revue des Deux Mondes*, 1861.

Singh, M I, *V.S. Naipaul*, New Delhi, 1998.

Tinker, H, *A New System of Slavery*, London, 1974.

Torabully, K, *Cale d'étoiles-coolitude*, Editions Azalées, Reunion, 1992.

Torabully, K, 'Les Enfants de la Coolitude', Courrier de l'Unesco, Paris, October 1996.

Torabully, K, 'Coolitude', *Notre Librairie*, CLEF, Paris, October 1996.

Torabully, K, *Chair Corail, Fragments Coolies*, Ibis Rouge Edns., Guadeloupe, 1999.

Torabully, K, *Dialogue de l'eau et du sel*, Le Bruit des Autres, Limoges, 1998.

Torabully, K, Palabres á parole, Le Bruit des Autres, Limoges, 1999.

Tredgold, J H, *The Export of Coolies, and other Labourers to Mauritius*, London, 1842.

Turcotte & Brabant, C, 'Ile Maurice: Nuvo Sime', *Peuples Noirs/Peuples Africains*, 31, 1983.

Vatuk, V P, 'Protest Songs of East Indians in British Guiana', *Journal of American Folklore*, 1964.

Vinson, A, *De l'Immigration Indienne*, Réunion, 1860.

Wanquet, C, (ed.), *Fragments Pour Une Histoire des Economies et Sociétés de Plantation à la Réunion*, St Denis, Réunion, 1989.

Yamin, G, 'The Character and Origins of Labour Migration from Ratnagiri District, 1840–1920', *South Asia Research*, vol. 9, no. 1, 1989.

Yang, A A, 'Peasants on the Move: A Study of Internal Migration in India', *Journal of Interdisciplinary History*, X, 1979.